AF790017

COMPREHENSIVE ASSURANCE & SYSTEMS TOOL

An Integrated Practice Set

FOURTH EDITION

COMPUTERIZED AIS MODULE

Comprehensive Assurance & Systems Tool

An Integrated Practice Set

FOURTH EDITION

Laura R. Ingraham

J. Gregory Jenkins
Virginia Polytechnic Institute and State University

Computerized AIS Module

Pearson

New York, NY

Vice President, Business, Economics, and UK Courseware: Donna Battista
Director of Portfolio Management: Adrienne D'Ambrosio
Director, Courseware Portfolio Management: Ashley Dodge
Senior Sponsoring Editor: Neeraj Bhalla
Editorial Assistant: Elisa Marks
Vice President, Product Marketing: Roxanne McCarley
Senior Product Marketer: Tricia Murphy
Product Marketing Assistant: Marianela Silvestri
Manager of Field Marketing, Business Publishing: Adam Goldstein
Executive Field Marketing Manager: Nayke Popovich
Field Marketing Assistant: Jessica Quazza
Vice President, Production and Digital Studio, Arts and Business: Etain O'Dea
Director of Production, Business: Jeff Holcomb
Managing Producer, Business: Melissa Feimer
Content Producer: Sugandh Juneja
Operations Specialist: Carol Melville
Design Lead: Kathryn Foot
Manager, Learning Tools: Brian Surette
Content Developer, Learning Tools: Sarah Peterson
Managing Producer, Digital Studio and GLP, Media Production and Development: Ashley Santora
Managing Producer, Digital Studio and GLP: James Bateman
Managing Producer, Digital Studio: Diane Lombardo
Digital Studio Producer: Mary Kate Murray
Digital Studio Producer: Alana Coles
Digital Content Team Lead: Noel Lotz
Digital Content Project Lead: Martha LaChance
Project Manager: Katherine Tiffany Ragay, SPi Global
Cover Design: Laurie Entringer
Cover Art: Jesus Cervantes/Shutterstock

Library of Congress Cataloging-in-Publication Data on File

1 18

Pearson

ISBN 10: 0-13-479064-2
ISBN 13: 978-0-13-479064-0

Table of Contents

Preface

The **C**omprehensive **A**ssurance and **S**ystems **T**ool (CAST) provides an integrated learning opportunity that encompasses financial statement assurance and accounting information systems issues. CAST uniquely exposes students to these issues at The Winery at Chateau Americana, a hypothetical company that is based on an actual domestic winery. Unlike traditional projects and assignments that may offer little or no context, students develop a rich knowledge and understanding of Chateau Americana and its industry as they provide assurance on the company's financial statements and address a variety of challenging accounting information systems issues.

For students to succeed in the rapidly changing fields of accounting and auditing, they need to think critically and analytically, understand and utilize information technology, and communicate clearly and effectively. We help students develop these skills in CAST in the following ways:

- Each of the modules that underlies CAST—the *Manual AIS module*, the *Computerized Accounting Information Systems module*, and the *Assurance module*—calls on students to apply critical and analytical thinking to understand and resolve problems and challenges related to internal controls, processing and reporting transaction data and financial statements, and the application of auditing standards.

- Students gain valuable hands-on experience in the Manual AIS module and the Computerized Accounting Information Systems module. Using realistic supporting documentation, students record transactions in both a traditional manual accounting system and a computerized accounting system. In addition, students analyze data and build a number of technology-based tools using *Microsoft's Excel* and *Access* and *Sage50.*

- Throughout each of the modules, clear and effective communication are reinforced. Students are called on to develop clear financial statements, explain the factors affecting an audit client's business, and document their performance of common audit procedures.

CAST can be implemented in either an undergraduate or graduate setting and is ideally suited for simultaneous integration across assurance and AIS courses. The Manual Module can also be implemented in an Introductory course. In addition, each of the modules can be completed either as an in-class or an out-of-class assignment. CAST affords students the opportunity to develop and strengthen their analytical thinking, written and oral communication, problem solving, and team building skills.

New to this Edition

The following items are new to the fourth edition of this text:

- Updated instructions and payroll information have been added to the Manual AIS Module.
- The Manual AIS Module contains three all new transaction sets.
- The spreadsheet application in the Computerized AIS Module has been updated to *Excel 2016* and contains additional screen shots and more complete instructions.
- The general ledger package utilized in the Computerized AIS Module has been updated to the 2018 version of *Sage 50 Accounting*.
- The database application in the Computerized AIS Module has been updated to *Access 2016* with provides additional screen shots and instructions.
- All references to the professional auditing standards in the Assurance Module have been revised to reflect the most recently issued standards.
- Industry data and terminology in the Assurance Module have been updated to provide more current information to students in completing the case.

Laura Ingraham
Greg Jenkins

We dedicate this book to our families:
Dan and Casey
Elaine, Anna, Claire and Will

SPREADSHEET APPLICATIONS USING MICROSOFT® EXCEL 2016: The Winery at Chateau Americana

LEARNING OBJECTIVES

After completing and discussing this module, you should be able to:

- Identify the managerial and technological issues and risks associated with designing and utilizing a spreadsheet application as the primary accounting information system
- Develop an understanding of and utilize various methods for evaluating formulas in a spreadsheet to determine where and what the formula errors are
- Develop an understanding of and evaluate data integrity issues associated with spreadsheet utilization
- Develop an understanding of and utilize data analysis techniques, such as ratio analyses and what-if analyses using spreadsheet applications
- Develop an understanding of how information needs for users of a spreadsheet might vary, what the advantages and disadvantages are in different presentation formats, and utilize tools to meet those needs
- Develop an understanding of the repetitive tasks that occur in the creation of a workbook and utilize basic and advanced macros to reduce the number of repetitive tasks and simplify complex tasks
- Develop an understanding of the advantages and disadvantages of database functions in spreadsheet applications and utilize the VLOOKUP function to import data from different tables
- Develop an understanding of and utilize pivot tables to examine the data in a spreadsheet from different perspectives

BACKGROUND

When Chateau Americana began operations in 1980, accounting records were maintained manually. As the winery grew, the former CFO decided it was time to computerize various aspects of the system. As an initial step, he decided to use a spreadsheet program to assist in preparing journal entries, the year-end worksheet, and the financial statements. He also wanted to be able to create a single set of financial statements that could be used to present differing amounts of information to the various users. His goal was to simplify the bookkeeping functions, while improving the accuracy and usefulness of the financial statements. He knew reducing the amount of redundancy inherent in manual recordkeeping could do this. If the data was entered once and was verified at that time, this data could then be transmitted to other spreadsheets without the risk of incurring clerical errors that might appear upon re-entering the same data. He, therefore, had created various spreadsheets for Chateau Americana that would assist in these goals.

Assume that you had been asked to create these spreadsheets for Chateau Americana, given the current year-end data. The following exercises were written assuming that you will be working in *Microsoft® Excel 2016*. Tutorials follow many of the sections, providing hints and additional explanations for some of the more advanced Excel skill requirements. As you read through the text, you will periodically come across the symbol ⌘. This symbol denotes areas for which additional tutorial explanation is provided.

NOTE: This book has consistently left the year as a variable. Your instructor will inform you as to the appropriate years to be used.

DOWNLOAD THE FILE

Download the Excel file entitled "CA Computerized Excel Workbook.xlsx" from the CAST web site (your instructor will provide you with the URL for this web site) and save it as "*yourlastname_your firstname.xls*"⌘. This workbook contains several worksheets that will be necessary for the completion of the various exercises contained in the Spreadsheet assignment. We will continue to refer to this file as the **CA Computerized Excel Workbook** file throughout the text, although you have now renamed it using your own name.

Save As
The **Save As** function in *Excel 2016* can be found by clicking on the **File** on the Excel spreadsheet.

As you have undoubtedly learned by now, one internal control for computerized accounting information systems is to maintain backups. Therefore, as with any other computer file, it is important to **save your work often** to avoid data loss in the event that your program should unexpectedly crash. In addition, it is strongly suggested that you **back up your file** to another storage medium frequently to avoid problems in the event that you do experience a crash, virus, etc.

PROTECTING THE DATA

Open the **CA Computerized Excel Workbook** file you have downloaded. This file contains several worksheets including a blank year-end worksheet similar to the one you may have completed in the Manual AIS Module of CAST entitled **Y-E Worksheet**. Examine the set-up of the year-end worksheet, familiarizing yourself with the ways in which the creation of formulas in Excel can be used to minimize the amount of data input.

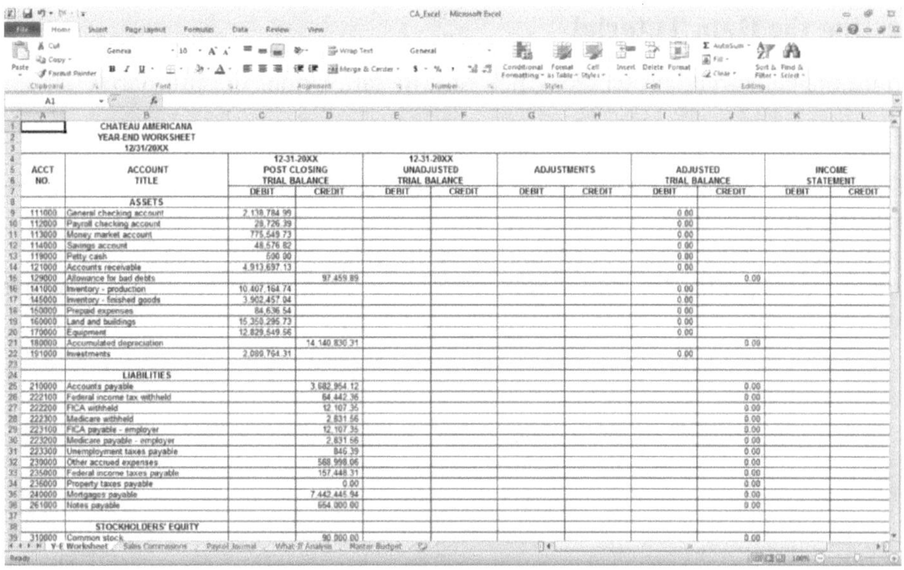

Figure 1

Requirements

1. With the file open to the **Y-E Worksheet**, enter the data for the 12-31-XX Unadjusted Trial Balance and the 12-31-XX Adjustments columns, allowing the formulas contained in the spreadsheet to calculate the totals and carry the figures from one column of the spreadsheet to the next (i.e., from those columns to the Adjusted Trial Balance, Balance Sheet, and Income Statement columns). Make sure that you change the years so that they reflect the appropriate date (ask your instructor if you are uncertain as to the years you should be using). The data for completion of this worksheet are available on the CAST web site.

2. Review the worksheet to be sure that your column totals are accurate and that you have entered the correct data for each account.

3. Once you have made certain that the embedded formulas are being calculated correctly, you should lock (or protect) the cells that contain them so that no one can change the formulas at a later date. To do this, highlight cells **I9** through **N93** and then protect them ⌘.

Protecting the Data Tutorial

Highlight the cells to be protected. Click on **File** tab. Under the Info tab 

, click on **Protect Workbook** 

. Now select "Protect Current Sheet" from the pull-down menu. Make sure that the boxes entitled "Protect Worksheet and Contents of Locked Cells," "Select locked cells," and "Select unlocked cells" are checked. You will need to enter a password to protect the cells. For purposes of this assignment, use "protect" as the password. You will then be prompted to confirm the password by reentering it. Note: The password is **case sensitive**!

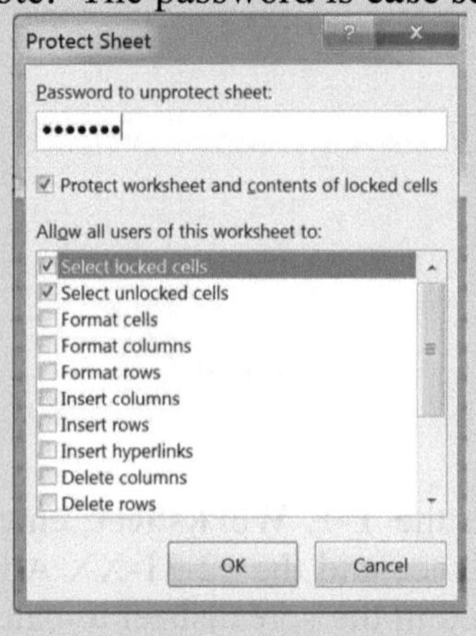

Alternatively, you can click on the **Review** tab and click on **Protect Sheet**.

4. Verify that the cells have been locked properly by attempting to alter any of the formulas contained in columns I through N. If the worksheet has been properly protected, you should get the following warning:

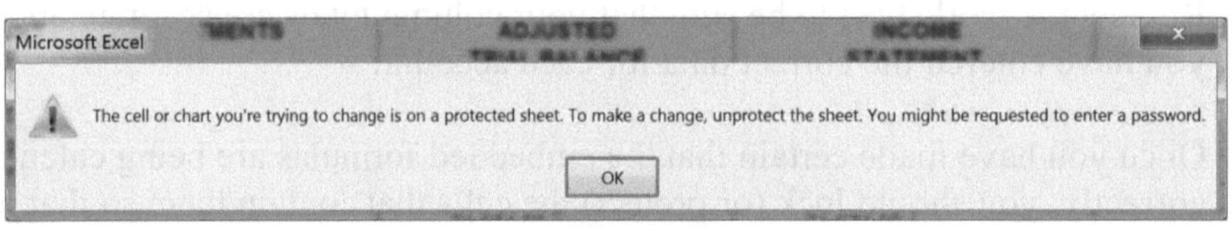

Figure 2

FORMULA AUDITING

The spreadsheet is now ready to be used for the creation of the financial statements and manipulation of the data for various managerial tasks. Before you begin, it is important to recognize that, despite the fact that you will be using a computer to deal with many of the clerical tasks previously done manually, the computer can do so accurately only insofar as the formulas are entered correctly. No one knowingly inserts errors in a worksheet. Unfortunately, however, errors often creep in with the result that these worksheets then end up giving incorrect results. Obviously, this can be a huge problem for business owners who are relying on accurate data so that they can create budgets, make pricing determinations, track accounts receivable, and more. Statistics show that the number of errors on computer worksheets exceeds 25%. Some of the more common errors are:

######	Occurs when a column is too narrow for the data contained therein. This error is easily fixed by expanding the column in question.
# NAME?	Occurs when Excel cannot evaluate a defined name used in the formula because the name may never have existed, may be misspelled, or may have been inadvertently deleted.
# N/A	Dependent upon the formula. It is most often found when using a vlookup function and it may mean that the value in question was not available.
#REF!	Indicates a problem with a cell reference due, perhaps, to deleting cells, rows or columns used in a formula.
# VALUE!	Typically due to trying to use a cell containing text in a calculation or entering incorrect arguments.

The **Formula Auditing** tool in Excel enables the user to audit the worksheet to find and correct many of the errors that inevitably occur.

Requirements

As you work through the following steps, you will occasionally be asked questions. Please respond to these questions in the space provided in the **Sales Commissions** worksheet.

1. Open the **CA Computerized Excel Workbook** file and click on the **Formula tab**. To the left of the toolbar you should now see the **Formula Auditing** section.

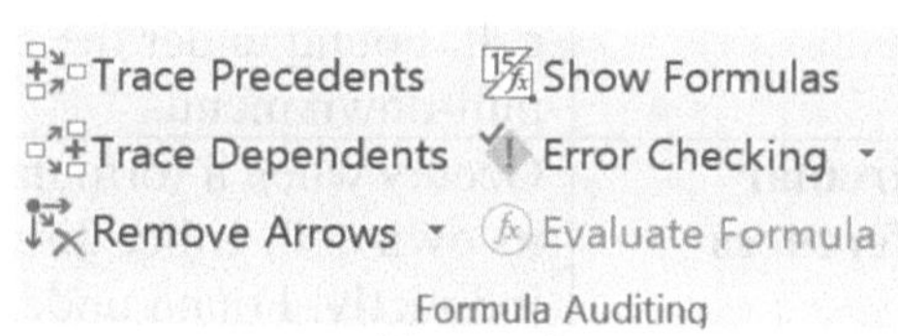

Figure 3

The following table describes some of the buttons on the toolbar:

Option	Description
Trace Precedents	Displays an arrow from all cells that supply data to the selected cell.
Trace Dependents	Displays an arrow to the cell that is dependent upon the selected cell for data.
Remove Arrows	Removes all tracer arrows throughout the worksheet.
Remove Precedent Arrows	Removes all precedent arrows for each level displayed. The button must be pushed for each level from which the data are supplied. Found under the Remove Arrows pull-down menu.
Remove Dependent Arrows	Removes all dependent arrows for each level displayed. The button must be pushed for each level to which the data are supplied. Found under the Remove Arrows pull-down menu.
Show Formulas	Displays the formulas in each cell rather than the resulting values.
Error Checking	Describes the error that has occurred and allows the user to obtain help on the error, to walk through the calculation steps, to ignore the error, or to edit the error in the formula bar.
Trace Errors	Allows the user to find the source of an error by displaying a blue arrow from the source of the error to the selected cell. Found under the Error Checking pull-down menu.
Circular References	Occurs when a formula refers back to its own cell, either directly or indirectly. Found under the Error Checking pull-down menu.
Evaluate Formula	Allows the user to display the result of any underlined or italicized portion of a formula.

2. Go to cell **G30**. Click on **Trace Precedents** on the **Formula Auditing** section. From what cell is cell **G30** obtaining its data? (Enter your response in cell **B48**.)

3. Now click on **Remove Precedent Arrows** on the **Formula Auditing** section.

4. While cell **G30** is highlighted, click on **Error Checking** on the **Formula Auditing** section (see *Figure 4*).

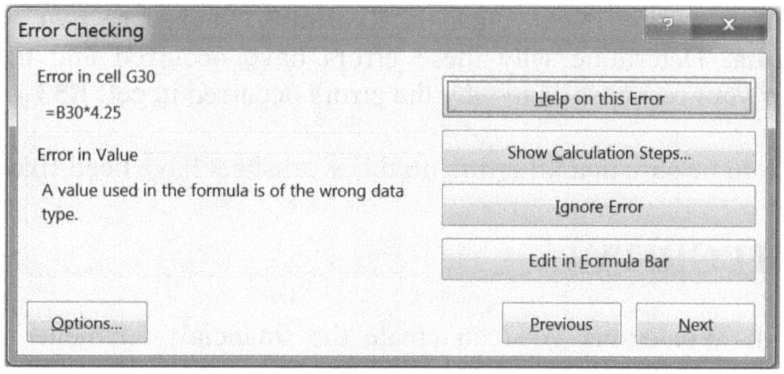

Figure 4

5. Note that an explanation for the error is provided for you in the window. More detailed explanations can be obtained by clicking on **Help on this error**. Obtain two other possible causes for the error by clicking on **Help on this error** and enter them in cell **B49**. Close the **Error Checking** window.

6. While cell **G30** is highlighted, click on **Evaluate Formula** on the **Formula Auditing** section. Next, click on **Evaluate**.

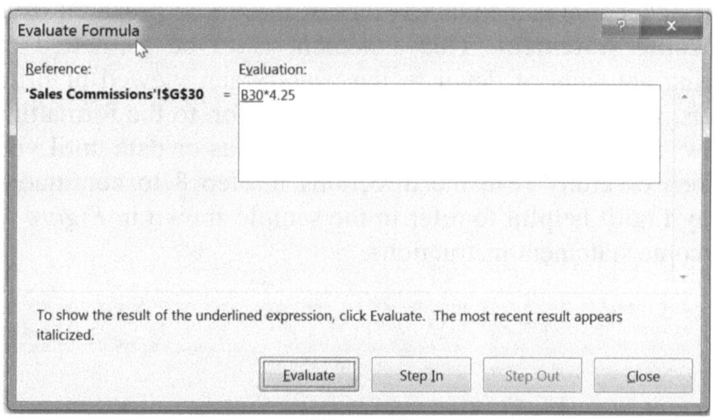

Figure 5

Based upon what you find when Excel evaluates this formula, explain why this has error occurred. Click on **Step In** if you are uncertain as to the reason why this has occurred. Now click on **Step** Out. Enter your response in cell **B50**. Close the **Evaluate Formula** window.

7. Examine the cells surrounding **G30** and then fix the error in cell **G30**.

8. Go to cell **F35**. Click on **Trace Precedents** on the **Formula Auditing** section. What happens? (Enter your response in cell **B51**.)

9. While cell **F35** is highlighted, click on **Trace Dependents** on the **Formula Auditing** section. What happens? (Enter your response in cell **B52**.)

10. While cell **F35** is highlighted, click on **Evaluate Formula** on the **Formula Auditing** section. Next, click on **Evaluate. There are two errors in this formula.** Determine why these errors have occurred and then fix them. (Enter your response as to why the errors occurred in cell **B53**.)

11. Check to be sure that all errors on this worksheet have been fixed.

DATA INTEGRITY

Using the **Y-E Worksheet** you can create the financial statements including the Statement of Income and Retained Earnings, the Balance Sheet and the Statement of Cash Flows with very little additional data entry. This is beneficial since you have already verified the accuracy of the data on the **Y-E Worksheet**, these statements will also be accurate if created with the correct formulas. Therefore, you will only need to verify the logic on the other spreadsheets you are preparing to be sure that they are operating as intended and achieving the correct results. One method by which this can be accomplished is to utilize the "=" sign to tell Excel that a particular cell is equal to the amount in another cell on another spreadsheet. Another method is to create a **Name** for a particular amount to be used later in a formula. You will utilize both of these methods in this section.

The Statement of Income and Retained Earnings is to be prepared as a **single-year, multi-step income statement**. This statement is to be formatted so that it can provide differing amounts of detail to the users when viewed or printed at a later date. To do this, you will need to pay careful attention to the formatting instructions provided below. Do not attempt to enter any formulas or data until you are finished formatting. Then carefully read the directions in step 8 to continue with the data entry. You may find it helpful to refer to the sample shown in *Figure 6* as you work through the income statement instructions.

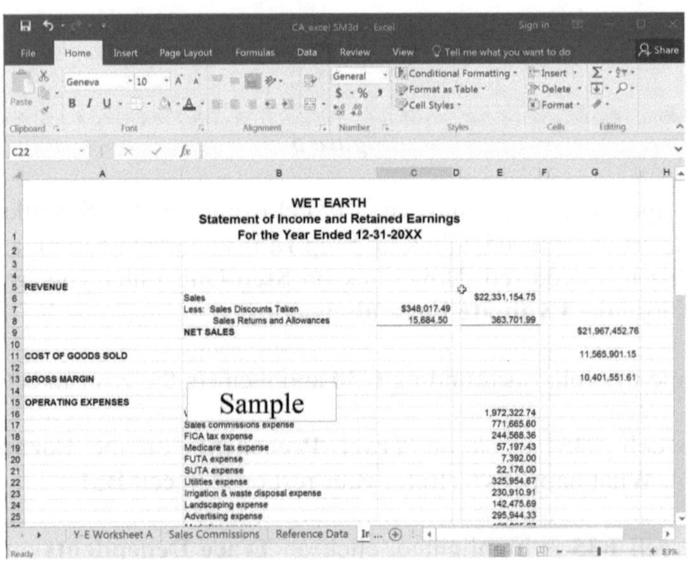

Figure 6

Requirements

1. Open the **CA Computerized Excel Workbook** file and insert a new worksheet by clicking on **Insert > Insert Sheet** (under the **Cells** section of the **Home** tab).

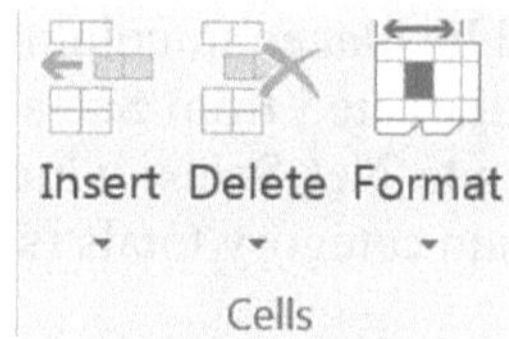

Figure 7

2. Format the columns for the following widths ⌘e:

A	B	C	D	E	F	G
31	38	14	3	14	3	17

Column A will contain the category headings. Column B will contain the account titles. Columns C, E and G will contain amounts.

Set the row height for row 1 at 71 ⌘. It is not necessary to adjust the heights of the remaining rows.

Rename the newly inserted worksheet "**Income Statement.**" ⌘

3. Column B will be used for individual revenue and expense account titles such as Sales, Wages and Salaries Expense, etc. Starting in **row 6** of **column B**, enter the revenue and expense account titles listed on the **Y-E Worksheet**. (**HINT**: Be sure that you have copied and pasted on the new worksheet all account titles needed to create the Statement of Income and Retained Earnings. The ordering and presentation of the account titles should be consistent with that commonly used on income statements, not that found on the **Y-E Worksheet**. When you past the cells into the **Income Statement Worksheet**, be sure to use the **Values** function so that you don't include the formatting from the prior worksheet.)

4. Column A will be used for category headings. Beginning on **row 5** of **column A**, enter the category heading "REVENUE." Enter the following headings in column A as follows. Enter "COST OF GOODS SOLD" on **row 11**, "GROSS MARGIN" on **row 13**, "OPERATING EXPENSES" on **row 15**, "INCOME FROM OPERATIONS" on **row 51**, "OTHER INCOME AND GAINS" on **row 53**, "OTHER EXPENSES AND LOSSES" on **row 58**, "INCOME (LOSS) BEFORE TAXES" on **row 61**, "FEDERAL INCOME TAX" on **row 63**, "NET INCOME (LOSS)" on **row 65**, "RETAINED EARNINGS - 12/31/20XW" on **row 67**, "RETAINED EARNINGS - 12/31/20XX" on **row 69**, and "EARNINGS PER SHARE" on row **71**.

5. Capitalize the main headings in column A using bold Arial 10. Use non-bold Arial 10 for the account titles in column B. Be sure to underline when appropriate using borders ⌘.

6. Columns C and E should be used for amounts that must be added to arrive at subtotals. For example, the amounts for Sales Returns and Allowances and Sales Discounts should be placed in column C. These are combined to arrive at the amount that is subtracted from Sales (both of these amounts should be in Column E) to compute Net Sales, which is then presented in column G along with the other main category totals (see *Figure 6*).

7. Copy the appropriate amounts to the **Income Statement** worksheet by typing an "=," locating the appropriate cell on the **Y-E Worksheet** (**HINT**: Most of these amounts should be taken from columns K through L), and hitting **Enter**. For example, when you have finished entering the value for Sales, the formula should read: "='Y-E Worksheet'!L45." This has the effect of returning the value located on the **Y-E Worksheet** to the **Income Statement** sheet. The benefit of doing this is that you know the numbers in the Income Statement are correct since you have already proofed the **Y-E Worksheet**. There is no redundancy or inconsistency in your workbook since you are pulling the data from its original source of data entry.

   Note, however, that Retained Earnings on the **Y-E Worksheet** has not yet been updated for the current year Net Income. Therefore, the amount in cell **N42** on the **Y-E Worksheet** represents Retained Earnings as of 12-31-XW. You will have to use a formula on the **Income Statement** worksheet to calculate Retained Earnings as of 12-31-XX.

8. Skip steps 9 through 13 if your instructor does not want you to calculate federal income taxes on the **Income Statement** worksheet using a nested "IF" statement ⌘. A nested "IF" statement is a powerful tool that allows Excel to evaluate several logical conditions in a single function. For example, it can be used for searching an Excel database or in complex calculations such as that of federal or state income tax where the calculation varies depending upon the level of net income before taxes, or payroll taxes where the calculation is dependent upon the amount of gross pay an individual earns.

9. You will need to calculate the amount to be entered into Federal Income Tax Expense using a nested "IF" statement. To minimize future changes to the nested "IF" statement, insert a new worksheet and name it "**Reference Data.**" Create a heading in this worksheet for Corporate Tax Brackets and Rates. You should provide any text necessary for the bracket descriptions in column A (e.g., "Greater than or equal to," etc.), the amounts for the brackets in column B (e.g., $50,000, etc.) and the rates in column C (e.g., 15%, etc.). Column D should contain any adjustments needed for your formula. Creating the brackets and associated rates will take some thought on your part as they are to be used in your nested IF statement for the corporate tax calculation to eliminate the need to recreate the formula if the brackets or rates are changed by Congress at a later date. (**Note:** Current tax rates may be found in any tax textbook or by referring to the instructions for Schedule J, Form 1120.)

10. It is much easier for both the creator and for later users of a worksheet to understand and maintain the worksheet if it is created using meaningful names for the data values contained in the cells rather than by using the cell references for those data values. For example, it would probably make more sense to you if you saw a formula written as =NetSales-CostOfGoodsSold instead of =G9-G11. For this reason, it is a good practice to use cell names whenever possible, but particularly when creating complex formulas.

    Create cell names ⌘ for the brackets, rates and adjustments (e.g., Bracket0, Rate0, Bracket1, Rate1, etc.) Be sure to consider the amount of tax if there is a Net Loss.

11. Create the nested IF ⌘ statement using the cell names on the Reference Data sheet.

12. Create the following cell names ⌘ for the Statement of Income and Retained Earnings:
    - Cost Of Goods Sold
    - Net Sales
    - Interest Expense
    - NIBT (i.e., net income before tax)
    - Federal Income Tax
    - Net Income

13. Properly format your amounts for currency (i.e., with dollar signs, commas, decimal points, etc.) ⌘ where appropriate. REMEMBER: Decimal points are supposed to line up!

14. Create a multiple-line heading ⌘ in cell **A1**. The information for this heading is as follows:

    Chateau Americana, Inc. (using bold Arial 14)
    Statement of Income and Retained Earnings (using bold Arial 12)
    For the Year ended 12/31/XX (using bold Arial 12)

    Center the heading across columns A through E.

15. Use formulas to calculate subtotals and totals on the income statement.

16. Be sure to include Earnings Per Share on your income statement. *There are 45,000 shares issued and outstanding.*

    NOTE: At this point, the only amount that you should have typed into your worksheet is the number of shares issued and outstanding needed to calculated earnings per share. All other amounts should be formula-driven.

17. Insert a new worksheet entitled "**Balance Sheet**" and create a **comparative, classified Balance Sheet** employing the same general formatting techniques and utilizing formulas as before (see *Figure 8*). Determine your column widths as you deem appropriate. Use a single column to present the various account balances for 20XW and a single column to present the account balances for 20XX.

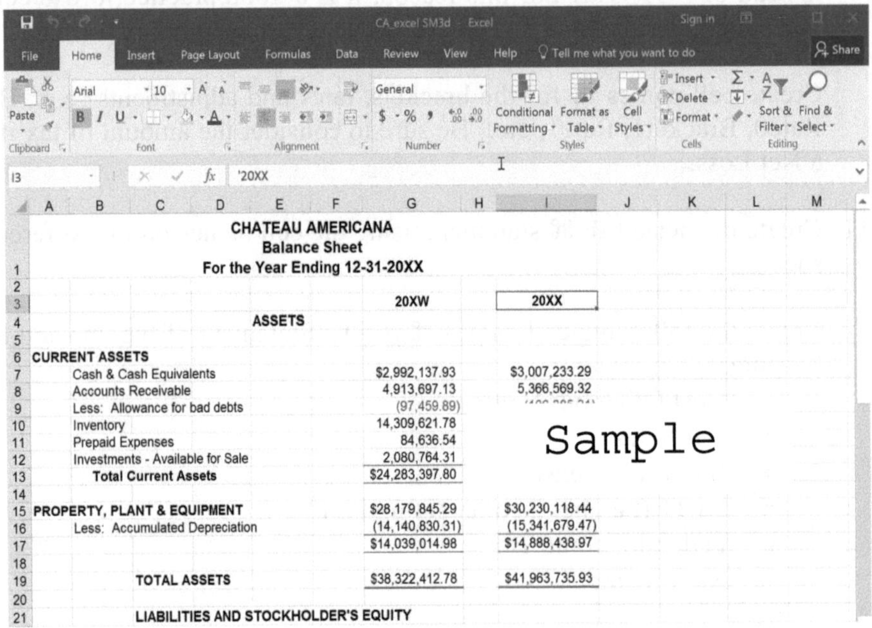

Figure 8

18. Create the following cell or range names for the Balance Sheet:
    - Beginning Inventory
    - Ending Inventory
    - Current Assets (for 20XX only)
    - Beginning Total Assets
    - Ending Total Assets
    - Current Liabilities (for 20XX only)
    - Ending Total Liabilities
    - Beginning Stockholders Equity
    - Ending Stockholders Equity

19. (***Optional***) Insert a new worksheet entitled "**Statement of Cash Flows**" and create a Statement of Cash Flows using the same general formatting techniques and utilizing formulas as before.

Data Integrity Tutorial

Adjust the column width. There are three ways in which you can adjust the column width. First, columns may be formatted by clicking on the applicable column letter. Then click on **Format > Column Width** (in the **Cells** section of the **Home** tab) and type in the desired column width.

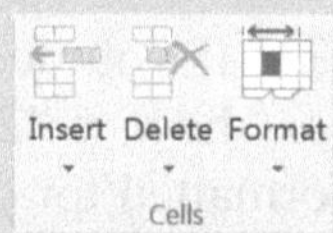

Alternatively, you can right-click on the appropriate column letter, select **Column Width** from the pull-down menu and enter the desired column width. Finally, you can adjust the column width by placing the cursor on the line separating the heading for columns A and B on the gray bar above the cells. You will notice that the cursor turns to a cross and the column width is displayed in the box above the column separator. Drag the cursor to the desired width. Repeat for every column whose width should be changed.

Adjust the row height. Similarly, you can use either of the three options above for rows. Click on the desired row number, click on **Format > Row Height** and type in the desired row height. Alternatively, you can click on the applicable row number and then clicking on **Format > Row Height** and type in the desired row height. Alternatively, you can right-click on the appropriate row number, select **Row Height** from the pull-down menu and enter the desired row height. Finally, you can adjust the row height by placing the cursor on the line separating two rows. Once you see that the cursor turns to a cross and the row height is displayed in the box above the row separator, drag the cursor to the desired height. Repeat for every row whose height should be changed.

Rename the worksheet. To rename a worksheet, left double-click on the worksheet's name tab and enter the new name. To illustrate, insert the first new worksheet into your workbook, left double-click on the tab at the bottom of the worksheet entitled 'Sheet 1' and enter the new worksheet title.

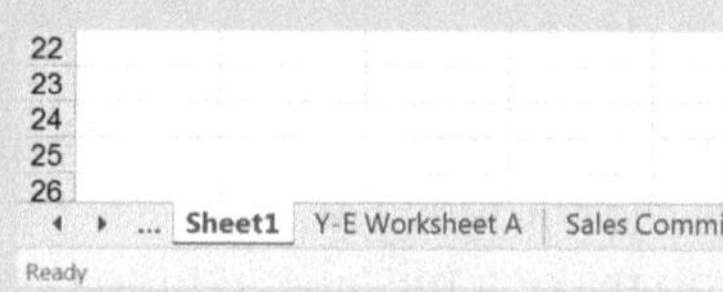

Underlining. To underline totals and subtotals use the border Icon 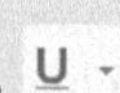 found in the **Font** section of the **Home** tab. For subtotals, after placing the cursor in the appropriate cell, pull down the border menu by placing the cursor on the arrow next to the Icon and select the **Bottom Border**. For totals, select **Bottom Double Border**.

Another way to place a border in a cell is to select the cell by clicking on it with the right mouse button to bring up the ShortCut Menu, select **Format Cells > Border**. Select the appropriate style and select the placement in the picture.

Data Integrity Tutorial (continued)

Formatting numbers and currency. Click **Format > Format Cells** found in the **Cells** section of the **Home** tab. Select **Number** and make sure the **Decimal places** box indicates "2" and the **Use 1000 Separator (,)** box has a check to format for commas with two decimal points. Be sure that you also select one of the choices that uses parentheses for negative numbers. If you desire a dollar sign, select **Currency** and make sure the **Decimal places** box shows a "2" in it and the **Symbol** box has "$" to ensure that your amounts will be formatted for currency with two decimal points.

Multiple line heading. To enter a multiple line heading in one cell, type the first line. Hold down the **Alt** key and hit the **Enter** key to go on to the second line, and repeat this process for the third line. To center the heading across columns, highlight the cells in which you would like to center the heading and click on the **Merge and Center** 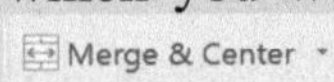

button. Increase the font on each line to the desired size. Resize the height of the row.

Entering and using formulas. A formula always begins with an "=" sign. Formulas use an operator (+ - / * > < % etc.) combined with values that can be cell references or range names. Note that the following are only examples of formulas you might need:

=Gross_Revenue-SUM(Sales_Adjustments)
=C15+C16
=$E9-$E19
=SUM(C24:C32)

Note the "**$**" in the third example above. This has the effect of holding the column **E** as an absolute reference. In other words, if this formula is moved to another place in the worksheet, it will still reference column **E** but the row number will change. If a dollar sign is placed on either side of the **E** (**E9**), both the column and row reference will be absolute. Without the dollar signs, EXCEL treats cell references as relative; that is, when they are moved, the references will change relative to the new cell position.

To enter a formula in a cell:

a) Select the cell into which you want to enter the formula.
b) Type an "=" to activate the formula bar.
c) Type the formula. If you make a mistake, edit to correct it.
d) Press Enter or click on the enter box (the green checkmark) next to the formula bar.

Nested "IF" statement. An "IF" statement returns one of two values based on a specified logical condition. They are what we call 'If, then, else' statements. For example, if *X* is less than *Y,* then return the value of 5, else return the value of 10. "IF" statements begin with the "=" sign and use comparison operators (=, >, <, >=, <=, <>) to specify the logical condition. The format for an "IF" statement is:

"=IF(**A1***comparison operator***B1**,**C1**,**D1**)."

For example, =IF(**A1**<=**B1**,**C1**,**D1**)

Data Integrity Tutorial (continued)

Nested "IF" statement (cont).
This "IF" statement specifies that if cell **A1** is less than or equal to cell **B1** (logical condition) then return the **A1**value in cell **C1** (the 'true' response), else return the **B1** value in cell **D1** (the 'false' response. Note that numerical values, cell references or range names can be used in "IF" statements.

A nested "IF" statement returns one of three or more values based on the specified logical conditions. For example, if *X* is greater than *Y* then return the value of 10 else if *X* is greater than *Z* then return the value of 5 else return the value of 1. The general format for a nested "IF" statement is:

"=IF(**A1**>=**B1**,**A2**, IF(**A1**>=**C1**,**B2**,**C2**))."

This "IF" statement specifies that if cell **A1** is greater than or equal to cell **B1** (first logical condition) then return the **A1** value in cell **A2**, else if cell **A1** is greater than or equal to cell **C1** (second logical condition) then return the **A1** value in cell **B2** else return the **C1** value in cell **C2**. The else condition represented by **C2** can be replaced by additional "IF" statements as necessary until all logical conditions have been met.

Naming cells. You can create a name for a single cell or an array (a range) of cells. Names cannot include special characters with the exception of an underscore (_), backslash (\), or period (.). In addition, cell names cannot contain spaces; instead you can capitalize the first letter of each word or use the underscore ("_") between words (e.g., either of the following are acceptable cell names: CostOfGoodsSold or Cost_of_goods_sold). Names are not case sensitive. Cost_of_Goods_Sold is read the same as 'cost_of_goods_sold'.Names can be up to 255 characters.

To create a cell name, first select the cell or cells that you wish to name. Use only those cells that contain the amounts you want to name. It is **not** necessary to include the cells with the text describing those numbers. Click on the **Name** box at the left side of the **Formula bar** 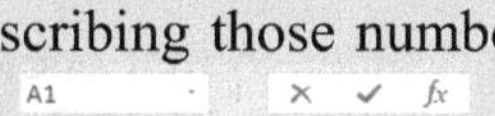

. Type the name for the cell(s) into the **Name** box to refer to your selection.

Alternatively, you can select the cell or cells that you wish to name. Click on **Define Name** in the **Defined Names** section 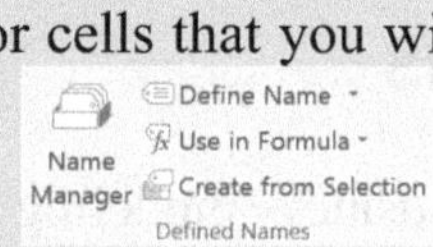

of the **Formulas** tab. Type the name for the cell(s) into the **New Name** window.

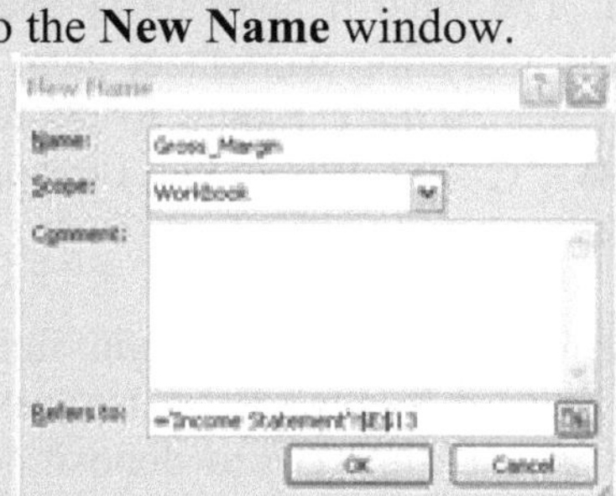

You can see a list of all named cells and edit them if you need to by clicking on **Name Manager** in the **Defined Names** section.

SIMPLE DATA ANALYSIS

With the data you now have in the financial statements and with the cell names that you have created in those financial statements, you can now easily explore the power of data analysis that a spreadsheet offers. For example, it is very easy to calculate some common ratios.

Requirements

1. Open the **CA Computerized Excel Workbook** file and insert a new worksheet entitled "**Ratio Analysis**."

2. On this new worksheet, calculate the ratios listed below by using formulas that refer to cell or range names that you have created. Do not use direct cell references (e.g., N42, G18, etc.) in these calculations.

   - Current ratio
   - Inventory turnover
   - Return on assets
   - Return on equity
   - Debt to equity ratio
   - Times interest earned

   In addition to increasing the understandability of your formulas, using cell names rather than cell references also increases the flexibility and auditability of your Excel workbook. At the same time, it decreases the maintenance necessary for your Excel workbook. For example, rows and columns can more easily be inserted and deleted without altering cell and range names, or formulas that refer to them. You may have to create new cell names to complete these formulas.

3. Format your Ratio Analysis worksheet so that one column contains the ratio name and one column contains the ratio itself. In addition, the spreadsheet should include an appropriate heading.

WHAT-IF ANALYSIS

There are also a variety of business modeling tools and analytic techniques that can be brought to bear on data. The what-if analysis is one of the most fundamental methods that can be used for analyzing worksheet data. In a what-if analysis, you calculate a formula and then change the variables to see what happens. For example, assume the formula is (A*B) + C = D. What would happen to D if you increase A? Or decrease C?

Assume that Chateau Americana is going to begin funding a pension plan. The president of the company, Edward Summerfield, has asked you to determine how much the fund would have in it if he were to deposit $250,000 initially and then make ten annual deposits of $100,000 each (at the end of each year), assuming an annual interest rate of 5%. You recognize this as a future value problem and turn to Excel knowing that can calculate this for you very quickly.

Requirements

1. Open the **CA Computerized Excel Workbook** file and click on the **What-If Analysis** worksheet.

2. Enter the interest rate in cell **C4**. The interest rate entered here will represent the interest rate per period in the future value formula.

3. Enter the time period in cell **C5**. The number entered here represents the total number of payment periods for the entire investment period.

4. Enter the annual deposit in cell **C6**. This amount is the payment made each period. It should be entered as a negative amount since this represents a cash disbursement (i.e., money paid out).

5. Enter the initial deposit in cell **C7**. The initial deposit is the present value of the investment, i.e., what it is worth now. Again this should be entered as a negative amount because we are disbursing this amount.

6. Enter the deposit type in cell **C8**. The type indicates the timing of the payment. If the payment is going to be made at the end of the period, enter a 0; if it will be made at the beginning of the period, enter a 1.

7. Go to cell **B10**. Click on **Financial > FV** in the **Function Library** section of the **Formulas** tab (*Figure 9*).

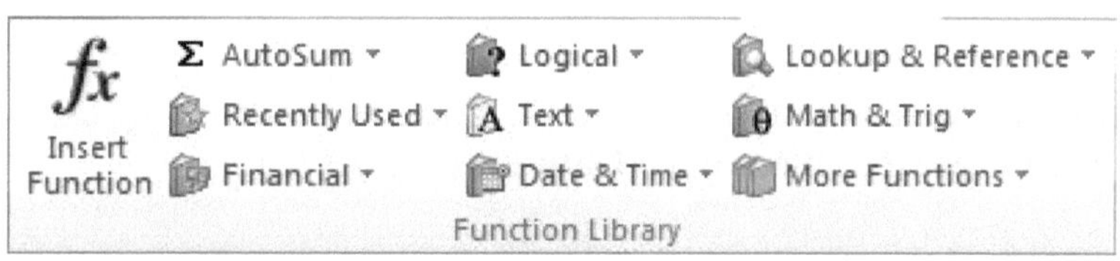

Figure 9

Enter the cells (from requirements 1-6) into the appropriate arguments and click **OK** (*Figure 10*).

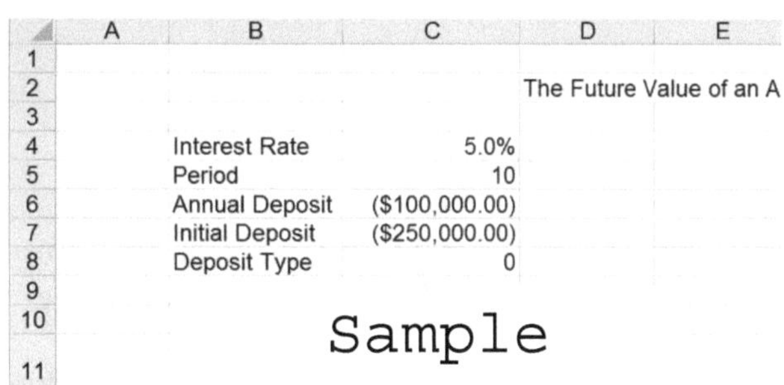

Figure 10

This gives you the amount that the pension plan will grow to if $250,000 is invested now and ten annual deposits are made, assuming 5% interest.

Now assume that Mr. Summerfield wants to know 'what-if' the interest rate is not 5% (rates ranging from 4.5% to 7%, in 0.5% increments) and 'what-if' the company decides to make a different annual deposit (anything from $70,000 to $130,000, in $10,000 increments). You can answer these questions quickly by creating a Data Table for the what-if analysis.

8. To set up the Data Table for the What-If Analysis, enter the interest rates in cells **C10** through **H10**. Enter the payment amounts in cells **B11** through **B17** (*Figure 11*).

	A	B	C	D	E	F	G	H
1								
2				The Future Value of an Annuity				
3								
4		Interest Rate	5.0%					
5		Period	10					
6		Annual Deposit	($100,000.00)					
7		Initial Deposit	($250,000.00)					
8		Deposit Type	0					
9								
10		$1,665,012.91	4.5%	5.0%	5.5%	6.0%	6.5%	7.0%
11		$70,000.00						
12		$80,000.00						
13		$90,000.00						
14		$100,000.00			Sample			
15		$110,000.00						
16		$120,000.00						
17		$130,000.00						
18								

Figure 11

9. Highlight cells **B10** through **H17**. Click **What-If Analysis > Data Table** in the **Forecast** section of the **Data** tab (*Figure 12*).

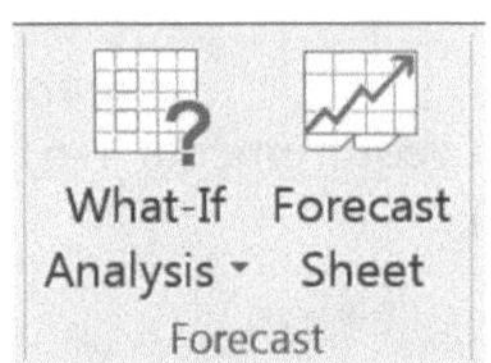

Figure 12

10. Enter the interest rate (**C4**) into the row input cell.

11. Enter the annual deposit (**C6**) into the column input cell. Click **OK**. The table is then populated with the future values of all the 'what-if' possibilities.

One final note: You can make changes to any of the variables in the formula and Excel will automatically recalculate the entire table IF the spreadsheet has been set to automatic recalculation. To do this, click on **Calculation Options** in the **Calculation** section of the **Formulas** tab (*Figure 13*) and make sure that it is set to **Automatic**.

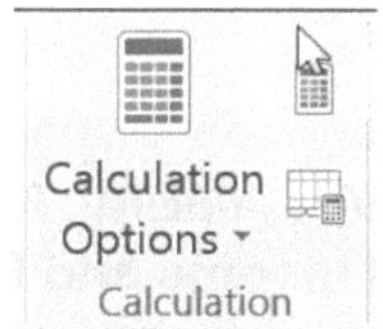

Figure 13

INFORMATION NEEDS

Information needs vary among the users of the accounting information system and information overload is a very real problem in businesses. Spreadsheets are very flexible and have very powerful reporting capabilities. Using the spreadsheets and the financial statements you have prepared, you can easily report information to each user according to his or her needs by grouping and ungrouping data from a single spreadsheet without changing the format of the spreadsheet. For example, a company's president may only want to see the overall picture, rather than the detail of the accounts, while the vice president of sales might want to see details related to a specific product or line of products and the production manager would need to see the manufacturing costs broken down, line item by line item.

Spreadsheets can also be used to sort and query large bodies of data to extract only the desired information. For example, the controller may want to see a listing of only those expense accounts that exceed a certain dollar amount.

The following requirements will help you create an outline for the income statement that will let you show or hide varying levels of detail without changing the income statement format itself.

Requirements

1. Open the **CA Computerized Excel Workbook** file and click on the **Income Statement** worksheet. Highlight columns B through F.

2. Click on **Group** in the **Outline** section of the **Data** tab (see *Figure 14*). Then click on **Group** in the pull-down menu.

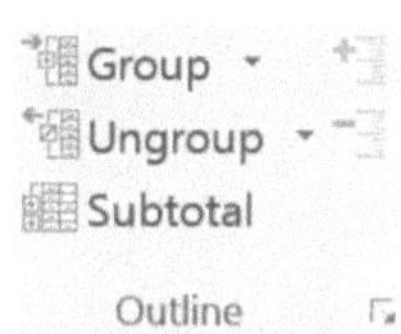

Figure 14

Notice that a bar with a minus sign appears above the column G.

3. Click on the minus sign to see what happens.

4. Highlight rows 6 through 9 and repeat the **Group** command.

5. Repeat the **Group** command for "OPERATING EXPENSES" and "OTHER INCOME AND GAINS" (see *Figure 15*).

	A	G	H
1	**CHATEAU AMERICANA** **Statement of Income and Retained Earnings** **For the Year Ended 12-31-20XX**		
2			
3		Sample	
4			
5	**REVENUE**		
9		$21,967,452.76	
10			
11	**COST OF GOODS SOLD**	11,565,901.15	
12			
13	**GROSS MARGIN**	10,401,551.61	
14			
15	**OPERATING EXPENSES**		
49		7,108,203.18	
50			
51	**INCOME FROM OPERATIONS**	3,293,348.43	

Figure 15

Now assume that the CFO has heard about your Excel skills and has asked you to help him determine which of the expense accounts for Chateau Americana, Inc. exceeded $200,000 for 20XX. Filter the expense accounts to provide this information as follows:

6. Insert a new worksheet entitled "**Operating Expenses**" into the **CA Computerized Excel Workbook** file. For all operating expenses copy the account title and amount from the **Y-E Worksheet** to the new worksheet.

7. Insert a row at the top of the data and enter the column headings "**Operating Expenses**" in cell **A1** and "**Amount**" in cell **B1**.

8. Extract, or filter, all operating expenses in excess of $200,000 ⌘. Insert a row at the top of the spreadsheet and create an appropriate heading for the worksheet (see *Figure 16*).

	A	B
1	**Chateau Americana** **Expenses In Excess of $200,000** **For the Year Ending 12/31/20XX**	
2		
3	*Preparer:*	Laura Ingraham
4	*Date:*	12/4/2017
5		
6	**Operating Expenses**	**Amount**
7	Wages and salaries expense	1,972,322.
8	Sales commissions expense	771,665.60
9	FICA tax expense	244,568.36
13	Utilities expense	Sample
14	Irrigation & waste disposal expense	
16	Advertising expense	

Figure 16

Information Needs Tutorial

Filtering data. Highlight the cells to be filtered including cells containing descriptions for other cells. Click on **Filter** in the **Sort & Filter** section of the **Data** tab.

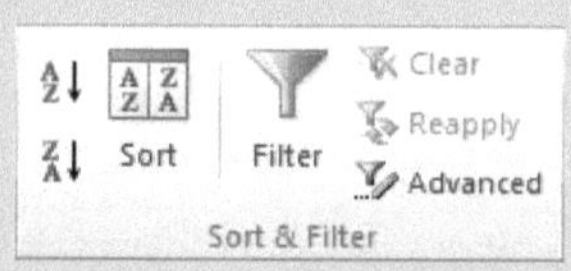

Notice that arrows for the pull-down menus appear in the top cells. Click on the arrow in the column to be filtered to obtain the appropriate pull-down menu (i.e., the column containing the amounts). Click on **Number Filters** and select **Custom Filter** from the pull-down menu. In the **Custom Filter** window, click on the pull-down menu next to the box containing "equal" to select the applicable logical condition and input the desired amount in the box to the right.

NOTE: You can restore the worksheet to its original format by selecting **Filter** and clicking on **Clear**. Therefore, it is not necessary to copy the data you are filtering to a new worksheet although it is advisable such that you are sure that you do not permanently alter the original format in any way.

MACROS

When preparing spreadsheets or workpapers, it is typical to add the name of the preparer and the date prepared to the work product. However, this is a repetitious task that can be automated through the use of macros. Excel macros are written in a programming language called Visual Basic for Applications (or VBA), which is a shorter version of the popular Visual Basic programming language.

There are two ways to create macros in Excel. The first is to learn VBA and write them in code. However, learning VBA takes a great deal of time and is outside the scope of this book. Fortunately, there is a much simpler way to create macros using an Excel tool called the **macro recorder**. This tool functions in much the same way as a tape recorder, recording each keystroke that you make once you turn the recorder on and continues recording until you turn the recorder off. You can then 'play back' the macro and it will repeat those keystrokes.

Requirements

1. Open the **CA Computerized Excel Workbook** file and click on the **Ratio Analysis** worksheet. Move to cell **A2**.

2. Select **Macros > Record Macro** under the **Macros** section of the **View** tab (*Figure 17*).

Figure 17

3. Type "**PreparerInfo**" in the **Macro name** section (*Figure 18*). Click **OK**.

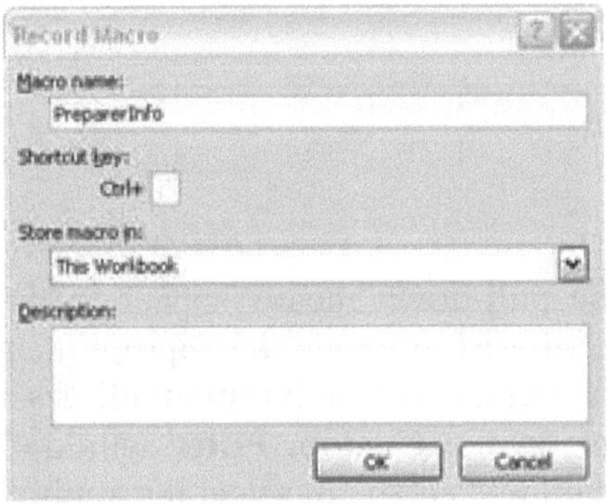

Figure 18

4. Keep in mind that entering preparer information is often an afterthought in the design of a spreadsheet:. Therefore, you will often have to make room for this data. Make sure that row 3 is blank; if it is not, insert a row(s) so that it is. Now begin the macro by highlighting the **3 through 5 simultaneously** in the row number column (using the left mouse button) and then right-click to reach the pull-down menu. Select **Insert** to insert two rows.

5. Move your cursor to **A3**. Type "**Preparer:**".

6. Move your cursor to **B3** and type your name (first and last name).

7. Go to cell **A4** and type "**Date:**".

8. The date that is entered should be entered automatically. This can be accomplished using the **TODAY** function in Excel. Go to cell **B4** and type "**=TODAY()**".

9. Highlight cells **A3** and **A4** and click on the Italics *I* icon in the **Font** section of the **Home** tab.

10. Click on **Macros > Stop Recording** in the **Macros** section of the **View** tab. Note that you might have to widen column B to view the date properly.

11. Save your file at this time. Note that you will get a warning that your file cannot be saved at this time (see *Figure 19*). Click on **No** and select **Excel Macro-Enabled Workbook** under the **Save as type** pull-down menu.

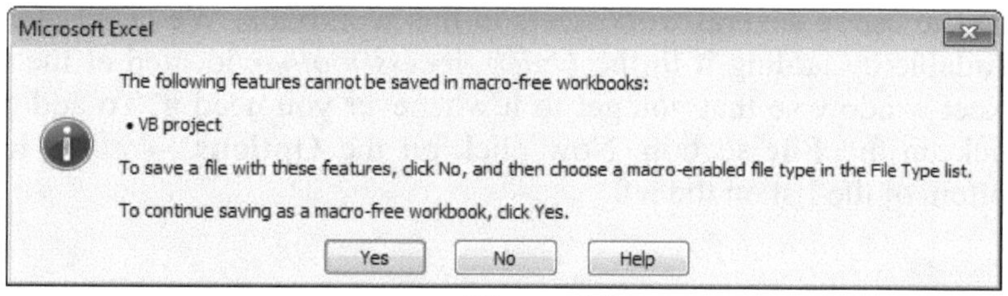

Figure 19

Macros can be a problem for your computer. They are potentially dangerous since they can be programmed to harm your computer. Many viruses and worms are based upon macros. As a result, you should not trust any file that contains macros unless it has been digitally signed or you created it yourself and you know what is in it. Excel files with an .xlsx extension can always be trusted since they are incapable of storing macros. The default setting in *Excel 2016* is to disable all macros with notification. Therefore, despite the fact that you saved the file as an **Excel Macro-Enabled Workbook**, the macros will be disabled before the file is opened again.

12. Open the file at this time. Note the Security Warning message under the Toolbar.

Figure 20

However, since this is a macro that you created and that you might want to use in several worksheets, you will want to click on **Enable Content**. You will also need to click **Yes** on the Security Warning window that pops up.

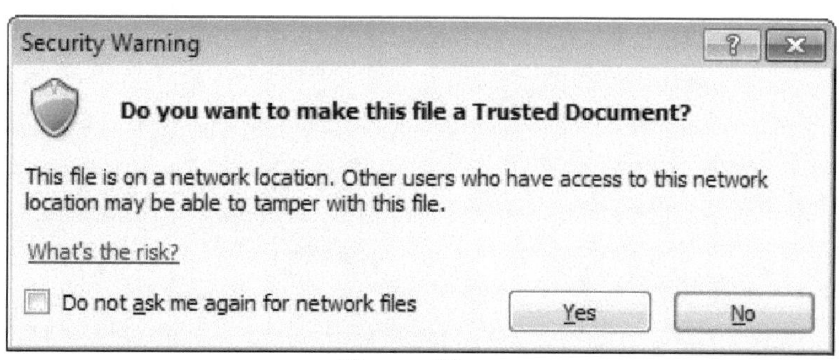

Figure 21

One way to get around this warning is to create a 'Trusted Files' folder on your computer. Then, in Excel, click on **File**, the click on **Options**, and finally click on **Trust Center**. Once in the **Trust Center** option, you can dlick on **Trust Center Settings > Trusted Locations > Add new location > Browse** and search your computer for the folder you set up. Once found, click the **OK** button three times to accept the location and close the dialog windows. Now any files saved in the 'Trusted Files' folder will be saved with their macros enabled and you won't have to deal with warnings.

13. As we said, the macro you created in the previous steps is one that you might want to use in several worksheets in this workbook. We can make it readily available by adding it to the *Quick Access toolbar* located at the top of the Excel window so that you get to it whenever you need it. To add the macro, click on the **File** section. Now click on the **Options** 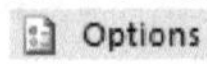

icon at the bottom of the list on the left.

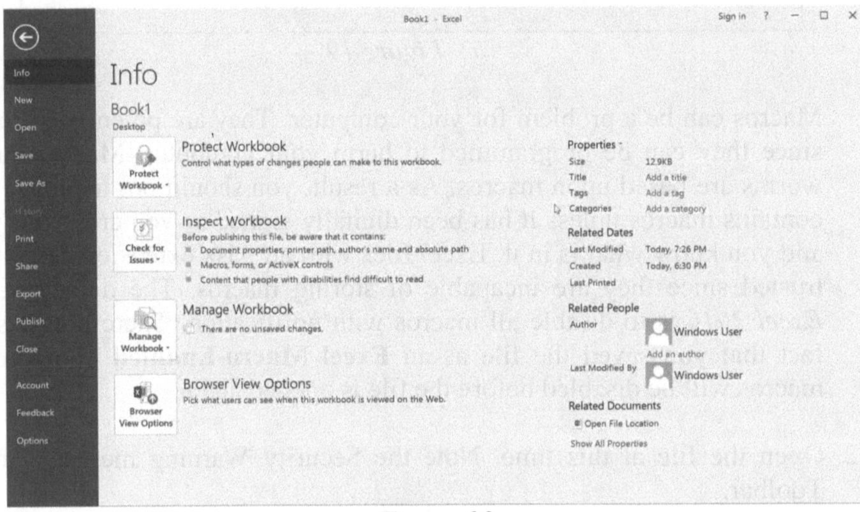

Figure 22

14. On the left-hand side of the Options window, click on the **Quick Access Toolbar** 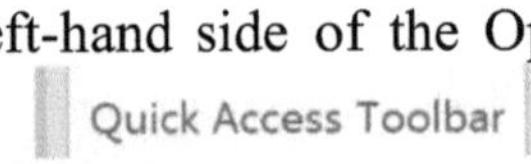

icon. The **Quick Access Toolbar** 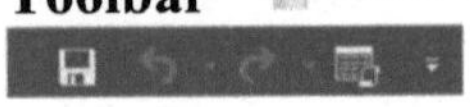 is the toolbar in the upper left corner of the Excel window.

15. Select **View Macros** from the **Choose commands from:** pull-down menu (*Figure 23*).

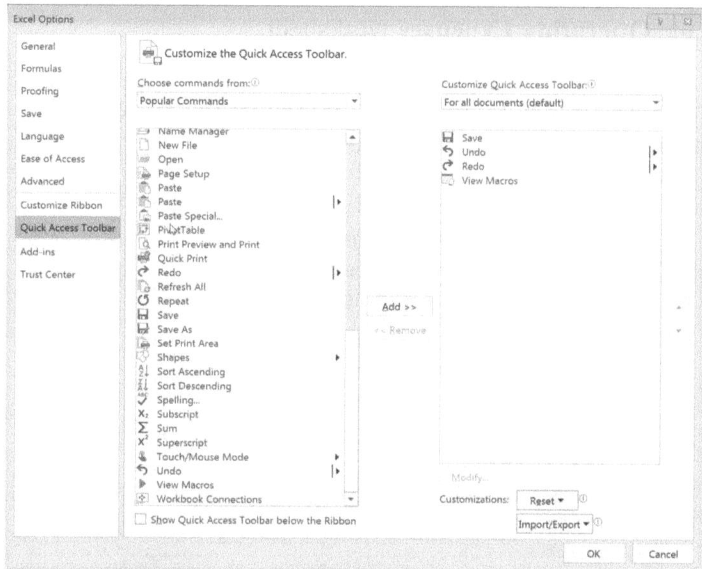

Figure 23

16. The **Quick Access Toolbar** now includes the **View Macro** icon . Click on this icon and you will find the **PreparerInfo** macro you have just created. This provides you with the ability to run this macro on any worksheet in your workbook.

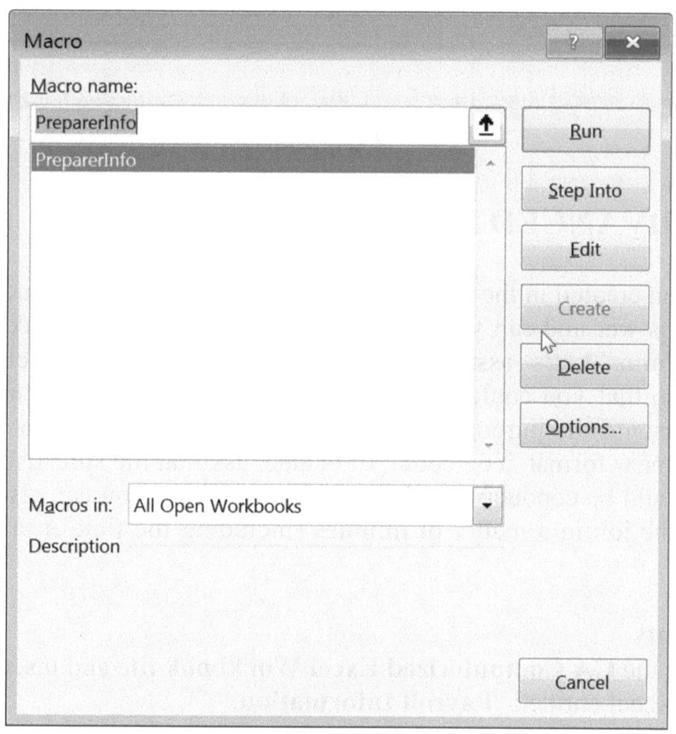

Figure 24

Now you can try out your newly created macro on another worksheet.

17. Select the **Operating Expenses** worksheet.

18. Move to cell **A3**. Click on the newly created macro icon . The preparer information is now inserted (*Figure 25*).

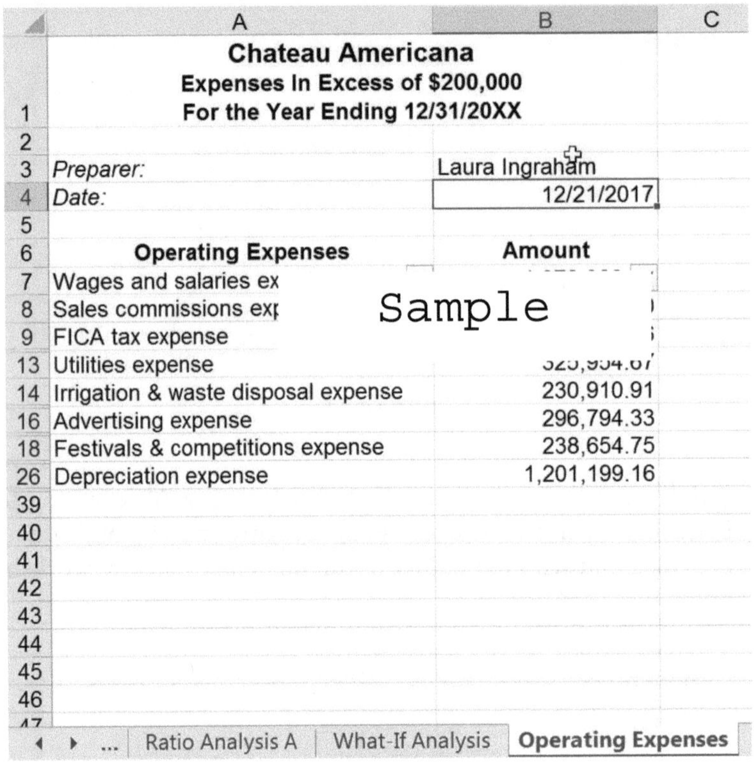

Figure 25

MORE ADVANCED MACROS

The macro you created in the previous section was a very simple one. Macros have a great deal of power and can simplify tasks that would otherwise take a great deal of time to perform. Let's assume that you asked the Payroll clerk for payroll information so that you could create a Master Payroll file. Unfortunately, the clerk did not understand the purpose of the request and the information was provided to you in a columnar format. You could, of course, ask that the spreadsheet be redone in the format would be conducive to your ultimate goal but you can also create a macro that will do the job in a matter of minutes (including the time it takes to create the macro).

Requirements

1. Open the **CA Computerized Excel Workbook** file and insert a new worksheet entitled "**Payroll Information.**"

2. Beginning in cell **A1** and continuing on down in column **A**, enter the Social Security Number, Employee Name, Pay Type and Regular Pay Rate. In cell **A5** (and for each subsequent employee), you will need to calculate Federal Income Tax Withheld based upon each employee's filing status and number of allowances. All of the necessary information has been provided for you in the table below.

Social Security Number	Employee Name	Pay Type	Regular Pay Rate	Filing Status	FIT W/H Allowance
124-11-7755	Rodriguez, José G.	Salaried	3500.00	Married	4
296-49-3438	Johnson, Anna C.	Salaried	1800.00	Married	3
349-43-6417	Hissom, Robert T.	Hourly	15.75	Single	0
014-39-4215	Bryan, Thomas P.	Hourly	17.50	Single	1

NOTE: The employee ID is the employee's social security number. The pay type is "S" for salaried employees or "H" for hourly employees. The FIT withholding should be the amount of federal income tax withheld for the pay period ending December 31, 20XX. If you have already completed the *Manual AIS Module*, you can refer to the Payroll Subsidiary Ledger in the *Manual AIS Module* for the withholding information. If you have not, you will need to determine the proper amount of federal income tax withheld for each employee by using the Percentage Method. You can simply look at the withholdings in the (**HINT:** You can find this information in Publication 15 from the IRS publications website. This form is also entitled "Circular E, Employer's Tax Guide.)

3. Insert a new row 1 into the worksheet. Click on cell **A1** and type "**ID**". Move cell to the right and type "**EMPLOYEE NAME**". Move one cell to the right and type "**PAY TYPE**". Move one cell to the right and type "**REGULAR PAY RATE**". Move one more cell to the right and type "**FIT W/H**".

4. Format the column widths so that column A is 11.86; column B is 18.43; column C is 7.29; column D is 9.43; and column E is 8.43.

5. Right click on row 1 and click on **Format Cells** in the pull-down menu. Click on the **Alignment** tab and select **Wrap text** under the **Text Control** section. Click **OK**. While the row is still highlighted, click on **Bold** in the **Home** section to bold the column headings you just created. Finally, click on **Center** to center these headings.

	A	B	C	D	E	F
1	ID	Employee Name	Pay Type	Regular Pay Rate	FIT W/H	
2	124-11-7755					
3	Jose G. Rodriguez					
4	S					
5	3500					
6	330.82					
7						
8						
9	296-49-3438					
10	Anna C. Johnson					
11	S					
12	1800					
13	101.14					
14						
15						
16	349-43-6417					
17	Robert T. Hissom					
18	H					
19	15.75					
20	193					
21						
22						
23	014-39-4215					
24	[illegible]					

Figure 26

6. When recording macros, Excel defaults to 'absolute referencing' of the cells. In other words, it records the cell you start in and will always default to that cell. Because of the format of this sheet, we will need to use relative referencing in our macro so that our payroll information for subsequent employees is not pasted again and again into the first cell of the first row. We can do this by telling the macro that we are using relative referencing when we set it up.

   Click on the **View** section and click on the **Macros** icon. Then select **Use Relative References**. Click on the **Macros** icon once more and select **Record Macro**. Name the macro **'MasterPayroll'**.

7. We will also set up a shortcut that will allow us to call up this macro with a click of the keyboard, rather than having to utilize the menu. Enter **p** in the **Shortcut key** box.

8. You can also provide a description for the macro to help subsequent users understand what the macro does. In this case, the description should read: 'This macro will take the columnar payroll information and create a Master Payroll table.' Click **OK**.

9. In our prior exercise we want cell **A3** to be the active cell and you were instructed to make sure that row 3 was blank and you were given instructions to insert a row if it was not. If you had to insert a row, those steps were recorded by the Macro Recorder in the **PreparerInfo** macro.

   In this exercise, we want to begin with cell **A1** as the active cell.

10. Right-click on cell **A3** and select **Cut**. Right-click on cell **B2** and select **Paste**. Continue this for the remaining information for the first employee (i.e., right-click on **A4** and cut, right-click on **C2** and paste, etc.)

11. Highlight rows 3 through 8. Right-click on the selected rows and select **Delete** from the pull-down menu.

12. Click in cell **A3**. This is now the active cell. Since this macro needs to be run for all employees, making cell **A3** puts the cursor in the correct position to convert the remaining employee information.

13. Click on the **View** section once more. Now click on **Macros** and select **Stop Recording**. We now have the macro set up for multiple usage.

14. While still in cell **A3**, hold down the **Control (Ctrl) key** and press **p**. You should now see the second employee's payroll information and the cursor should now be in cell **A4** (the new active cell).

15. Repeat step 13 for the two remaining employees.

16. Highlight columns D and F and select **Format Cells**. Click on **Number**, make sure that the **Decimal places** is set to 2 and click **OK**.

17. Rename the worksheet **Payroll Master File**.

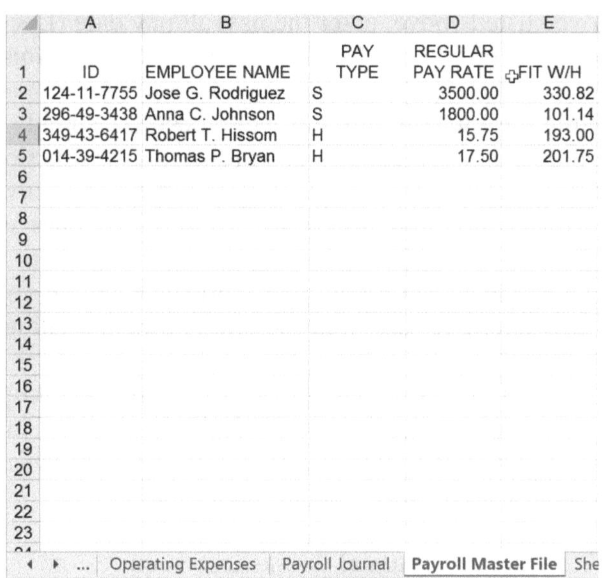

	A	B	C	D	E
1	ID	EMPLOYEE NAME	PAY TYPE	REGULAR PAY RATE	FIT W/H
2	124-11-7755	Jose G. Rodriguez	S	3500.00	330.82
3	296-49-3438	Anna C. Johnson	S	1800.00	101.14
4	349-43-6417	Robert T. Hissom	H	15.75	193.00
5	014-39-4215	Thomas P. Bryan	H	17.50	201.75

Figure 27

DATABASE FUNCTIONS

One of the benefits of a database is the reduction or elimination of data redundancy, which in turn, reduces or eliminates data inconsistency. As we stated earlier, this is one of the reasons you have been instructed to use formulas whenever possible. Excel contains a variety of functions that allow you to query or search for data in the worksheets. **VLOOKUP** is one of these Excel functions. **VLOOKUP** searches for a value that is located in the first column of a table array and, based upon the criteria requested, returns a value in the same row from another column in that table array. As a result, there is no need to reenter the data in a new worksheet. For example, you can enter employee data into a master payroll file and then pull that data into a payroll journal.

Requirements

1. Open the **CA Computerized Excel Workbook** file and insert a new worksheet. Name the new worksheet **"Payroll Master File"**.

2. The **Payroll Master File** worksheet will be used as a database for the **Payroll Journal** worksheet provided for you in the **CA Computerized Excel Workbook** file. To accomplish this, you must designate an array for the database (i.e., create a range name). To do this, highlight cells **A2:E5** and designate the range name (i.e., the table array) as **Payroll_Master**.

3. Click on the **Payroll Journal** worksheet provided for you in your file. For each employee listed above, enter the payroll pay date (December 31, 20XX) and employee ID in cells **A3** through **B6** on the **Payroll Journal** worksheet.

   NOTE: While the **Payroll Journal** worksheet has already been created and formatted, it does not contain any data, formulas, or functions. ***However, the worksheet does contain various cell names that you must use in creating the required formulas and functions***. These cell names were saved in the worksheet before you received it. Take some time now to acquaint yourself with all the cell names that are in your worksheet so that you will be familiar with what is available for use in this portion of the assignment.

4. Click on **Formulas** tab and pull down the **Lookup & Reference** Lookup & Reference ▾ menu. Use the **VLOOKUP** function ⌘ in cells **C3** and **D3** in the **Payroll Journal** worksheet to return the employee's name and pay type to these cells.

   NOTE: The **Payroll Journal** worksheet requires no entry for salaried employees in columns **E** or **H**. However, both Thomas Bryan and Robert Hissom worked 96 hours of regular time and Thomas worked 2.25 hours of overtime.

5. Use the **VLOOKUP** function to return the pay rate in cell **F3** in the **Payroll Journal** worksheet.

6. In the **Payroll Journal** worksheet, create formulas to calculate the regular pay and overtime pay for cells **G3** and **I3**, respectively. **HINT:** Keep in mind that you are trying to create a Payroll Journal that will calculate the payroll for both salaried and hourly individuals based upon formulas. Therefore, we must create a formula (i.e., an **IF** statement) that will calculate pay for an employee regardless of their pay type. This formula should accommodate salaried employees whether or not they have entries for the number of hours worked. Otherwise, it would be easy for someone to commit fraud by, for example, paying a salaried individual overtime.

7. In the **Payroll Journal** worksheet, create formulas in cells **J3** and **K3** to calculate gross pay and FICA, respectively. Recall that Medicare is 1.45% of gross pay and Social Security is 6.2% of gross pay. Together, the deduction for FICA is 7.65%.

8. Use the **VLOOKUP** function in cell **L3** in the **Payroll Journal** worksheet to return the amount of federal income tax to be withheld.

9. In the **Payroll Journal** worksheet, create a formula in cell **M3** to calculate net pay and enter the appropriate check number in cell **N3** beginning with check number **7111**.

10. For internal control purposes, a formula should also be created in cell **N4** in the **Payroll Journal** worksheet as a sequential number check for the check number (i.e., "=**N3** +1").

11. To facilitate the entry of payroll data for any other employees, you will need to copy the formulas and functions you created. For this assignment, you only need to copy them into the next 3 rows.

12. Note that the final column is reserved for the Subsidiary Journal Posting Reference. You do not need to enter anything in this column for this exercise. However, if you were completing the posting of this data to the payroll subsidiary ledgers, you would fill in this column.

Database Functions Tutorial

VLOOKUP function. The VLOOKUP function in EXCEL searches a previously defined database (i.e., array designated by an appropriate range name) for a specified value and returns a desired field (i.e., a data value) from that database. The syntax for the VLOOKUP function is

=VLOOKUP(lookup_value,table_array,col_index_num,range_lookup)

where

lookup_value names the value to that you want to search for that is located in the first column of the table array. The **lookup_value** is typically a value that is unique to each row of data. For example, in a customer database, the **lookup_value** might be the Customer ID number. Therefore, in an employee database, the **lookup_value** would be the Employee ID number.

table_array contains two or more columns of data. It provides the name of the database that stores the data you want to bring into the current worksheet.

col_index_num specifies the number of the column in the database in which the desired data value is located. For example, if the data value is located in column C, column C is the third column and, therefore, the col_index_num would be 3. (NOTE: you must count the columns beginning with A=1, etc., and enter the appropriate column number).

range_lookup is a logical value specifying whether or not you want an exact match; FALSE indicates an exact match must be returned; TRUE indicates that an approximate match may be returned.

INTRODUCTION TO PIVOTTABLE REPORTS

Budgeting is a critical managerial accounting tool and Excel has a variety of tools that make it very easy to work with large bodies of data for budgeting purposes.

You have been asked to prepare Chateau Americana's budget for next year. Obviously, Excel can be used to assist in the preparation of the budget. You can set up a worksheet providing columns for the accounts, year, month, and amount. You can further break down the accounts by providing columns for type, code, and titles. You can also provide columns for departments and cost centers. And, lastly, you can provide a column that provides explanations for any months in which there are amounts that are out of the ordinary. Such a worksheet, entitled "**Master Budget**" has been prepared for you in the **CA Computerized Excel Workbook** workbook.

If all the data for the budget for an entire company is entered into one worksheet, you could easily end up with hundreds, if not thousands of rows of data; in other words, a worksheet that has become so large that working with the data has become slow, unwieldy and impractical. It becomes difficult to find the data you are looking for quickly and analyses on the data are slow and cumbersome. Fortunately, as we have discussed, Excel has powerful data analysis capabilities and we can employ these tools on large worksheets through the use of a PivotTable Report.

A PivotTable Report is an interactive table that enables you to quickly sift through and summarize large amounts of data. You can rotate rows and columns to see different summaries of the source data, filter the data by displaying different pages, or display details for certain areas of interest. You can do all this without writing a single formula or copying a single cell. In addition, these PivotTables are dynamic. In other words, once you have created them, you can rearrange the table so that it summarizes the data based on another grouping. For example, if you create a PivotTable for sales broken down by each quarter, you can then rearrange the data so that it focuses on sales by product, by salesperson, or by territory.

Before creating a PivotTable, you must prepare the data source. An excerpt from the Chateau Americana budget has been provided for you. You will find it on the "**Master Budget**" worksheet contained in the **CA Computerized Excel Workbook** file. Certain assumptions have been made and constraints have been imposed to facilitate your handling of the budget and the PivotTable, as detailed below.

The budget is for the entire year but contains only selected accounts. For purposes of this assignment, only three departments have been selected and the number of employees per department has been limited, as follows:

Administration (Edward and Rob)
Marketing (Taylor, Daniel and Cameron)
Operations (Jacques and Sam)

Review the **Master Budget** worksheet. Notice that the worksheet has the following headings: **ACCT_TYPE**, **ACCT_CODE**, **ACCT_TITLE**, **DEPT**, **COST_CENTER**, **YR**, **MON**, **BUDGET**, **EXPLANATIONS**. These represent the fields that you will use to create the PivotTable.

Requirements

1. Open the **CA Computerized Excel Workbook** file and click on the **Master Budget** worksheet. Be sure that the cursor is placed somewhere in the data on the worksheet. From the **Tables** section of the **Insert** tab, click on **PivotTable > PivotTable**.

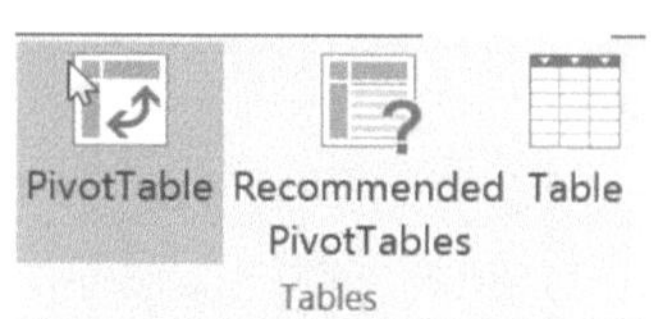

Figure 28

2. The Create PivotTable window (*Figure 29*) appears.

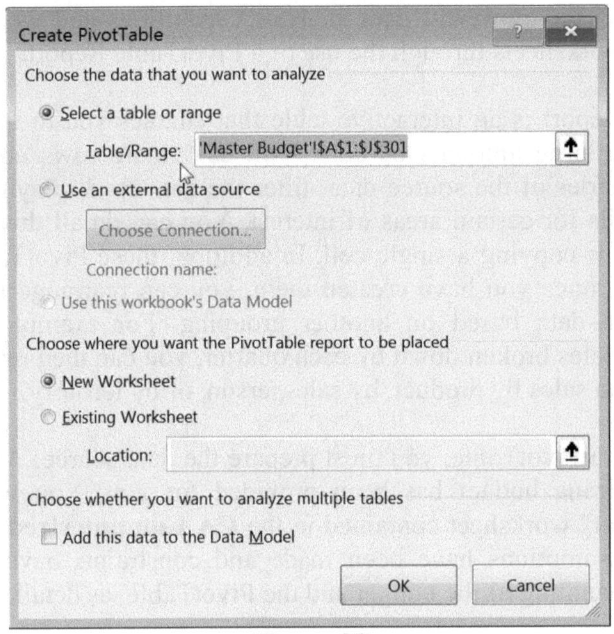

Figure 29

Be sure that the entire master budget has been selected (the range should be **A1** to **I301**). Also be sure that the radio button for "New worksheet" is selected. Click on **OK**.

3. Notice that Excel has generated (and moved you to) a new worksheet to create the PivotTable. You should see a **PivotTable1** table and a **PivotTable Field List** window that contains the column headings from your **Master Budget** spreadsheet (see *Figure 30*).

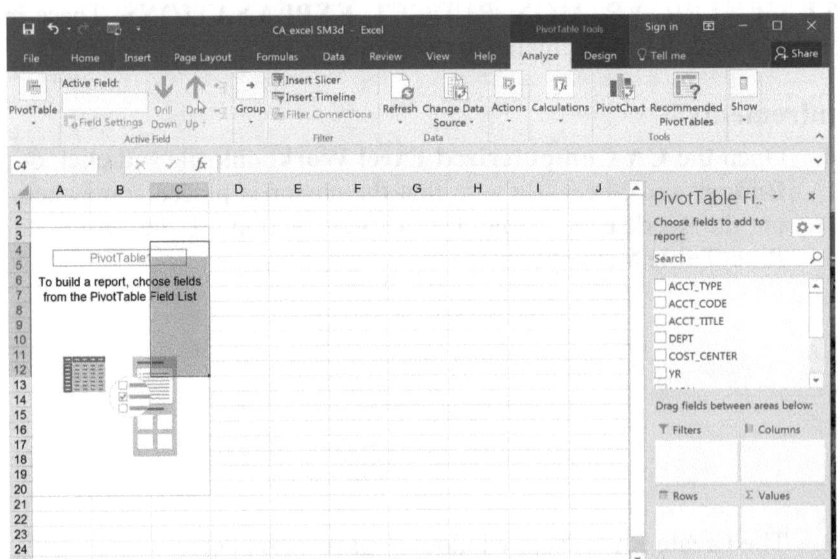

Figure 30

Drag the **ACCT_CODE** into the **Row Labels** area located in the lower left hand side of the **PivotTable Field List** window. Notice that the Account Codes are now listed in **Column A**.

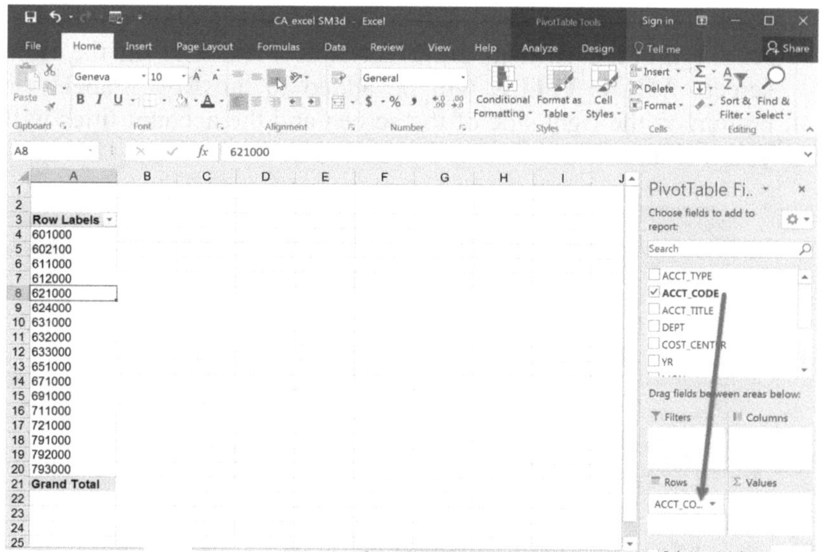

Figure 31

4. Now drag the **BUDGET** into the **Σ Values** area. Notice that the sums of the various account codes are now totaled in **Column B** and that the label for **BUDGET** has now changed "**Sum of BUDGET**." The **Grand Total** at the bottom of the sheet should be $4,321,018. Excel has now generated a PivotTable that summarizes the master budget by GL code.

5. Notice that the **Master Budget** worksheet is still intact. Now rename the new worksheet "**Pivot**".

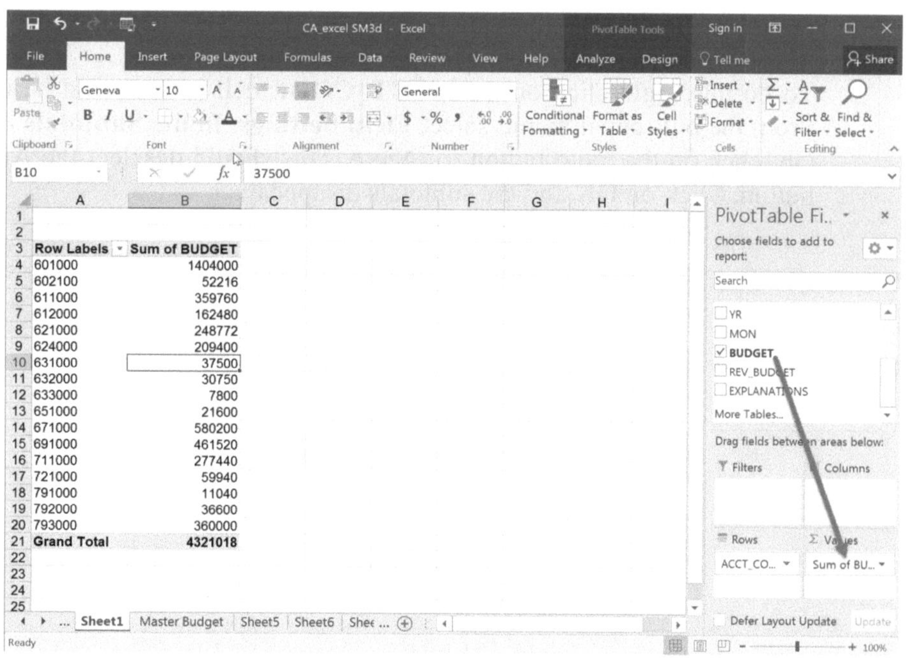

Figure 32

6. General ledger codes do not provide much information without the account titles. To add the general ledger account titles, click on the box next to the **ACCT_TITLE** field in the PivotTable Field List on the right side of the screen. **ACCT_TITLE** will be added to the Row Labels window at the bottom on the right side of the screen and the account titles will be added to your PivotTable.

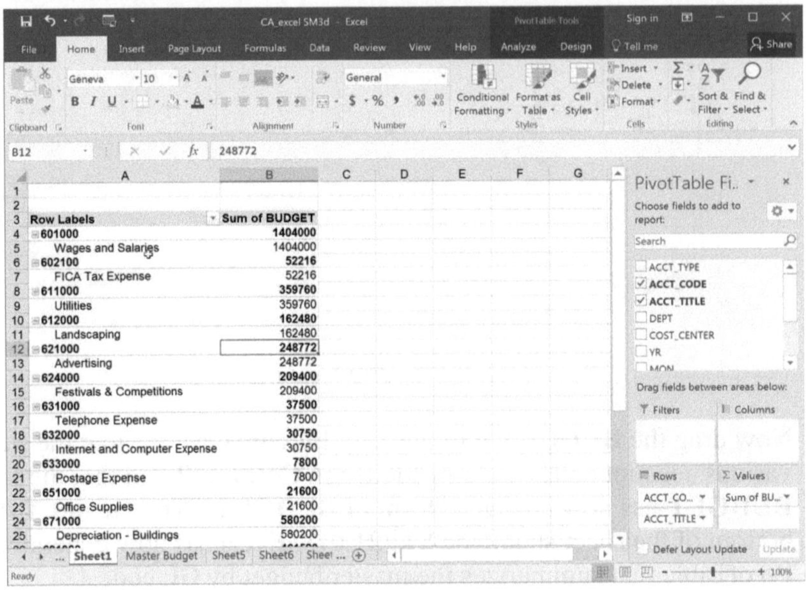

Figure 33

7. Note that the general ledger codes, descriptions and their totals are now in the PivotTable. This contains much more detail than we need in the budget. For example, the total lines are repetitious and should be removed.

   To do this, right-click on the **ACCT_CODE** cell (this should be Cell **A4**). From the pull-down menu, select **Field Settings**. In the **Subtotals & Filters** tab, click on the radio button for **None.** This should deselect the **Automatic** button. Click on **OK** and the subtotals disappear.

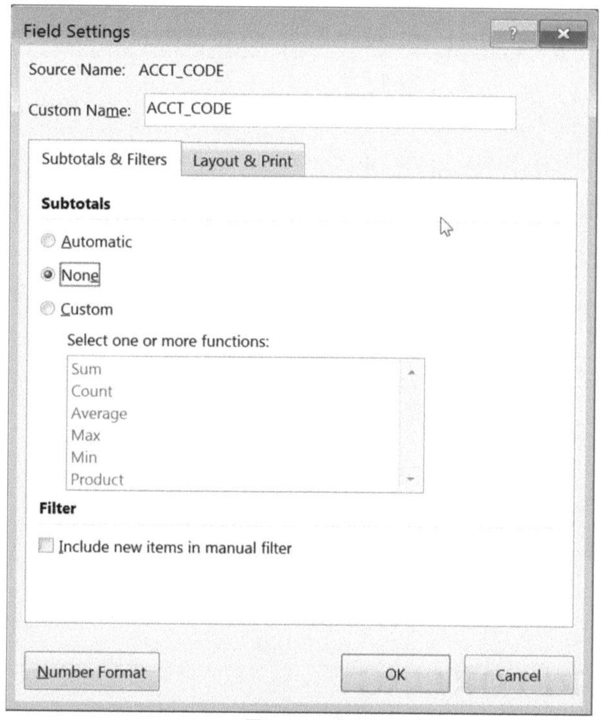

Figure 34

8. To provide managers with more detailed budget information, the time periods should be added to the PivotTable. Click anywhere within the PivotTable. Select **MON**. Again, notice that it automatically drops into the **Row Labels**. This is not particularly useful for analyzing the data. It would be preferable to have the months appear as Column labels. Drag **MON** into the **Column Labels** area. The PivotTable should now break down the GL account totals by month.

9. Now add **ACCT_TYPE** to the list of **Row Labels**. In terms of hierarchy, **ACCT_TYPE** should come before **ACCT_CODE**. However, when it is added, it appears below **ACCT_TITLE**. Click on the pull-down menu for **ACCT_TYPE** and click on **Move to Beginning**. The **Row Labels** window now contains **ACCT_TYPE**, **ACCT_CODE** and **ACCT_TITLE**. The PivotTable should now be divided into "**601 – Salaries**", "**602 – Payroll Taxes**," "**610 – Occupancy**," etc, each with a total.

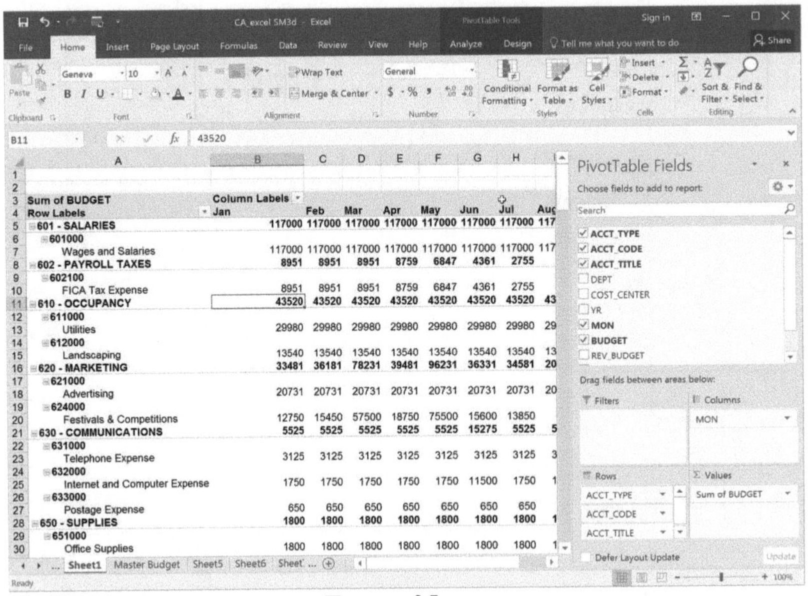

Figure 35

DETAIL IN REPORTING

The PivotTable allows the user to query or "drilldown" into a particular value in the PivotTable report to examine that item more closely. This provides a great deal of power and flexibility to the PivotTable report, whether the report is for budgeting applications, reporting monthly costs to department managers, or for reporting the results of sales to territory managers. The user can query a balance to view any of the underlying detail by simply double clicking on the entry in question.

The CFO has asked you to identify any unusual items in the budgeted amounts and report them to him. A quick review of the budget reveals *two months* under **Festivals and Competitions** and *one month* under **Internet and Computer** that appear to have higher than usual amounts of expenditures, when compared to other months.

Requirements

1. Open the **CA Computerized Excel Workbook** file and click on the **Pivot** worksheet. To determine what has caused this spike in costs, query one of the amounts in question by double clicking on an amount in question. A new worksheet appears that provides all the detail for the amount queried (*Figure 36*).

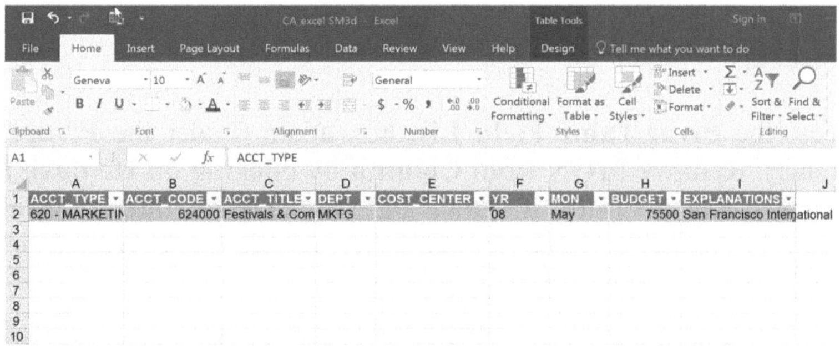

Figure 36

2. Return to the **Pivot** worksheet. Drill down on each of the other amounts to investigate the nature of their variance in cost.

   Return to the **Pivot** worksheet again. There may be occasions when you would want to limit other users' abilities to drill down into the data, particularly if the costs deal with payroll. This is done by right-clicking anywhere in the PivotTable report, selecting **PivotTable Options** from the shortcut menu, clicking on the **Data** tab, and deselecting the **Enable show details** box.

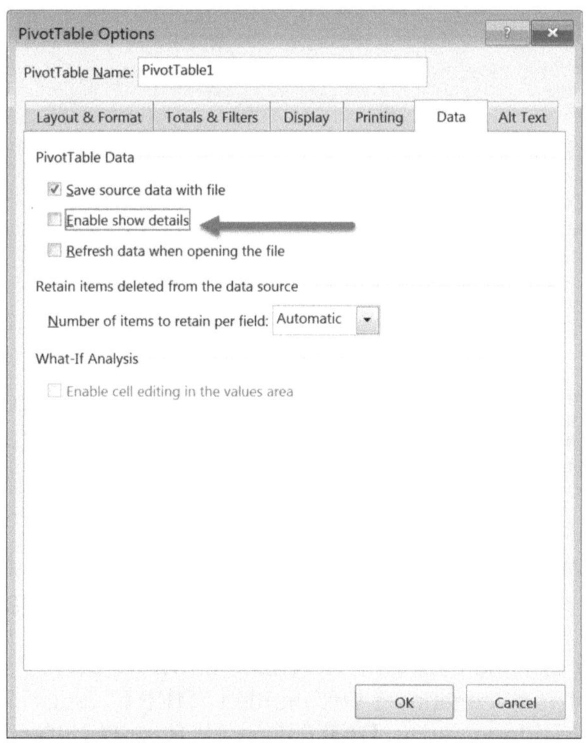

Figure 37

3. As you have seen, the PivotTable can be used to display only the data of interest. You might, for example, want to view the data for a particular department rather than for all departments or view data by cost centers. Either of these views can be obtained by dropping a particular field of interest in the **Column** area of the PivotTable or by filtering the entire

PivotTable report to display data for a single item or all the items, using the **Page** field.

Access the **Pivot Table Field List** box again (under the **PivotTable Tools** Toolbar). Remove **MON** from **Column** by clicking on **Remove Field** in the pull-down menu beside it. Drag and drop **DEPT** into the **Column** area. Notice that the departmental totals for the Administrative, Marketing, and Operations departments now appear.

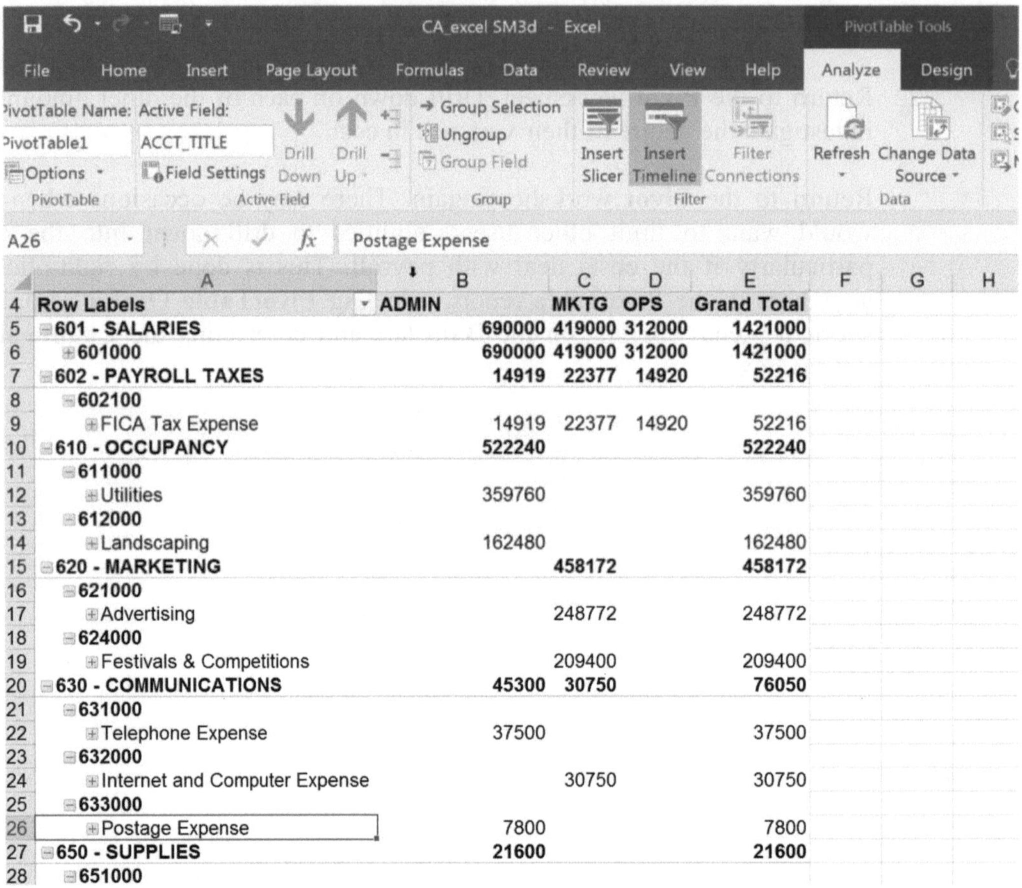

Row Labels	ADMIN	MKTG	OPS	Grand Total
601 - SALARIES	690000	419000	312000	1421000
601000	690000	419000	312000	1421000
602 - PAYROLL TAXES	14919	22377	14920	52216
602100				
FICA Tax Expense	14919	22377	14920	52216
610 - OCCUPANCY	522240			522240
611000				
Utilities	359760			359760
612000				
Landscaping	162480			162480
620 - MARKETING		458172		458172
621000				
Advertising		248772		248772
624000				
Festivals & Competitions		209400		209400
630 - COMMUNICATIONS	45300	30750		76050
631000				
Telephone Expense	37500			37500
632000				
Internet and Computer Expense		30750		30750
633000				
Postage Expense	7800			7800
650 - SUPPLIES	21600			21600
651000				

Figure 38

4. You can also view the data by department and month by using the **Report Filter** area in the lower right area of the screen. Drag **DEPT** to the **Report Filter** area and drop it. Drag and drop **MON** back into the **Column** area. Notice that the data is now broken down by period again. Notice also that cell **A1** now contains a box entitled "**DEPT**" and cell **B1** says, "**(All)**" and has a pull-down menu. **DEPT** is now a **Report Filter** field. It allows the user to see the information for the entire organization or by department (see *Figure 39*).

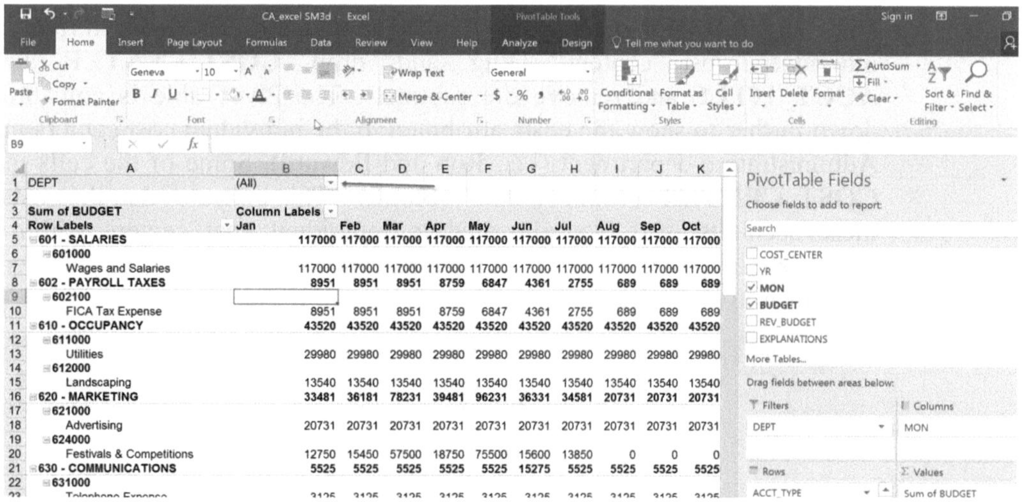

DEPT	(All)									
Sum of BUDGET	Column Labels									
Row Labels	Jan	Feb	Mar	Apr	May	Jun	Jul	Aug	Sep	Oct
601 - SALARIES	**117000**	**117000**	**117000**	**117000**	**117000**	**117000**	**117000**	**117000**	**117000**	**117000**
601000										
Wages and Salaries	117000	117000	117000	117000	117000	117000	117000	117000	117000	117000
602 - PAYROLL TAXES	**8951**	**8951**	**8951**	**8759**	**6847**	**4361**	**2755**	**689**	**689**	**689**
602100										
FICA Tax Expense	8951	8951	8951	8759	6847	4361	2755	689	689	689
610 - OCCUPANCY	**43520**	**43520**	**43520**	**43520**	**43520**	**43520**	**43520**	**43520**	**43520**	**43520**
611000										
Utilities	29980	29980	29980	29980	29980	29980	29980	29980	29980	29980
612000										
Landscaping	13540	13540	13540	13540	13540	13540	13540	13540	13540	13540
620 - MARKETING	**33481**	**36181**	**78231**	**39481**	**96231**	**36331**	**34581**	**20731**	**20731**	**20731**
621000										
Advertising	20731	20731	20731	20731	20731	20731	20731	20731	20731	20731
624000										
Festivals & Competitions	12750	15450	57500	18750	75500	15600	13850	0	0	0
630 - COMMUNICATIONS	**5525**	**5525**	**5525**	**5525**	**5525**	**15275**	**5525**	**5525**	**5525**	**5525**
631000										

Figure 39

5. Click on the down arrow in the right of cell **B1** and notice that, in addition to **(All)**, the choices **ADMIN**, **MKTG**, and **OPS** appear. Click on **ADMIN** and click **OK**. The PivotTable now shows the costs for the Administrative department.

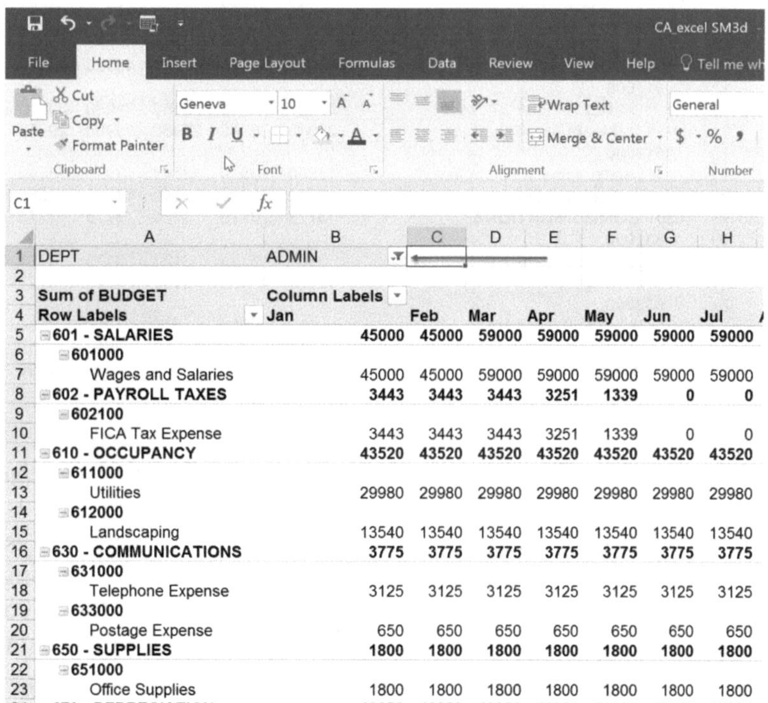

DEPT	ADMIN						
Sum of BUDGET	Column Labels						
Row Labels	Jan	Feb	Mar	Apr	May	Jun	Jul
601 - SALARIES	**45000**	**45000**	**59000**	**59000**	**59000**	**59000**	**59000**
601000							
Wages and Salaries	45000	45000	59000	59000	59000	59000	59000
602 - PAYROLL TAXES	**3443**	**3443**	**3443**	**3251**	**1339**	**0**	**0**
602100							
FICA Tax Expense	3443	3443	3443	3251	1339	0	0
610 - OCCUPANCY	**43520**	**43520**	**43520**	**43520**	**43520**	**43520**	**43520**
611000							
Utilities	29980	29980	29980	29980	29980	29980	29980
612000							
Landscaping	13540	13540	13540	13540	13540	13540	13540
630 - COMMUNICATIONS	**3775**	**3775**	**3775**	**3775**	**3775**	**3775**	**3775**
631000							
Telephone Expense	3125	3125	3125	3125	3125	3125	3125
633000							
Postage Expense	650	650	650	650	650	650	650
650 - SUPPLIES	**1800**	**1800**	**1800**	**1800**	**1800**	**1800**	**1800**
651000							
Office Supplies	1800	1800	1800	1800	1800	1800	1800

Figure 40

You can click on the pull-down arrow again to look at the budgets for the Marketing department and for Operations. Note that the **(All)** option allows you to view the company totals.

6. View the **ADMIN** data again. This data can broken down further into individual cost centers. Drag and drop **COST_CENTER** below **ACCT_TITLE** and remove the subtotals. The PivotTable is now broken down further to show the costs attributed to the individual cost centers in the Administrative department (i.e., Rob and Edward). Some of the cells in the **COST_CENTER** column contain "**(blank).**" This indicates that the costs for these accounts were not allocated to individual cost centers within the Administrative department, but were allocated instead to the entire Administrative department.

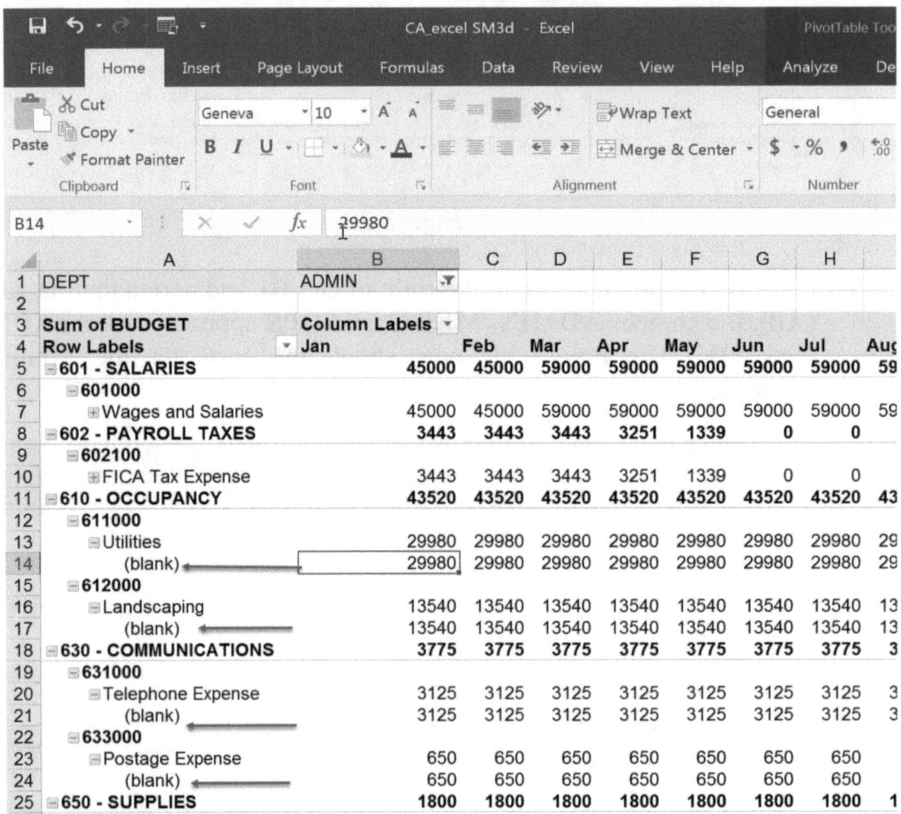

Figure 41

7. As more data is included in a worksheet, the threat of *information overload* or *analysis paralysis* increases. In addition, as more data is included, the PivotTable will likely require more levels to facilitate analysis of the data. However, increasing levels also increases complexity making data analysis more difficult. To address the issue of complexity, the PivotTable can be expanded or collapsed between different levels of detail using the **Expand Field** and **Collapse Field** commands found in the **Active Field** section of the **PivotTable Options** toolbar.

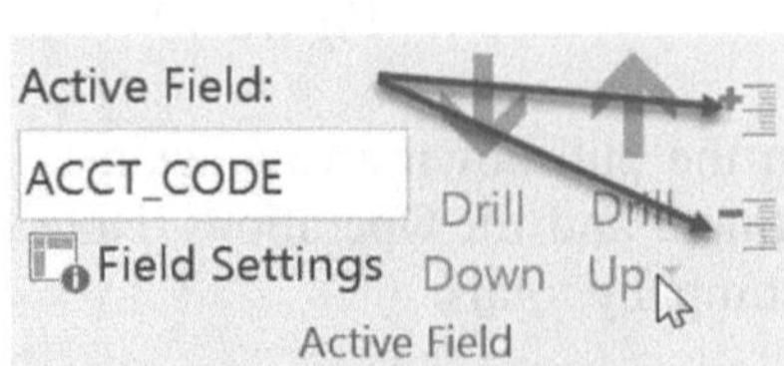

Figure 42

8. Click on cell **B1** and select **(All)** and click **OK**. The entire budget is now displayed.

9. Click on cell **A5** and then check to make sure that **ACCT_TYPE** is the **Active Field** in the **Active Field** section.

10. Select **Collapse Field** in the **Active Field** section of the **PivotTable Tools** toolbar. Only the top level data (i.e., the account types) should now be visible (*Figure 43*).

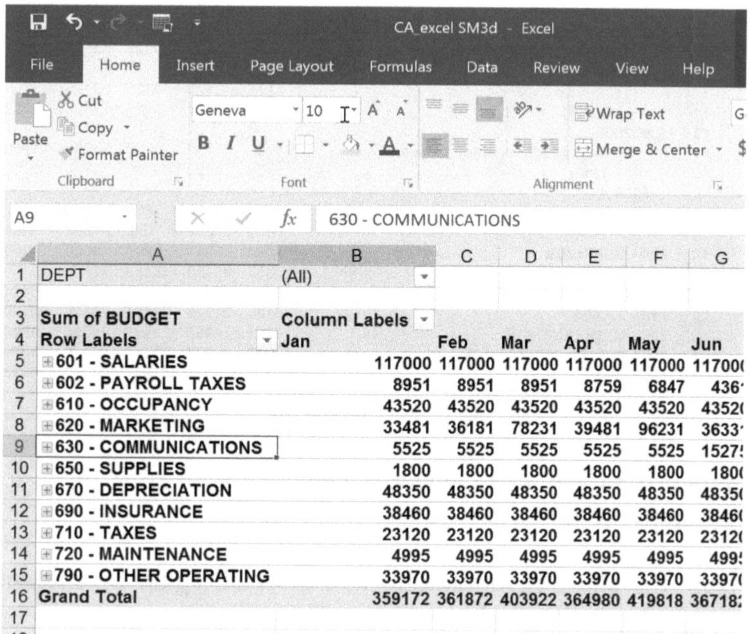

	A	B	C	D	E	F	G
1	DEPT	(All)					
2							
3	Sum of BUDGET	Column Labels					
4	Row Labels	Jan	Feb	Mar	Apr	May	Jun
5	601 - SALARIES	117000	117000	117000	117000	117000	11700(
6	602 - PAYROLL TAXES	8951	8951	8951	8759	6847	436
7	610 - OCCUPANCY	43520	43520	43520	43520	43520	4352(
8	620 - MARKETING	33481	36181	78231	39481	96231	3633
9	630 - COMMUNICATIONS	5525	5525	5525	5525	5525	1527
10	650 - SUPPLIES	1800	1800	1800	1800	1800	180(
11	670 - DEPRECIATION	48350	48350	48350	48350	48350	4835(
12	690 - INSURANCE	38460	38460	38460	38460	38460	3846(
13	710 - TAXES	23120	23120	23120	23120	23120	2312(
14	720 - MAINTENANCE	4995	4995	4995	4995	4995	499
15	790 - OTHER OPERATING	33970	33970	33970	33970	33970	3397(
16	Grand Total	359172	361872	403922	364980	419818	36718
17							
18							

Figure 43

11. The detail can then be expanded for one or more account types. However, if you deselected the drilldown option in step 2 above, you will need to re-enable it before you go on. Show the detail for the costs associated with Communications by clicking on the "+" next to "**630 – Communications**" in column **A**. The Communications detail is now shown down to the **COST_CENTER** level (see *Figure 44*).

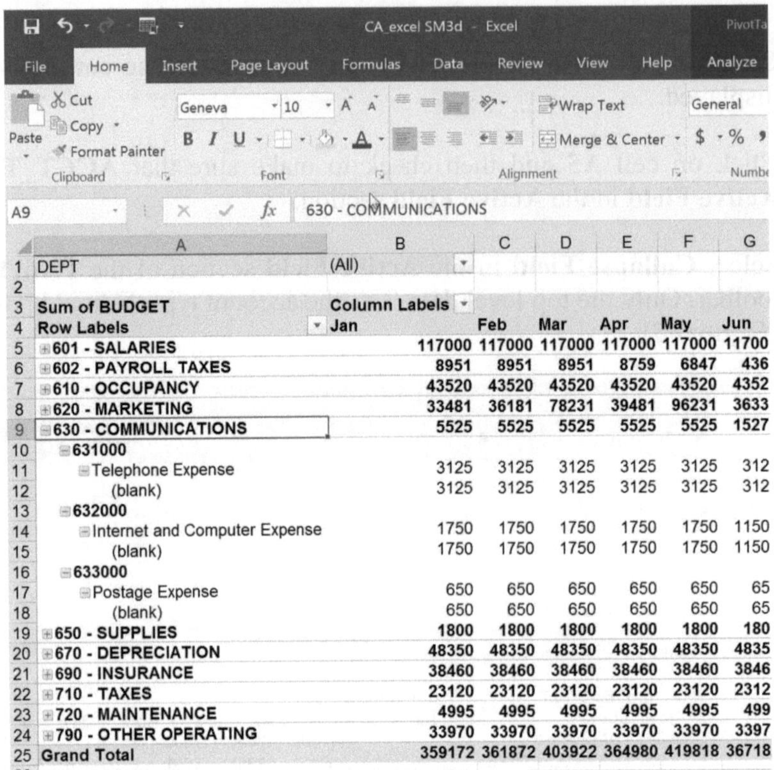

	A	B	C	D	E	F	G
1	DEPT	(All)					
2							
3	**Sum of BUDGET**	**Column Labels**					
4	**Row Labels**	**Jan**	**Feb**	**Mar**	**Apr**	**May**	**Jun**
5	**601 - SALARIES**	**117000**	**117000**	**117000**	**117000**	**117000**	**11700**
6	**602 - PAYROLL TAXES**	**8951**	**8951**	**8951**	**8759**	**6847**	**436**
7	**610 - OCCUPANCY**	**43520**	**43520**	**43520**	**43520**	**43520**	**4352**
8	**620 - MARKETING**	**33481**	**36181**	**78231**	**39481**	**96231**	**3633**
9	**630 - COMMUNICATIONS**	**5525**	**5525**	**5525**	**5525**	**5525**	**1527**
10	**631000**						
11	Telephone Expense	3125	3125	3125	3125	3125	312
12	(blank)	3125	3125	3125	3125	3125	312
13	**632000**						
14	Internet and Computer Expense	1750	1750	1750	1750	1750	1150
15	(blank)	1750	1750	1750	1750	1750	1150
16	**633000**						
17	Postage Expense	650	650	650	650	650	65
18	(blank)	650	650	650	650	650	65
19	**650 - SUPPLIES**	**1800**	**1800**	**1800**	**1800**	**1800**	**180**
20	**670 - DEPRECIATION**	**48350**	**48350**	**48350**	**48350**	**48350**	**4835**
21	**690 - INSURANCE**	**38460**	**38460**	**38460**	**38460**	**38460**	**3846**
22	**710 - TAXES**	**23120**	**23120**	**23120**	**23120**	**23120**	**2312**
23	**720 - MAINTENANCE**	**4995**	**4995**	**4995**	**4995**	**4995**	**499**
24	**790 - OTHER OPERATING**	**33970**	**33970**	**33970**	**33970**	**33970**	**3397**
25	**Grand Total**	**359172**	**361872**	**403922**	**364980**	**419818**	**36718**

Figure 44

12. To return to the more concise view, click the "-" next to the "**630 – Communications**" title.

13. Return the entire PivotTable to its full detail again by clicking on **Expand Field** in the **Active Field** section.

14. It is also sometimes desirable to focus on certain periods in a budget. The PivotTable enables you to hide the detail for some periods while leaving the detail for others showing and simultaneously recalculate the cumulative totals to show totals for just the periods of interest. Look at the data for the second quarter only by pulling down the **Column Labels** menu. Uncheck the **Select All** box and check the boxes for April, May and June and click **OK**. The PivotTable now contains the data only for April, May and June and the cumulative totals for each **ACCT_CODE** have been recalculated to include only the amounts from the second quarter months (see *Figure 45*). Notice also that a filter icon has appeared next to **Column Labels** to indicate that the columns have been filtered.

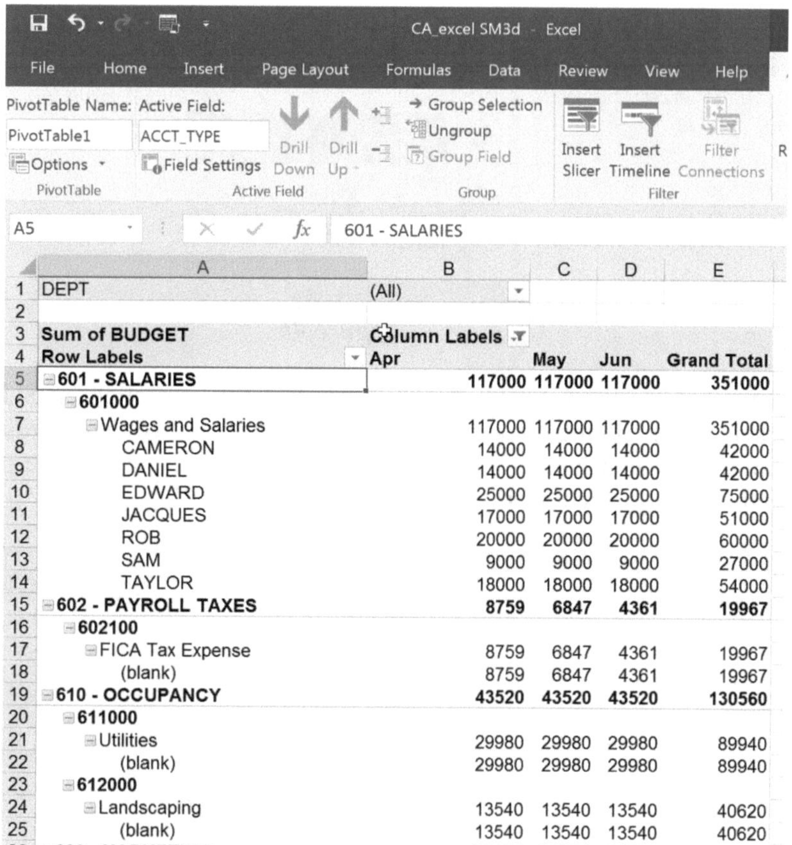

	A	B	C	D	E
1	DEPT	(All)			
2					
3	**Sum of BUDGET**	**Column Labels**			
4	**Row Labels**	**Apr**	**May**	**Jun**	**Grand Total**
5	**601 - SALARIES**	**117000**	**117000**	**117000**	**351000**
6	**601000**				
7	Wages and Salaries	117000	117000	117000	351000
8	CAMERON	14000	14000	14000	42000
9	DANIEL	14000	14000	14000	42000
10	EDWARD	25000	25000	25000	75000
11	JACQUES	17000	17000	17000	51000
12	ROB	20000	20000	20000	60000
13	SAM	9000	9000	9000	27000
14	TAYLOR	18000	18000	18000	54000
15	**602 - PAYROLL TAXES**	**8759**	**6847**	**4361**	**19967**
16	**602100**				
17	FICA Tax Expense	8759	6847	4361	19967
18	(blank)	8759	6847	4361	19967
19	**610 - OCCUPANCY**	**43520**	**43520**	**43520**	**130560**
20	**611000**				
21	Utilities	29980	29980	29980	89940
22	(blank)	29980	29980	29980	89940
23	**612000**				
24	Landscaping	13540	13540	13540	40620
25	(blank)	13540	13540	13540	40620

Figure 45

15. Unhide the rest of the year by clicking on the pull-down menu for **Column Labels** and checking the **Select All** box again and click on **OK**.

FLEXIBLE BUDGETING USING PIVOTTABLES

Flexible budgets are an important tool in accounting. PivotTables facilitate flexible budgeting. It is very easy to make changes, the results appear immediately, and any formulas that are affected are automatically updated. To see how revisions work, perform the following *independent* steps.

1. Open the **CA Computerized Excel Workbook** file and click on the **Master Budget** worksheet.
   After the budget was established, it was decided that some changes would be made. To allow for these changes, insert a new column before the **EXPLANATIONS** column by right-clicking on column **H** and selecting **Insert** from the pull-down menu. Copy the **BUDGET** values into the new column **I** by selecting the entire **BUDGET** column and copying and pasting it to the new column. Change the column heading **BUDGET** in Column **I** to **REV_BUDGET**. You should now have the original and revised budgets side by side. Daniel will be transferring from Marketing to Administration as of March 1. At that time, his salary will increase by $1,000. To adjust the budget for this change, click onto the **Master Budget** worksheet. Be sure the

entire budget is highlighted (from A1 to J301). Click on **Filter** in the **Sort & Filter** section of the **Data** tab.

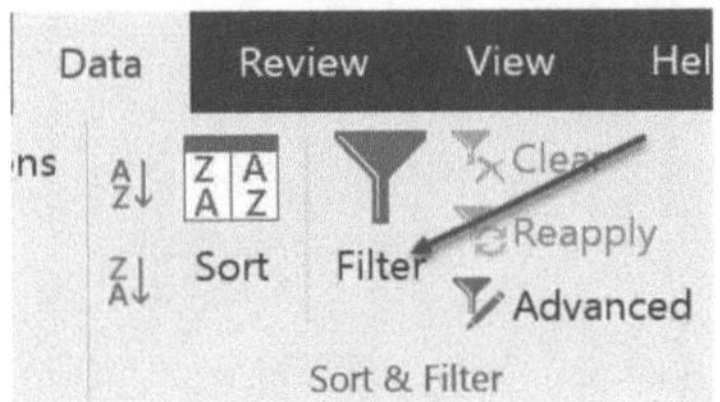

Figure 46

2. Now click on the **Cost Center** pull-down menu and click on **Select All** (to deselect all) and the click on **Daniel** to select him. Twelve records for Daniel should appear. Change Daniel's department for the appropriate periods and increase his salary for only those periods (*Figure 47*).

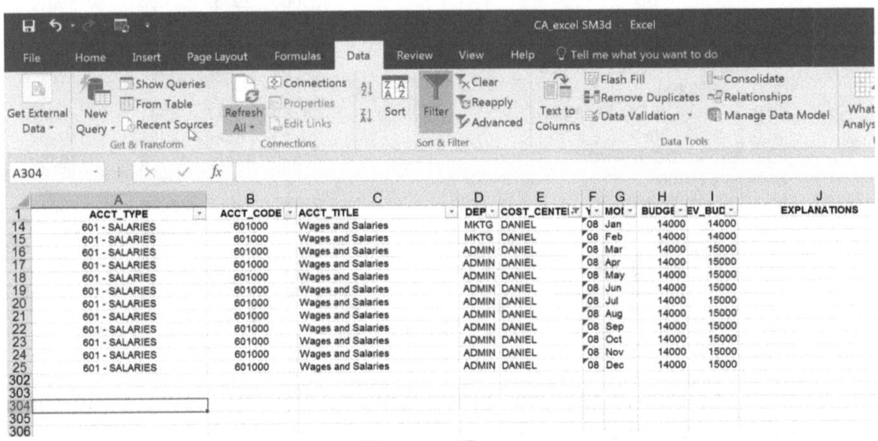

Figure 47

3. Go to the **Pivot** worksheet. Notice that Daniel's salary has not changed. Make sure that **the PivotTable Options** toolbar is active and click on **Refresh** in the **Data** section of the **PivotTable Tools** toolbar.

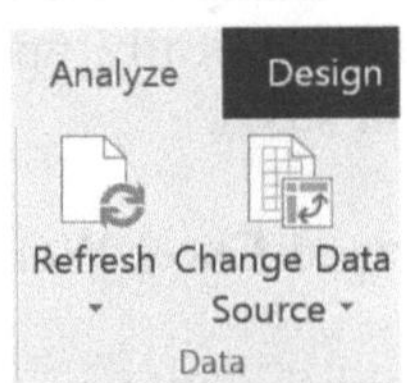

Figure 48

4. Drag **Sum of Budget** from the **Σ Values** section of the **Pivot Table Field List** and drag **Rev_Budget** to that section (*Figure 46*)**.** Daniel's salary should now be updated.

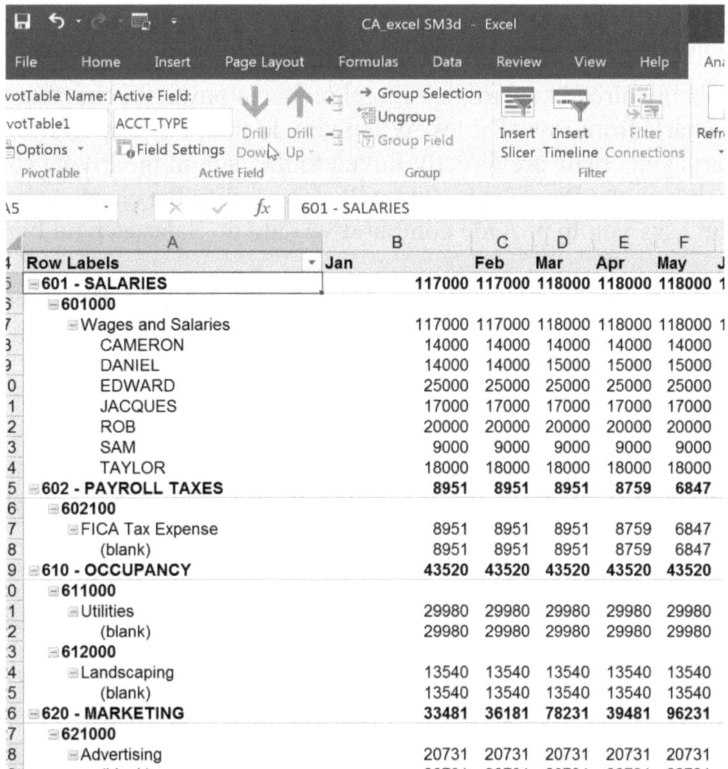

Figure 49

5. Go back to the **Master Budget** worksheet. Turn off the filter by clicking on the **Filter** icon next to **COST_CENTER** and clicking on **(Select All)**.

6. Turn on the **Filter** again. Select Cameron and update her salary to reflect a $1,000 raise in the **REV_BUDGET** column beginning in June and extending into the subsequent months. Click onto the **Pivot** worksheet. Click **Refresh** in the **Data** section of the **PivotTable Options** toolbar.

7. Once the first budget has been created using PivotTables, it can be used to produce others very quickly. In the **Pivot** worksheet, show all departments. Pull down the **Options** menu in the **PivotTable** section of the **PivotTable Options** toolbar and select **Show Report Filter Pages**.

Figure 50

The three departmental budget PivotTables (one for **ADMIN**, one for **MKTG** and one for **OPS**) are created as three new worksheets in your workbook.

CREATING CHARTS FROM PIVOTTABLES

You are probably already aware that Excel contains powerful charting tools. You can also create charts from PivotTables. When you do this, it is important to remember that the charts you create are directly linked to the data in the PivotTable. If you change the data in the PivotTable, you will also modify the chart. Assume that management asks you to provide comparative data on Salaries paid by Department.

1. You already know that you can view the data in the three departmental worksheets. You could pull the information requested from each of these three sheets and provide that to management. However, you also know that charts are an excellent way to view comparative data.

2. Go to the **Pivot** worksheet. Click on the **Row Label** pull-down menu and deselect **Select All**. Click on **Salaries** and click **OK**. You should now see only the data for **Salaries**.

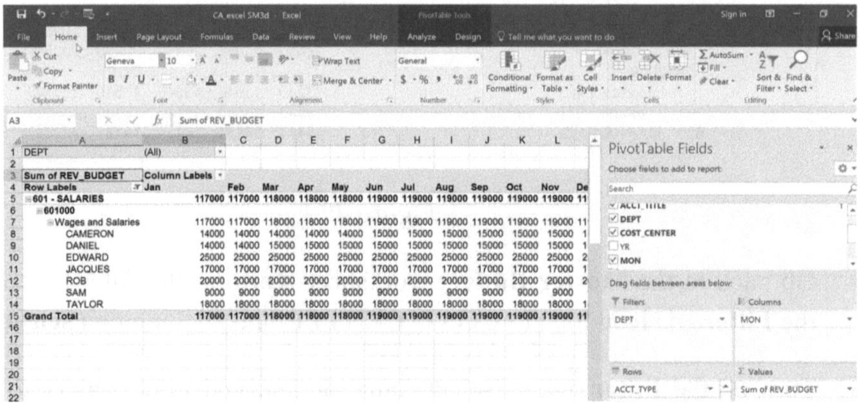

Figure 51

3. Drag **Cost_Center** from the **Row Labels** window and drop it in the **PivotTable Field List** window.

4. Drag **Dept** from the **Report Filter** window and drop it in the **Row Labels** window.

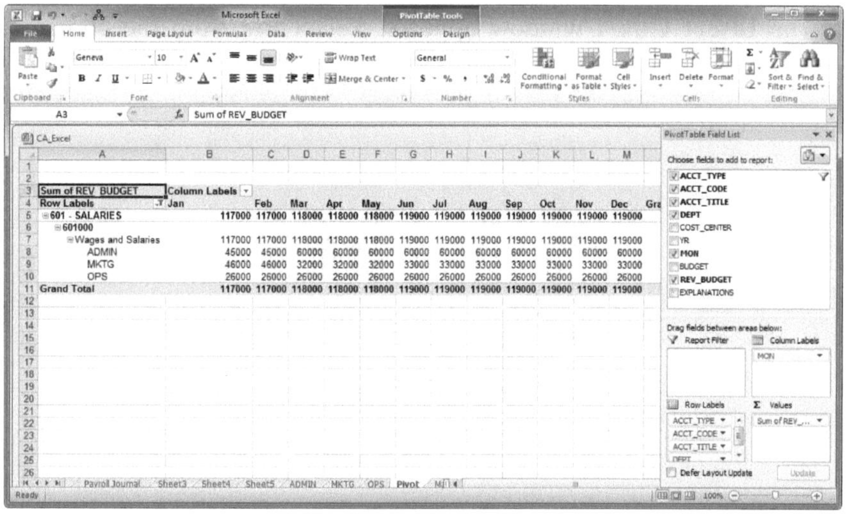

Figure 52

5. You do not need the **ACCT_CODE** so you can drag the field from the **Row Labels** window to the **PivotTable Field List** window. In addition, you have not been asked for a breakdown by month so drag **MON** from the Column **Labels** window to the **PivotTable Field List** window.

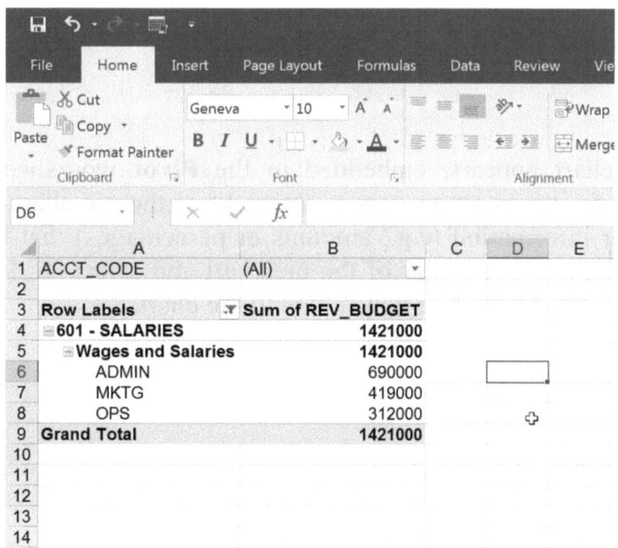

Figure 53

6. Click inside the PivotTable and click on the **Options** tab of the **PivotTable Tools** menu. Click on the **PivotChart** icon in the **Tools** section.

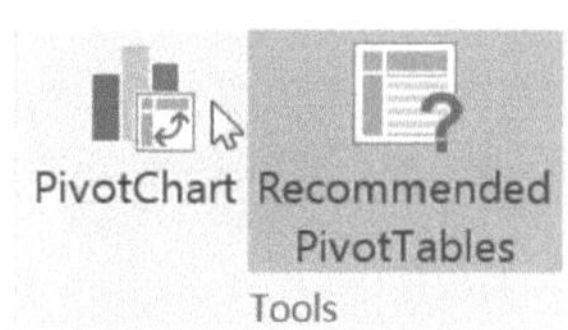

Figure 54

7. The **Insert Chart** window appears. Select **Pie** from the choices and click **OK**.

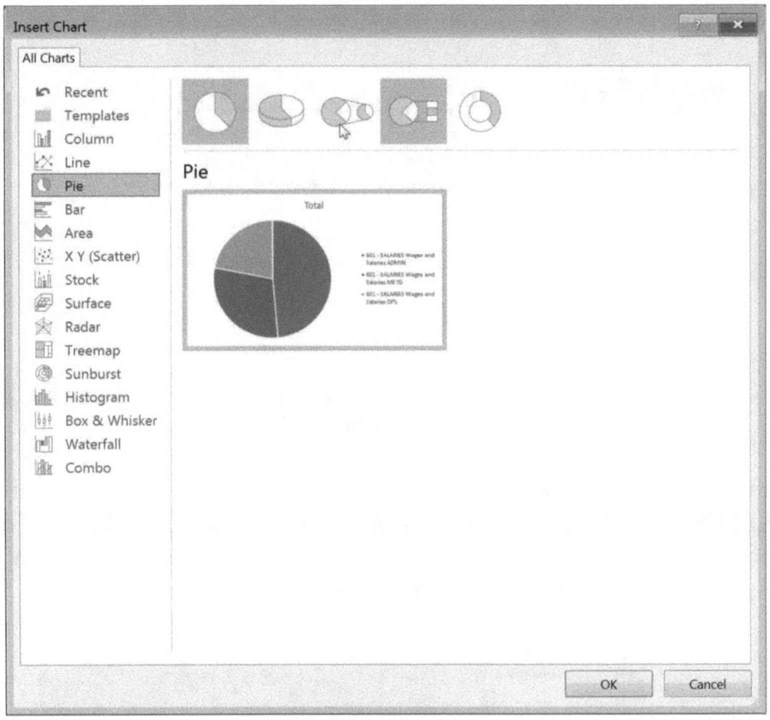

Figure 55

8. A pie chart appears, embedded in the **Pivot** worksheet. Notice that the Legend for the chart appears to the right of the pie chart. However, there is no other information (e.g., amounts or percentages) that has been provided. Right click on the center of the pie chart and select **Add Data Labels**. The totals by department are now added to the chart.

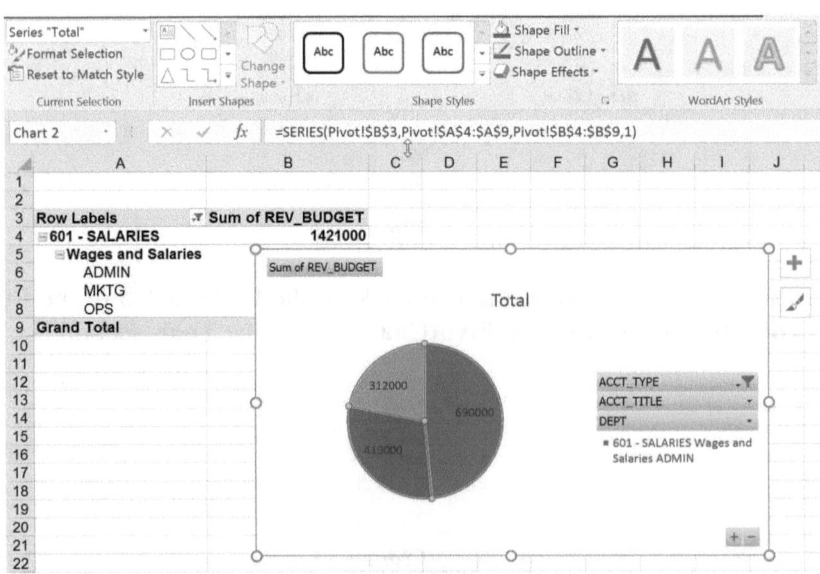

Figure 56

9. You can add more information by right clicking on the pie chart again and clicking on **Add Data Labels**. Right click on the chart once more and select **Format Data Labels**. Notice that a **Format Data Labels** section is added to side of the window. Category Name and Percentage and deselect **Value** in the **Format Data Labels** window.

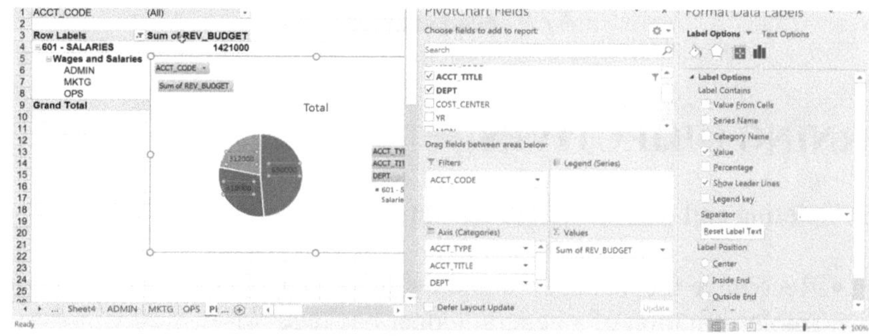

Figure 57

10. The placement of the chart in the middle of the **Pivot** worksheet is not optimal. Click on the **PivotChart Tools** toolbar and click on **Move Chart** in the **Actions** section of the toolbar.

Figure 58

11. In the **Move Chart** window, click on **New Sheet** and name the sheet **Salary by Department**.

12. Notice that the newly created pie chart is entitled "**Total**". This is not very descriptive if you were to print the pie chart. Select the chart title by double clicking on it and change the title to "**Salary Expense by Department**".

13. Finally, note that if you were to return to the **Pivot** worksheet and restore the **DEPT**, **MON**, **ACCT_CODE**, and **COST_CENTER** fields to their appropriate places (in their proper order) and then click on the worksheet containing your pie chart, the formatting of the chart will change. As mentioned at the beginning of this exercise, the chart is linked to and matches the data shown in the PivotTable. If you change that data, the chart changes with it. If you experiment with the PivotTable from this point on, be sure to restore the settings for the chart discussed above.

WRAP-UP

You have now completed the Excel assignment. Be sure to save your work. Your instructor may provide you with an appropriate file naming convention, in which case you will have to rename your file.

GENERAL LEDGER APPLICATIONS USING *SAGE 50 ACCOUNTING 2018* ®: The Winery At Chateau Americana

LEARNING OBJECTIVES

After completing and discussing this assignment, you should be able to:

- Recognize the managerial and technological issues associated with the implementation of a general ledger package
- Complete sample transactions
- Understand the implications of the design of the user interface
- Recognize and evaluate the strengths and weaknesses of controls embedded in a general ledger package
- Compare and contrast a general ledger package with a manual accounting information system

BACKGROUND

As the winery has grown, Rob Breeden, the chief financial officer, has realized that management does not have timely information about the financial condition of the company. This has resulted in several instances in which the decisions made were not optimal. Therefore, he has determined that it is time to convert the current system to a general ledger package. After investigating the possibilities, he has decided to utilize *Sage 50 Accounting 2018*®. Chateau Americana has hired you to convert the system.

REQUIREMENTS

Using the *Sage 50 Accounting 2018*® software program contained in your *CAST* package or in your school computer lab, you are to convert Chateau Americana from a manual system to a general ledger software package. In order to obtain the *Sage 50 Accounting 2018*® software, go to https://www.sage.com/en-us/about-us/education-instructor/ and scroll down until you see 'For Students' and click on the 'Students click here' button.

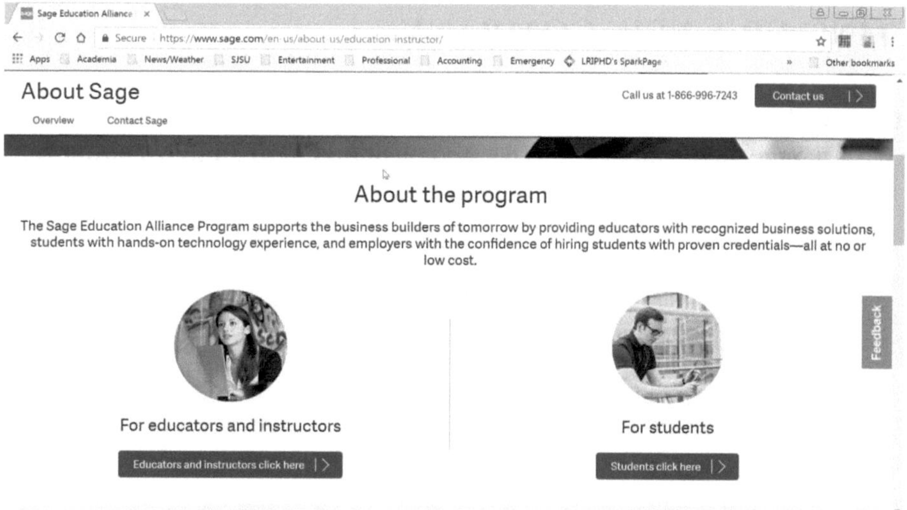

Under the Sage 50 Accounting – U.S. Edition, click on 'Register now'. Fill in the required information on the form and click 'Submit'.

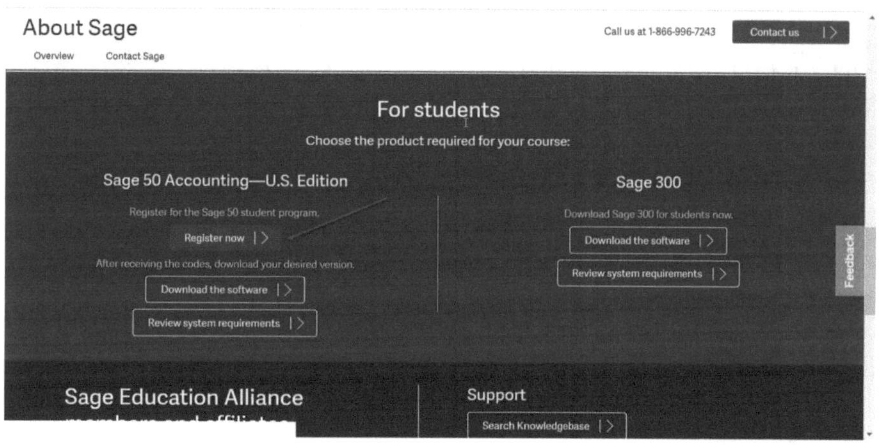

After you have submitted this form and Sage verifies your information, you should receive a serial number for use in registering the software. You can now click on 'Download the software', choose the 2018 version of the software and install it using the serial number you have received.

Note that with any other computer file, it is important to **back up frequently** to another storage medium as you are working through the following assignment.

SETTING UP A NEW COMPANY

Requirements

1. Start *Sage 50 Accounting 2018®* and click on **Create a new company**.

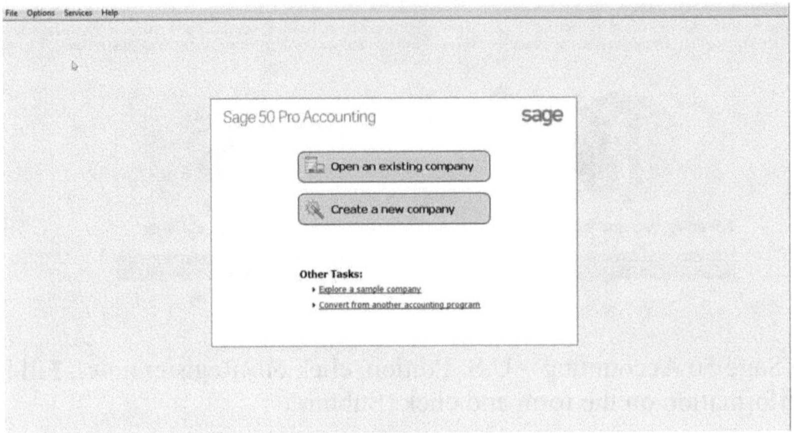

Figure 1

2. The Introduction screen that appears next alerts the user to information that will be required throughout the set-up procedure. Click on **Next**.

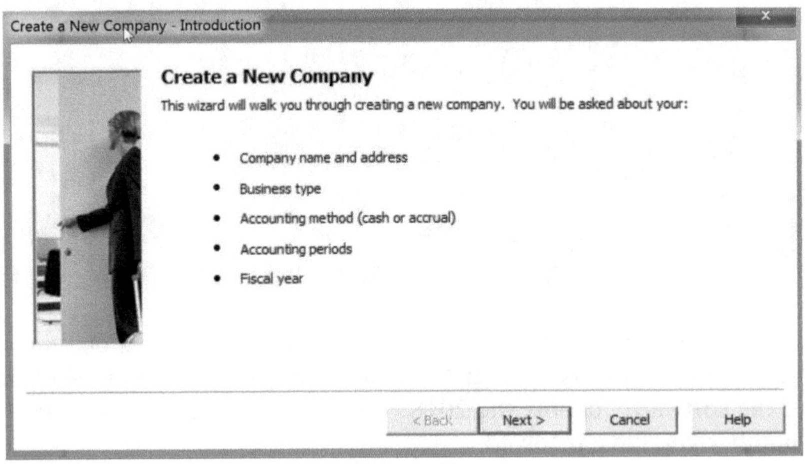

Figure 2

3. Enter the following company information and then click on **Next:**

.

> The Winery at Chateau Americana, Inc.
> 3003 Vineyard Way
> Huntington, CA 95394
> Phone: (707) 368-8485
> Fax: (707) 368-8486

Do not enter any information in the remaining input boxes. Click on **Next**.

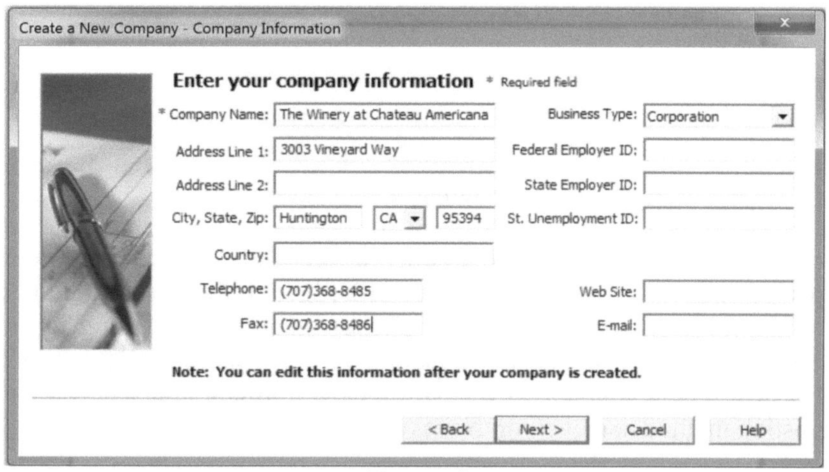

Figure 3

4. You are now asked to select a method for setting up the Chart of Accounts. *Sage 50* provides you with sample charts of accounts in the event that you are setting up a start-up company. However, because Chateau Americana already has a Chart of Accounts, select **Build your own chart of accounts** and click on **Next**.

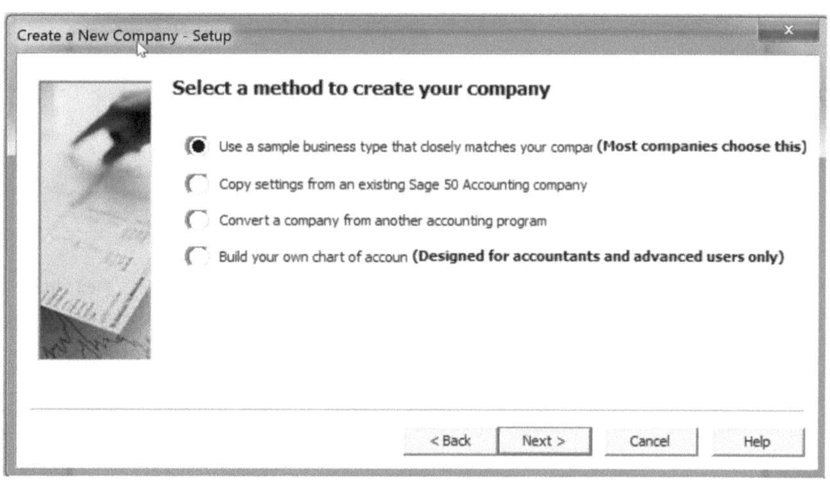

Figure 4

5. The next screen provides options for the company's accounting method. If you examine the Chart of Accounts you will notice various accounts that

provide evidence that Chateau Americana utilizes the accrual method of accounting. Identify what these accounts are. Then click on **Next**.

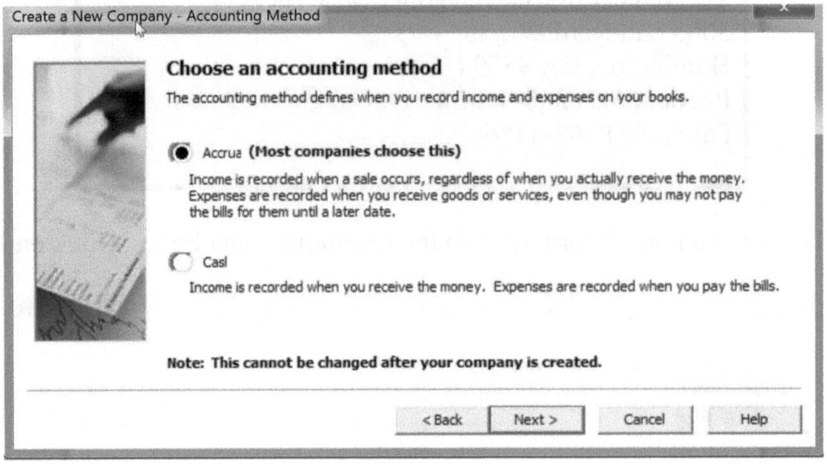

Figure 5

6. *Sage 50* offers two posting methods. In Real Time mode, each transaction is posted as it is written and the General Ledger is always up to date. In Batch mode, transactions are posted in batches or groups, resulting in processing efficiencies but delaying the updating of the General Ledger. Since one of Rob Breeden's concerns is that of timely information, select the **Real Time** posting method and click on **Next**.

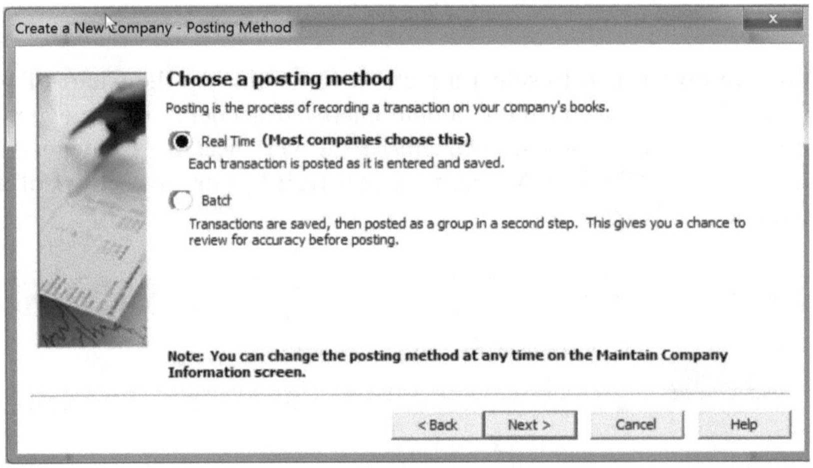

Figure 6

7. The next two screens address the company's accounting period. The first asks you to select the number of accounting periods within a year. The company's fiscal year is a calendar year with 12-monthly accounting periods. Make sure the correct accounting period is selected and click on **Next**.

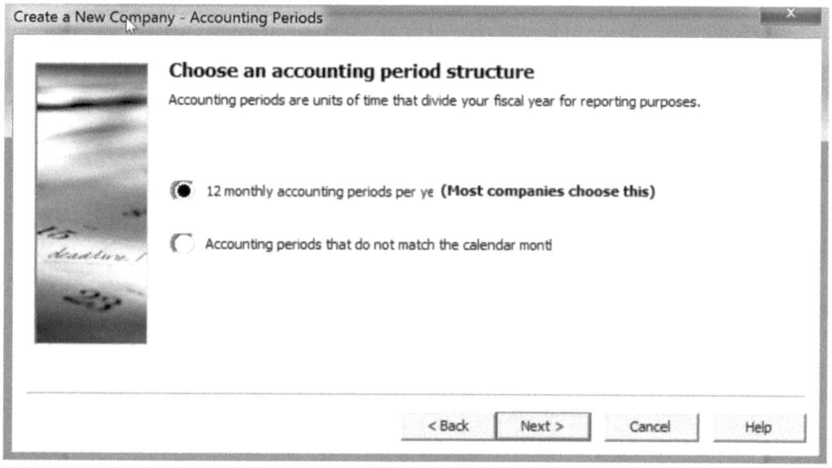

Figure 7

8. Now you are prompted to provide the month and year that the fiscal year begins (i.e., January 20XX). We will refer to the current year as 20XX but your instructor will provide you with the year you are to use. You have been given the general ledger balances as of December 15, 20XX. Note that this implies that the fiscal year begins as of January 20XX. Make sure the correct information is input and click on **Next**.

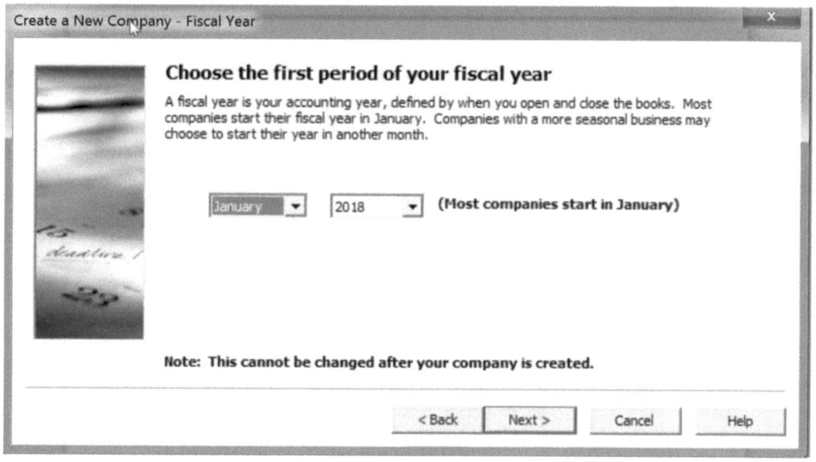

Figure 8

9. You have now completed the set-up procedures for converting Chateau Americana to *Sage 50*. Click on **Finish**.

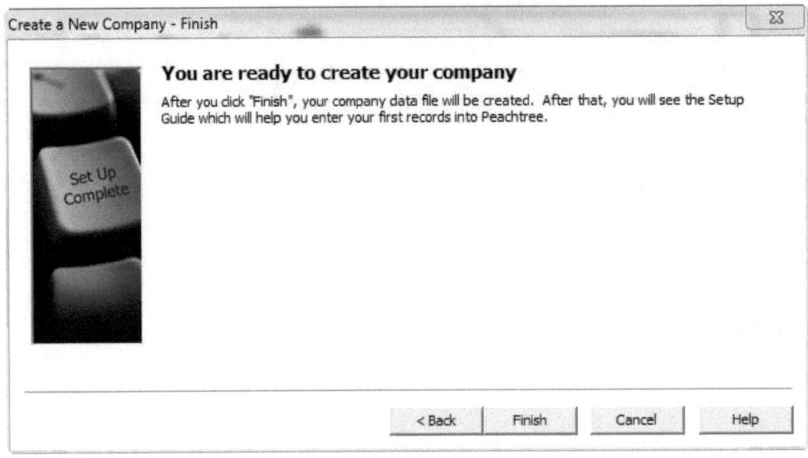

Figure 9

10. Close the **What's New in *Sage 50* 2018** window. (Before closing the window, you might also want to check the "Do not show this screen again" box.)

11. The **Setup Guide** window appears with the **Chart of Accounts** highlighted.

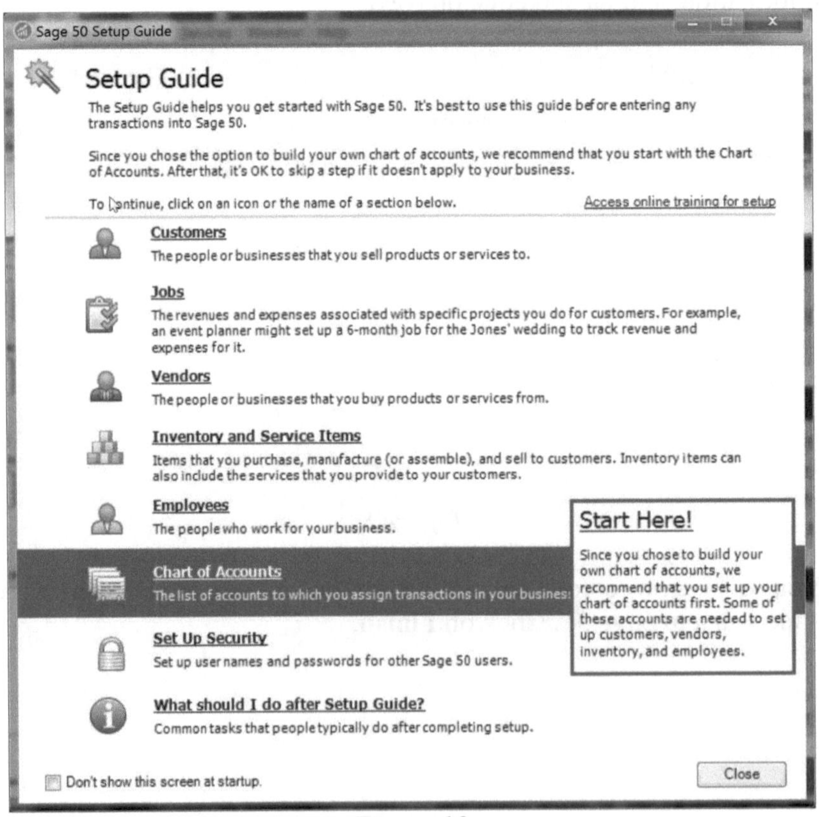

Figure 10

If you wish, you may close the file at this time and *Sage 50* will automatically save the contents. If you do so, the **Setup Guide** can be obtained the next time you start up *Sage 50* by clicking on **File**.

SETTING UP THE GENERAL LEDGER

Requirements

1. If you have closed the file, reopen the Chateau Americana file. Click on the **Chart of Accounts** now. After familiarizing yourself with the information on this window, you can click the **Next** button in the lower right-hand corner of the window.

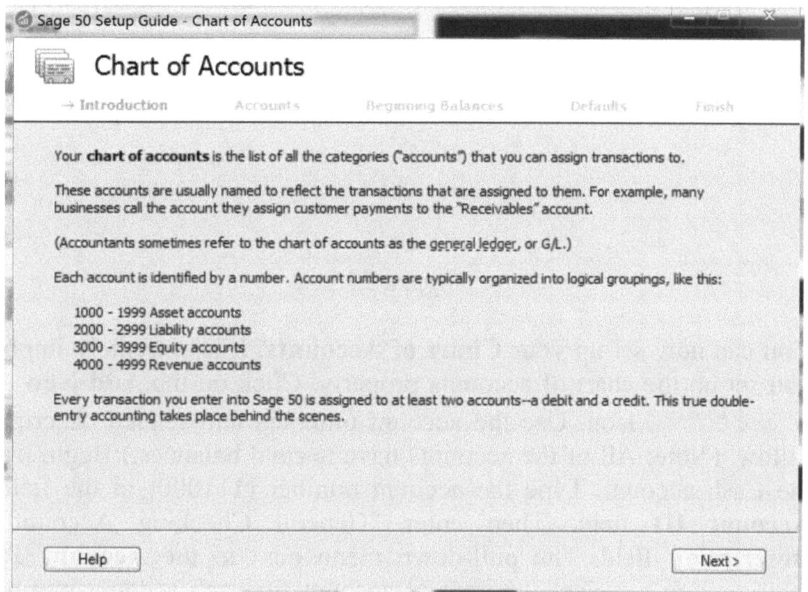

Figure 11

2. The next window describes the process for adding new accounts. Once you have read this information, you may click **Add New Accounts**.

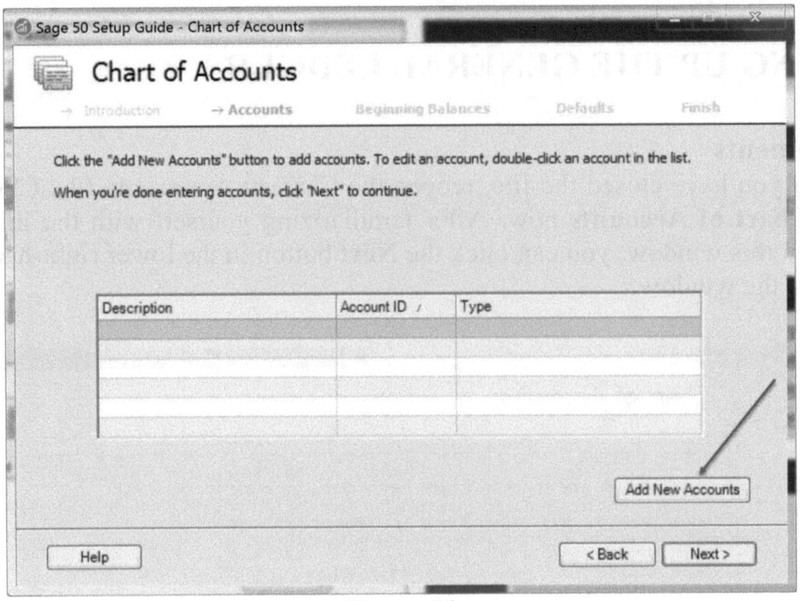

Figure 12

3. You can now set up your **Chart of Accounts**. It is extremely important that you set up the chart of accounts properly. Click on the **Add New Accounts** [Add New Accounts] icon. Use the account numbers and related descriptions that follow. (Note: All of the accounts have normal balances.) Begin by entering the Cash account. Type the account number (111000) in the field entitled **Account ID** field. Then enter "General Checking Account" in the **Description** field. The pull-down menu next to the **Account Type** field requires you to select the type of account for each account number. Scroll through the various Account Types to acquaint yourself with the listings there but leave the Account Type as Cash. **Do not enter balance information** for the accounts at this time.

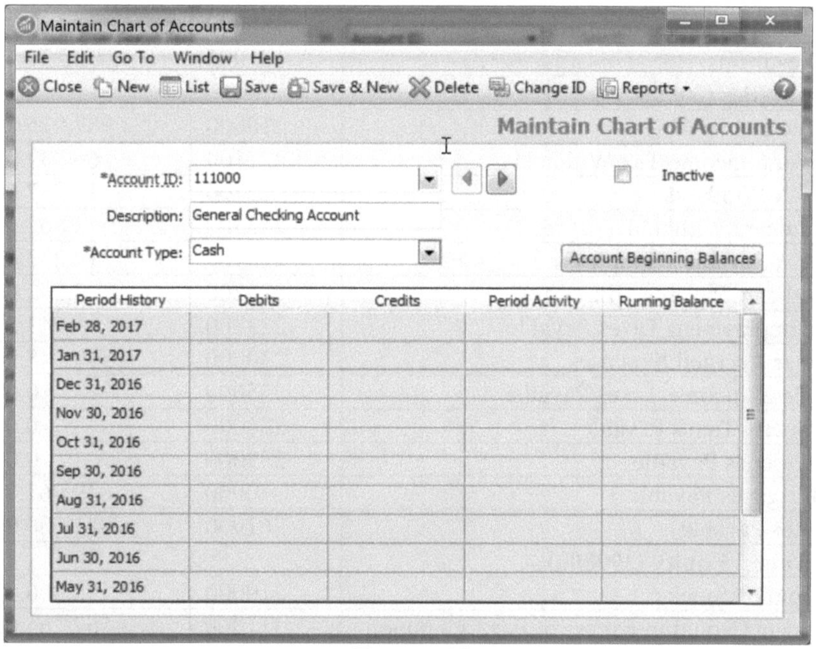

Figure 13

Click the **Save & New** 

button after you enter each account's information**.** As you enter the account titles, notice that the full title does not always fit in the space provided and you will, therefore, need to abbreviate the descriptions slightly. In addition, the **Account Type** for many of these accounts is obvious. For those that are not obvious, you will need to refer to the information provided below.

- Common Stock and Paid-In Capital in Excess of Par are "Equity-doesn't close" accounts
- Dividends is an "Equity-gets closed" account type
- "Income" accounts include Sales, Sales Returns and Allowances, Sales Discounts Taken, Gain/Loss on Sale of Assets, Gain/Loss on Sale of Securities, Interest/Dividend Income, and Miscellaneous Revenue

Account Title	**Account #**	**12/15/XX Balance**
Assets (100000)		
General Checking Account	111000	$ 2,222,927.47
Payroll Checking Account	112000	1,000.00
Money Market Account	113000	782,546.49
Savings Account	114000	51,745.56
Petty Cash	119000	500.00
Accounts Receivable	121000	5,366,670.86
Allowance for Bad Debts	129000	95,401.58
Inventory – Production	141000	$ 11,564,851.56
Inventory – Finished Goods	145000	4,044,046.31
Prepaid Expenses	150000	142,465.96
Land and Buildings	160000	16,358,487.34
Equipment	170000	13,844,881.10

Accumulated Depreciation	180000	15,233,662.97
Investments	191000	3,070,227.56
Liabilities (200000)		
Accounts Payable	210000	4,987,975.79
Federal Income Tax Withheld	222100	66,739.08
FICA Withheld	222200	12,237.64
Medicare Withheld	222300	2,862.01
FICA Payable – Employer	223100	12,237.64
Medicare Payable – Employer	223200	2,862.01
Unemployment Taxes Payable	223300	943.57
Other Accrued Expenses	230000	599,348.98
Federal Income Taxes Payable	235000	0.00
Property Taxes Payable	236000	0.00
Dividends Payable	239000	0.00
Mortgages Payable	240000	7,639,067.73
Notes Payable	261000	841,000.00
Owners' Equity (300000)		
Common Stock	310000	90,000.00
Paid-in Capital in Excess of Par – Common	311000	3,567,265.00
Dividends – Common	312000	0.00
Retained Earnings	390000	22,064,134.78
Income (400000)		
Sales	410000	22,264,431.15
Sales Discounts	420000	346,741.36
Sales Returns and Allowances	430000	15,588.47
Gain/Loss – Fixed Assets	451000	0.00
Gain/Loss – Marketable Securities	452000	0.00
Dividend Income	491000	4,000.00
Interest Income	492000	23,482.56
Cost of Goods Sold	510000	11,514,092.11
Expenses (600000 – 700000)		
Wages and Salaries Expense	601000	1,965,164.11
Sales Commission Expense	601500	771,665.60
FICA Tax Expense	602100	244,124.52
Medicare Tax Expense	602200	57,093.62
FUTA Expense	602300	7,392.00
SUTA Expense	602400	22,176.00
Utilities Expense	611000	307,067.05
Irrigation & Waste Disposal Expense	611300	230,910.91
Landscaping Expense	612000	142,475.69
Advertising Expense	621000	296,794.33
Marketing Expense	623000	192,865.67
Festivals & Competitions Expense	624000	238,654.75
Telephone Expense	631000	37,584.73
Internet & Computer Expense	632000	14,475.00
Postage Expense	633000	35,117.66
Legal & Accounting Fees	641000	88,425.50
Other Consulting Fees	643000	12,500.00
Office Supplies Expense	651000	58,689.68
Data Processing Expense	660000	9,743.89
Depreciation Expense	670000	1,092,832.66

Travel and Entertainment Expense	680000	169,405.86
Other Insurance	691000	115,058.55
Medical Insurance	692000	192,154.80
Workmen's Compensation Insurance	693000	139,750.00
Other Employee Benefits Expense	699000	175,643.90
Dues and Subscriptions Expense	700000	32,076.00
Federal Income Tax Expense	711000	857,595.76
Property Tax Expense	712000	19,875.00
Repairs and Maintenance Expense	721000	71,974.93
Automobile Expense	731000	81,493.45
Lease Expense	740000	113,607.56
Bad Debt Expense	791000	0.00
Miscellaneous Expense	792000	26,575.63
Interest Expense	793000	359,915.53

You can go back and forward to view or edit your work at any time by clicking on the **Arrow**  buttons next to the **Account ID** and selecting the account that you want to edit.

4. When you have finished entering all of the accounts, review the Chart of Accounts by clicking on **List** 

to make sure you haven't made any errors. If you find any problems, double-click the account in question and correct it. When you are finished, close the **Maintain Chart of Accounts** window and click the **Next** button.

You are now asked if you want to enter the beginning balances. **WARNING**: Begin this process only if you have enough time to enter all the balances. If you are ready to proceed, click **Next**.

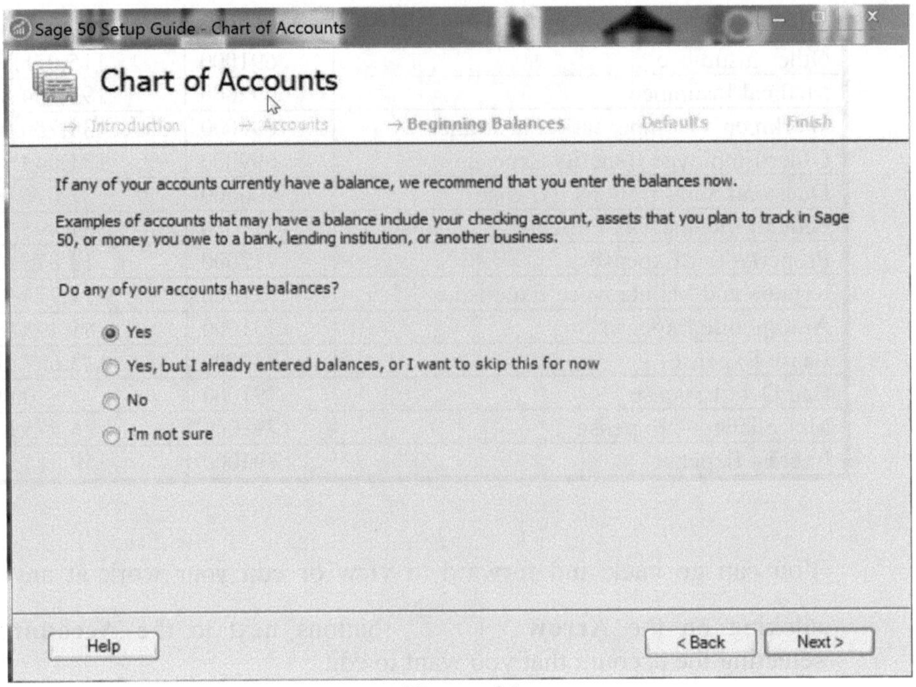

Figure 14

SETTING UP BEGINNING ACCOUNT BALANCES

Requirements

1. To set up your beginning balances, you first need to decide upon the accounting period. Begin by clicking on the **Enter Account Beginning Balances** button.

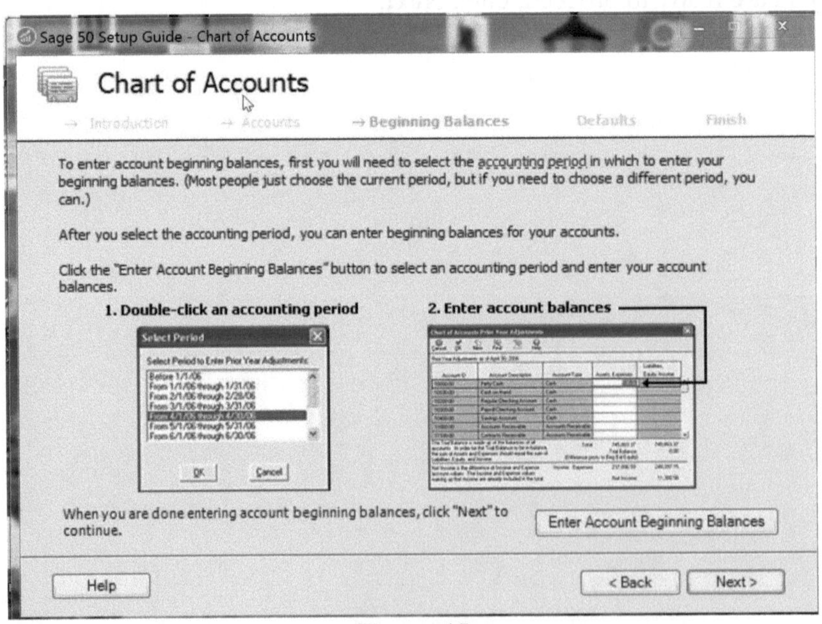

Figure 15

2. Since our books for Chateau Americana begin in the middle of December, we will select the period **From 12/1/XX through 12/31/XX**. Click **OK**.

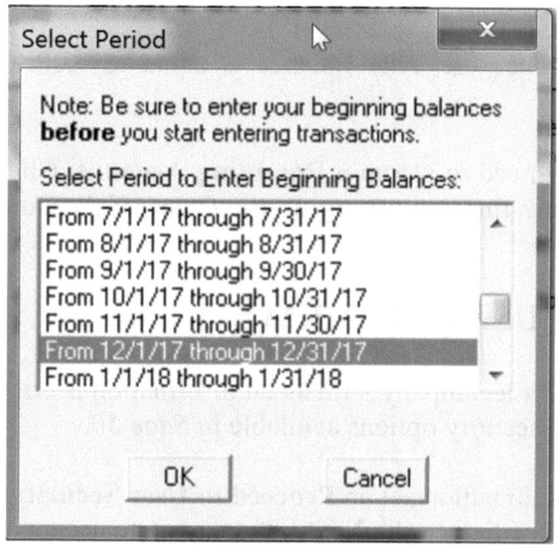

Figure 16

IMPORTANT: When entering beginning balances, Sage 50 classifies the balances as either "Assets, Expenses" accounts that have debit balances or "Liabilities, Equities, Income" accounts that have credit balances. Thus, it is imperative that you watch for contra accounts (e.g., allowance for bad debts) and enter them as negative numbers if necessary since, in most instances, *Sage 50* will not recognize them as contra accounts.

3. When you are finished entering the beginning balances for all accounts, you should see that the trial balance equals "**0.00**".

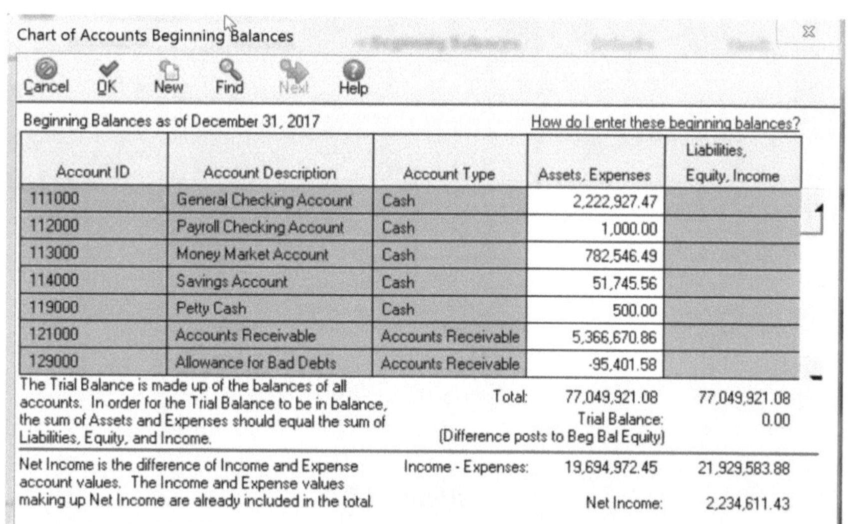

Account ID	Account Description	Account Type	Assets, Expenses	Liabilities, Equity, Income
111000	General Checking Account	Cash	2,222,927.47	
112000	Payroll Checking Account	Cash	1,000.00	
113000	Money Market Account	Cash	782,546.49	
114000	Savings Account	Cash	51,745.56	
119000	Petty Cash	Cash	500.00	
121000	Accounts Receivable	Accounts Receivable	5,366,670.86	
129000	Allowance for Bad Debts	Accounts Receivable	-95,401.58	

Figure 17

If the sum of Assets and Expenses does not equal the sum of Liabilities, Equity, and Income, *Sage 50* will create a temporary equity account for any unaccounted for difference. This amount will have to be investigated and adjusted for at a later time. However, the account created (**Beg Bal Equity**) will not go away after the adjustment has been made. It will remain in the Chart of Accounts.

4. Click **OK** once the Trial Balance is equal to 0.00 and click on the **Next** button.

5. There is no need to set up a **Rounding Account**. Click on the **Next** button. You are now finished setting up the Chart of Accounts. Click on the **Next** button.

SETTING UP USER SECURITY

1. Security over a company's financial information is critical. We will now explore the security options available in *Sage 50*.

2. With the radio button set on **Proceed to User Security Setup**, click on the **Next** button. Click on the **Next** button again to accept **Yes, I want to set up users now**.

3. You must begin by setting up a company or system administrator. This individual has complete access to *Sage 50*. In addition, this individual will be in charge of adding users and maintaining their passwords. Click now on **Set Up Users** 

icon to set up the administrator, as well as other user names and passwords. Note that the **User List** is blank in *Figure 18*.

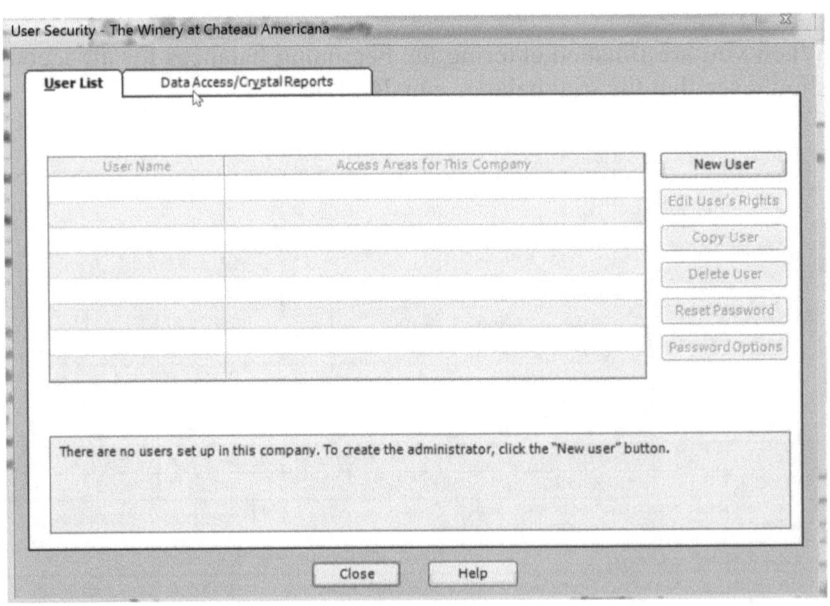

Figure 18

4. Click on the **New User** 

icon. The default **User Name** is **Admin**. This is the default used by most programs and would be easily hacked. It should be changed to something that is not obvious and a strong password should be chosen. **IMPORTANT**: Keep in mind that once you set a **User Name** and **Password** for the Administrator you will then be prompted to login whenever you open *Sage 50* from now on. *REMEMBER IT!!*

5. Now we will set up another security for another employee. Anna Johnson is the Accounting Supervisor. Her **User Name** is *ajohn* and her **Password** is *password1*. Click on **Selected access** and click **Next**.

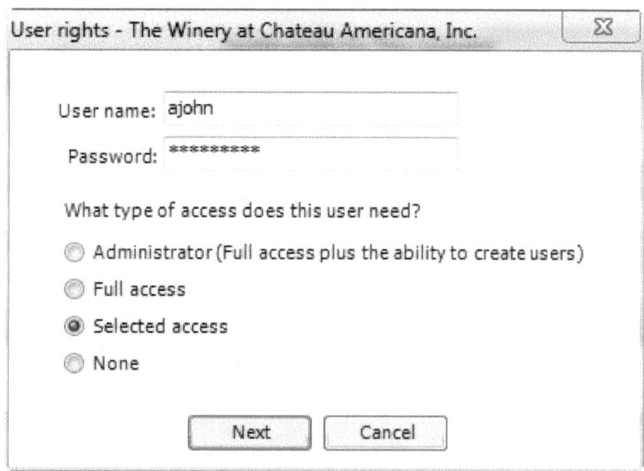

Figure 19

6. Scroll through the categories of access. Think about whether the Accounting Supervisor should have Full Access to each area. Keep in mind that this person is not the same person as the **Administrator** and should not have access to all areas.

7. Sue Jones is the Payroll Entry Clerk. Her **User Name** is *sjones* and her **Password** is *password2*. Set Sue Jones up so that she only has access to Payroll entry and no access to anything else by clicking **Selected Access**.

8. Once you have finished setting up user security for these three individuals, click on the **Close** button and then click on the **Next** button. Leave the radio button on the "**Show me what I might do next**" option and click **Next**.

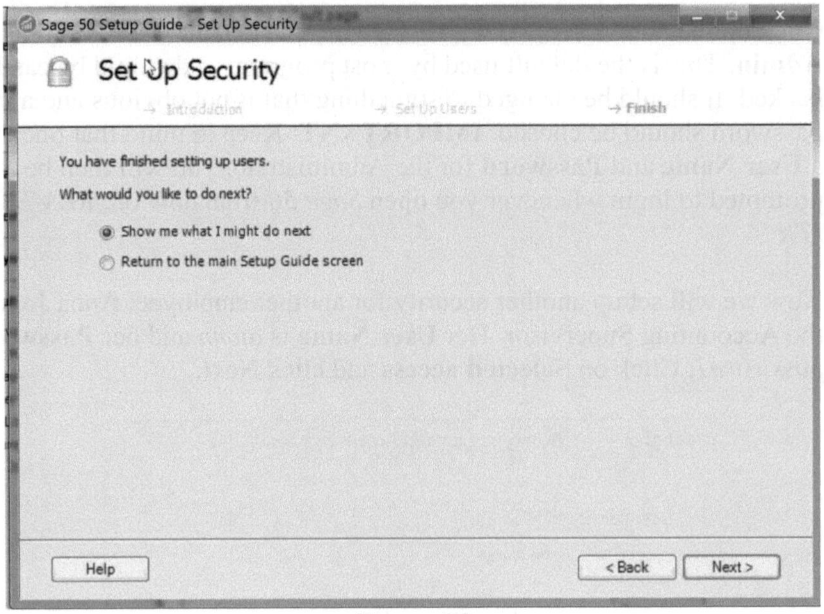

Figure 20

9. Look through the list of Next Steps. We are not ready to perform any of these steps. We can't create invoices, pay vendors or pay employees yet because we have not yet entered any customers, vendors or employees into our system. Click **Close** so we can enter these entities into *Sage 50.*

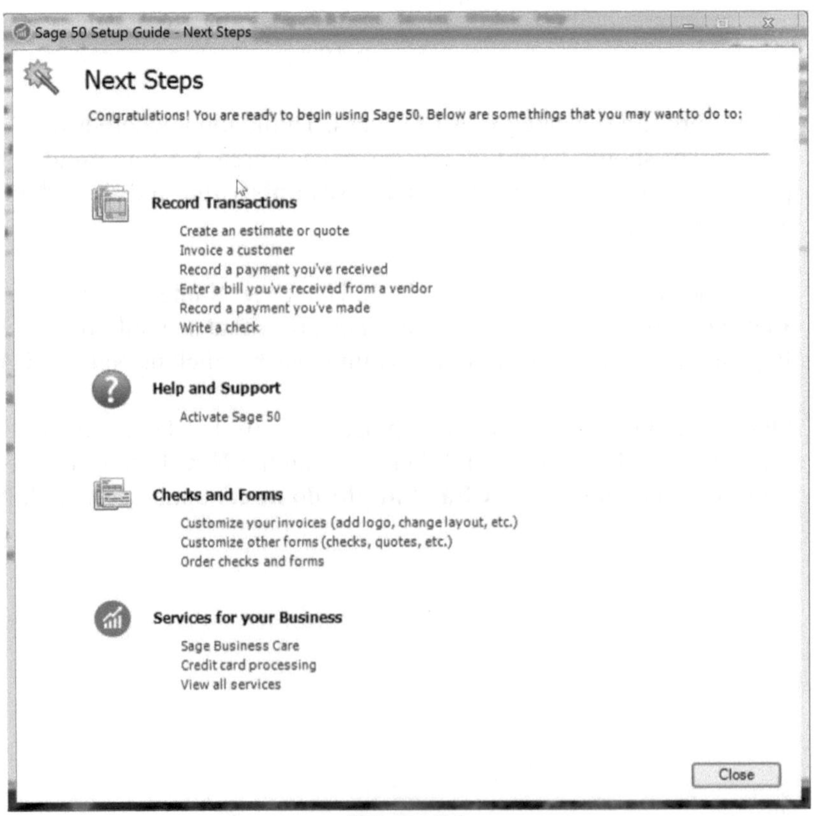

Figure 21

SETTING UP ACCOUNTS RECEIVABLE

Requirements

1. Before you begin, make sure that the **Period** in the icons near the top of the page is set to 12/1/XX to 12/31/XX. You also want to change the **System Date** to 12/15/XX. Open the Chateau Americana file if it's not already open. Make sure you are in the **Customers & Sales Task** window.

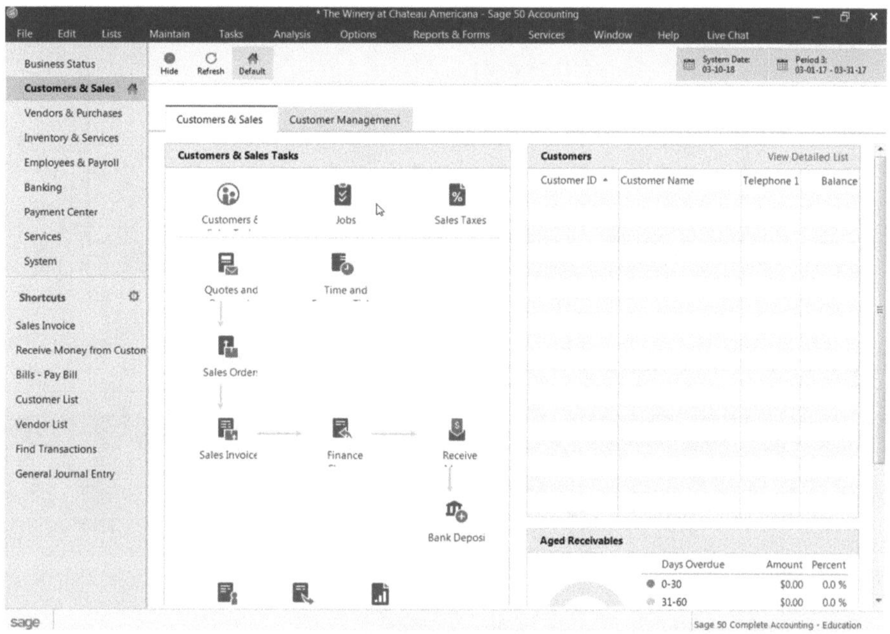

Figure 22

2. Click on **Customers**. Click on **Set Up Customer Defaults** in the pull-down window. Leave the Standard Terms as "Due in number of days." Remove the Credit Limit since you have not been provided credit limits for any of Chateau Americana's customers. Change the Discount Terms to "3" percent and "15" number of days. Set the defaults for the Sales account and the Sales Discounts account using the pull-down menu. Set the Credit Status to "No Credit Limit."

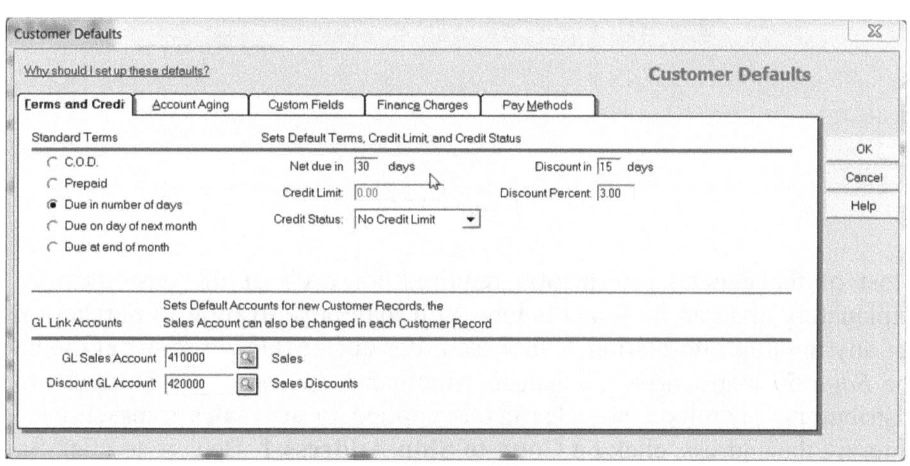

Figure 23

3. Click on the **Account Aging** tab. Change the aging method to **Invoice date** and click **OK**. There is no need to modify any information on the remaining tabs.

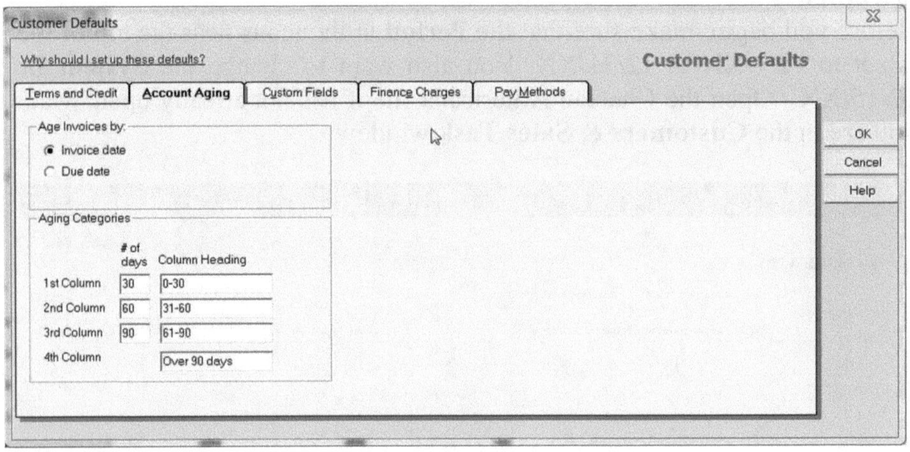

Figure 24

4. Click on **Customers** again but now click on **New Customer**.

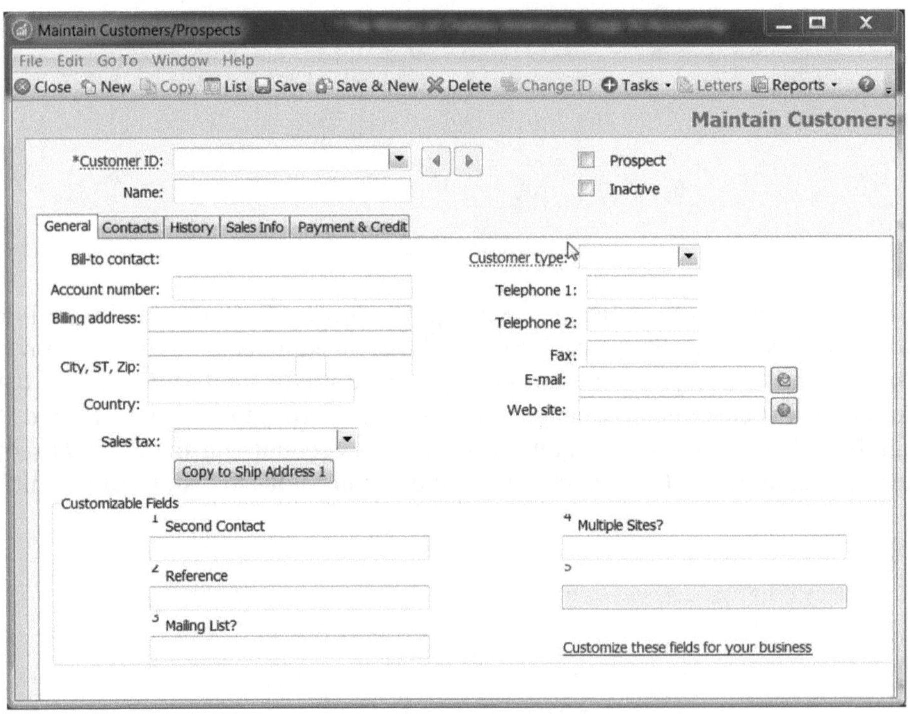

Figure 25

Most of the general information required for each of the customers is self-explanatory and can be found below. You may have to refer to purchase orders for any missing information. (Purchase order documents are found at the back of the *Sage 50* instructions.) Chateau Americana makes only wholesale sales to distributors. Therefore, no sales tax is applied to any sales transactions. After entering the address, click on **Copy to Ship Address 1**. Be sure to click **Save & New** for each customer as they are entered.

Customer Name	Customer ID	Address/Phone	Terms
Alota Wine Distributors	0509	Pier 32, The Embarcadero San Francisco, CA 94111 Phone: (415) 975-8566	3/15, net 30
Bock Wines and Vines	0501	Pier 19, The Embarcadero San Francisco, CA 94111 Phone: (415) 834-9675	3/15, net 30
California Pacific Wine	0555	Pier 81, The Embarcadero San Francisco, CA 94111 Phone: (415) 827-8455	3/15, net 30
California Premium Beverage	0504	39848 South Street Santa Rosa, CA 95402 Phone: (707) 555-7451 Fax: (707) 555-7452	3/15, net 30
Diversita Wine and Beer Distributors	0511	1328 L Street Sacramento, CA 95814 Phone: (916) 441-5517	3/15, net 30
Pacific Distribution Co.	0505	10034 Westborough Boulevard San Francisco, CA 94080 Phone: (415) 555-1532	3/15, net 30
Seaside Distributors, Inc.	0506	9835 West Hills Road Ukiah, CA 94080 Phone: (707) 555-3102	3/15, net 30
Ukiah Beer, Wines and Vines	0527	782 Talmadge Street Ukiah, CA 95482 Phone: (707) 555-8247	3/15, net 30

5. Using the blue arrow keys next to the **Customer ID** or the pull-down menu, scroll back and click on Alota Wine Distributors and click on the **History** tab**.** Then click on **Customer Beginning Balances**. Enter the beginning balance (as of December 15). You will need to enter an invoice number. For most customers, it will be sufficient to enter Balance Forward as the invoice number. If you are provided with specific information about invoices that are included in the balance forward, however, you can break those amounts out and enter them separately. When you have entered all the beginning balance data, click **Save** and then click **Close**. Continue this process for each of the customer accounts. Note that you can also use the **Customer ID** pull-down menu to find the customer for which you wish to enter data.

Customer Name	Invoice Number	Invoice Date	Amount
Alota Wine Distributors	Bal Forward	12/15/XX	$3,340,283.15
Bock Wines and Vines	Bal Forward	12/15/XX	$39,824.24
California Pacific Wine	Bal Forward	12/15/XX	$47,147.71
California Premium Beverage			
Diversita Wine and Beer Distributors	Bal Forward	12/15/XX	$1,885,031.06
Pacific Distribution Co.	Bal Forward	10/31/XX	$39,153.60
Seaside Distributors, Inc.			
Ukiah Beer, Wines and Vines	Bal Forward	12/15/XX	$15,231.10

6. There is no need to modify any information on the remaining tabs. You are now finished setting up Accounts Receivable. Click **Close** Close.

7. You can verify that you have input the correct numbers by clicking on **Forms & Reports** in the top menu of the **Customers & Sales Tasks** screen. Then click on **Accounts Receivable** and open the **Aged Receivables** report. Make a note of the balance at the end of this report. Close the **Aged Receivables** report.

8. Now click on the **Reports & Forms** in the menu bar.

In the **Select a Report or Form** screen, double click **General Ledger.**

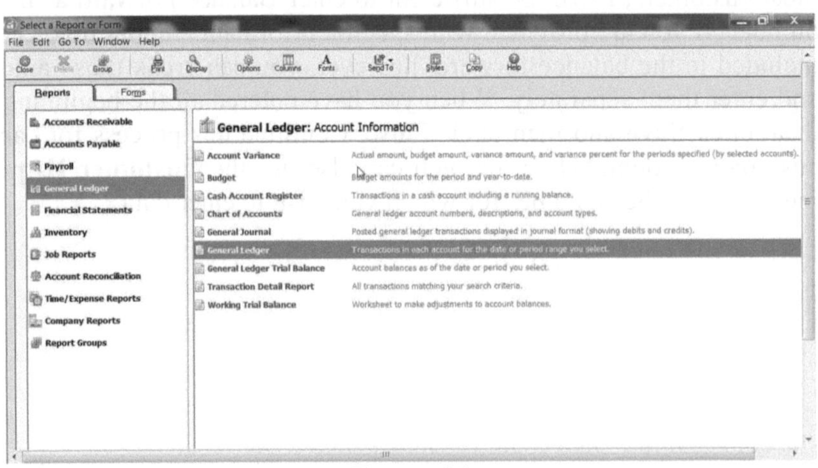

Figure 26

9. Click on General Ledger and examine the balance under General Ledger account **121000 Accounts Receivable**. Compare it to the balance you saw in the **Aged Receivables** report. They should be the same. If they are not, click on **View Detailed List** at the upper right of the **Customers & Sales Tasks** screen and compare the beginning balances to those that were provided to you above. When you find a balance that is incorrect, you can double-click on that customer and it will take you to the **Maintain Customers/Prospects** input screen for the customer in question. You can then click on **History** and then on **Customer Beginning Balances** to correct your mistake.

10. If you wish, you may close the file at this time.

SETTING UP ACCOUNTS PAYABLE

Requirements

1. Open the Chateau Americana file if it's not already open. Click on the **Vendors & Purchases** tab.

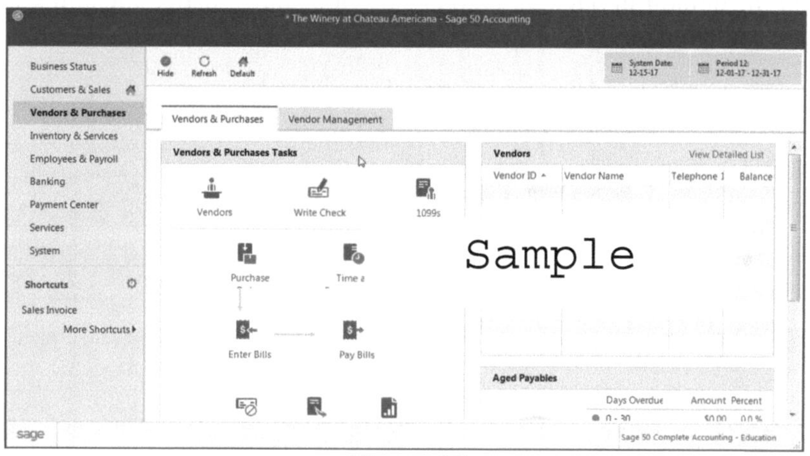

Figure 27

2. Click on **Vendors** and click on **Set Up Vendor Defaults**. Since the terms vary for each vendor, leave the default set to "Due in number of days." Using the pull-down menu, select the Inventory - Production account for the default Expense account. Despite the fact the Inventory – Production is not an Expense account, it is the account that is debited when the company credits most Purchases. The default Discount GL account should also be set to the Inventory - Production account since the company is using the perpetual inventory method. This sets up the debit for purchases to default to Production Inventory and will similarly credit any discounts to Production Inventory. Clear all remaining default values on the **Payment Terms** tab with the exception of the **Net due in** box, which should be left at **30 days** so that the company keeps track of its payables.

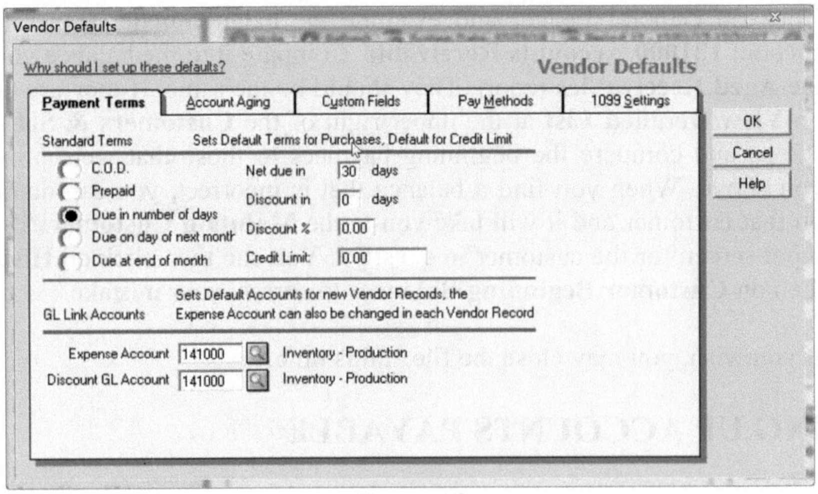

Figure 28

3. Continuing with the vendor defaults menu, click on **Account Aging**. Notice that the default in *Sage 50* is to age by due date. Change the aging to invoice date and click **OK**.

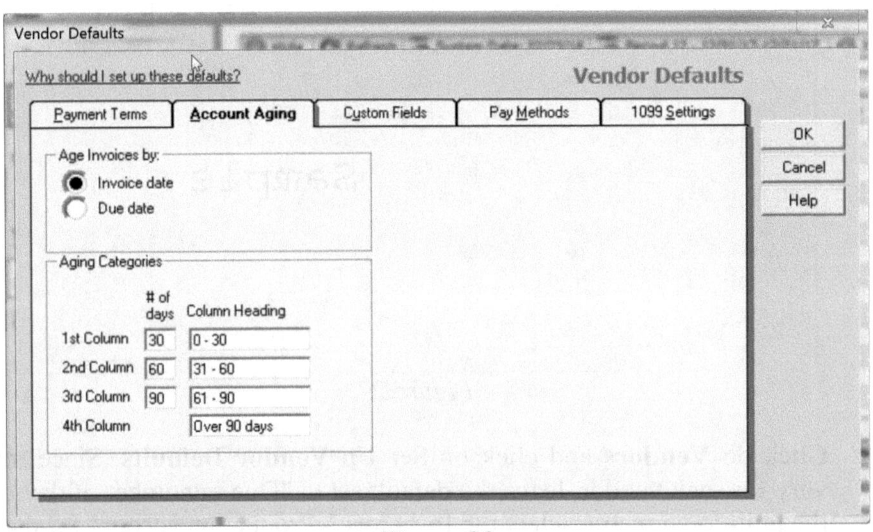

Figure 29

4. Click on **Vendors** again and click on **New Vendor**.

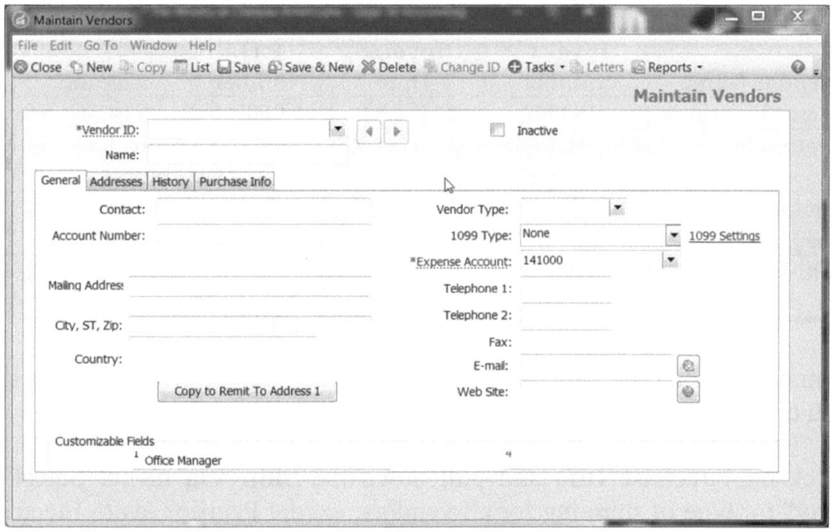

Figure 30

Set up the following five vendor accounts using the following information along with the vendor invoices provided at the end of this module:

Vendor Name	Vendor ID	Address/Phone
Delicio Vineyards	D2538	12701 South Fernwood Livermore, CA 94550 (925)555-1890
Diversi Vineyards	D0999	8713 Montauk Drive Napa, CA 94558 (707)515-8575
Mendocino Vineyards	M0652	8654 Witherspoon Way Hopland, CA 95449 (707)555-1890
Molti Vineyards	M5170	12773 Calma Court Geyersville, CA 95441 (707)956-8626
Pacific Gas & Electric	P0341	P.O. Box 2575 San Francisco, CA 94103 (415)973-8943

The **General** data is self-explanatory. If information is not provided above or on the vendor invoices leave the cell blank. Be sure to click on **Copy to Remit To Address 1** after entering the address for each vendor. Be sure that the correct **Expense Account** (on the right side of the window) has been selected for each vendor before continuing on from this screen. Pull down the menu and you will find the entire Chart of Accounts. For example, Production Inventory is already selected as the default and is valid for the Delicio, Diversi, Mendocino and Molti Vineyards. However, this is not the correct Expense Account for Pacific Gas & Electric.

5. As you did with Customers, click on the **History** tab and click on **Vendor Beginning Balances** to enter the beginning balance.

Vendor Name	Invoice Number	Invoice Date	P.O. Number	Amount
Delicio Vineyards	45354	11/04/XX	9607	$14,563.56
Diversi Vineyards	Bal Forward	12/15/XX		$2,675,814.93
Mendocino Vineyards	Bal Forward	12/15/XX		$28,942.78
Molti Vineyards	Bal Forward	12/15/XX		$2,268,654.52

6. You can check to be sure that you have entered this information correctly, as you did with Accounts Receivable.

7. Click on **Purchase Info** and pull down the **Ship Via** menu. Select "Best Way" for type of shipping for all vendors, except Pacific Gas & Electric. For the vendors with beginning balances, click on the pull-down menu in **Terms and Credit** and select **Customize terms for this vendor**. Click **Use discounts** and change the **Discount in** to **10 days**. Change the **Discount Percent** to **2%**. If there is a credit limit, remove it at this time.

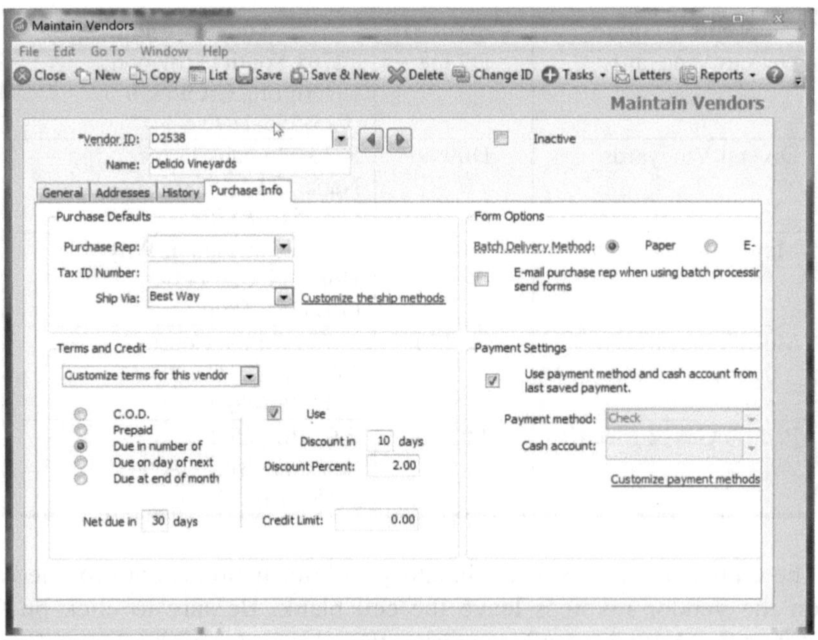

Figure 31

8. Click **Save** after entering each new vendor. Click **Close** Close.

9. You are now finished setting up Accounts Payable. If you wish, you may close the file at this time.

SETTING UP INVENTORY

Requirements

1. Open the Chateau Americana file. Click **Inventory & Services** and click on the **Inventory Items** and select **Set Up Inventory Defaults**. Set the **Item Class** default as Stock item.

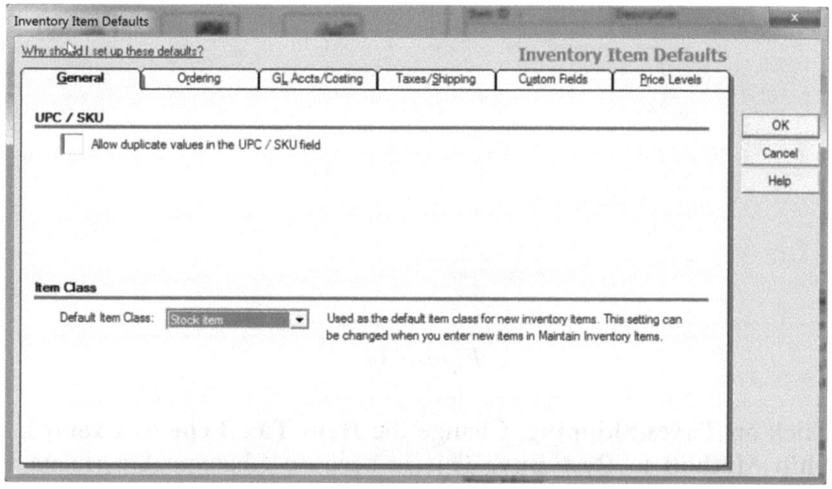

Figure 32

2. Under the **Ordering** tab, change the **Sales Invoice** Out of Stock warning and the **Sales Order** Out of Stock Warning to "**Warn if inventory item is out of stock based on quantity on hand.**" Leave the other defaults in the **Ordering** tab as they are.

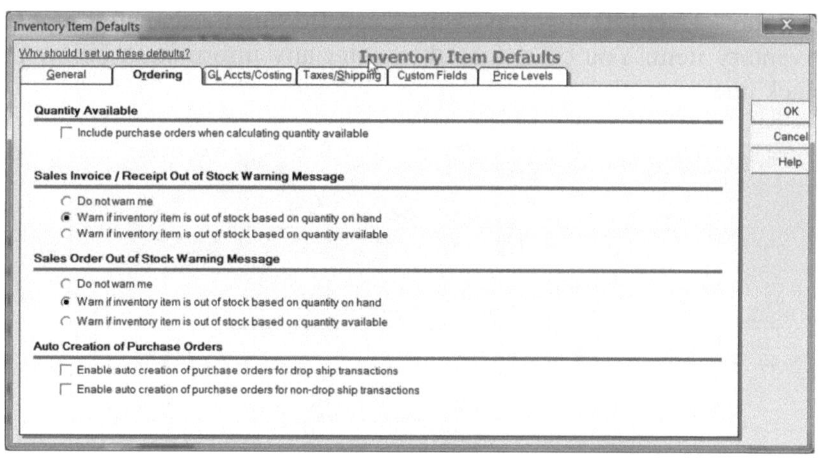

Figure 33

3. Click on the **GL Accts/Costing** tab. Set up the default accounts as follows: GL/Sales Inc should be set to Sales - 410000, GL Invtry/Wage should be set to Inventory – Finished Goods - 145000, and GL Cost Sales should be set to Cost of Goods Sold – 510000. We need to set up these accounts for stock

items only. Change the Costing to LIFO. You will also need to set the GL Freight Account to Cost of Goods Sold - 510000.

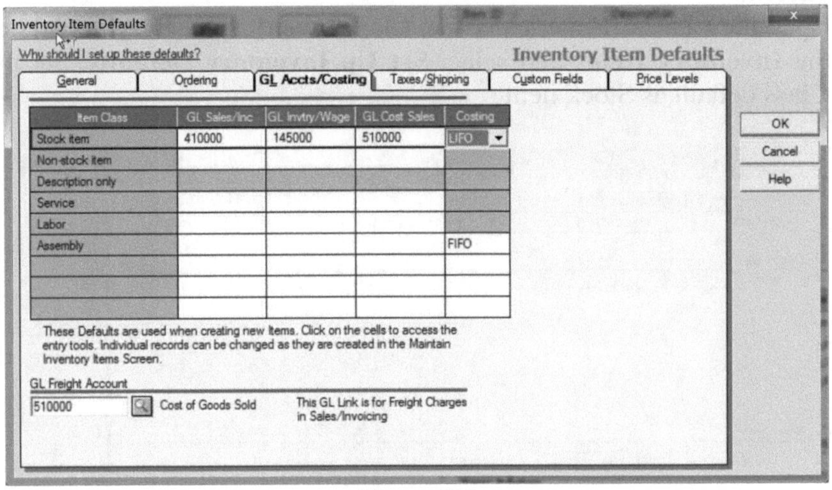

Figure 34

4. Click on **Taxes/Shipping**. Change the **Item Tax Type** to **Exempt**. And the **Ship Method** to **Best Buy**. This is because Chateau Americana typically sells to distributors and, therefore, sales are tax exempt. Click **OK**. You do not need to modify settings on the other tabs.

5. Click on **Inventory Items** again and click on **New Inventory Item**.

   On the **General** tab enter the following information for each inventory item: **Item ID**, **Description**, **Price (Price Level 1)**, **Item Tax Type (select 1 – Regular - Exempt)**, and **Last Unit Cost**. Be sure to save after inputting each inventory item. You do not need to enter any information below the heavy black line.

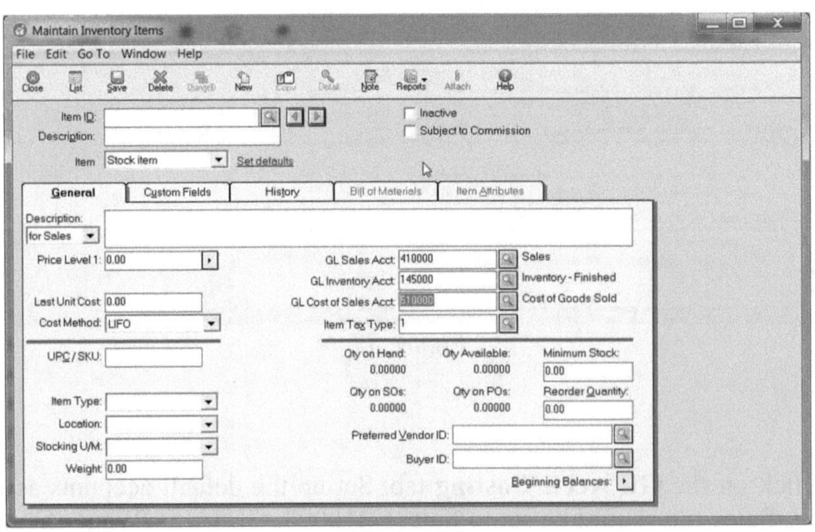

Figure 35

After you have entered the general information for an inventory item, click on **Beginning Balances** in the lower right-hand corner of the window. **Be sure you have referred to your instructor to determine which Transaction Set you are to use before you continue to set up inventory!!** Click on the item and enter its **Quantity** and **Unit Cost**. *Sage 50* will automatically calculate the **Total Cost**. Note that when you are through, the **Total Beginning Balances** will not reconcile to the amount that you input into the **General Ledger** when you were setting up the Chart of Accounts for the company. This is a problem with *Sage 50*. If you were to have put in the **Unit Cost** for each wine that was used previously during the year, that **Unit Cost** would then override the **Last Unit Cost** amount that you entered in the **Maintain Inventory Items** window (see *Figure 35*). The **Unit Cost** fluctuates during the year but *Sage 50* provides no way to properly represent the previous unit cost without impacting the **Last Unit Cost**. Click **OK** to close the Beginning Balances window and enter the information for the next inventory item.

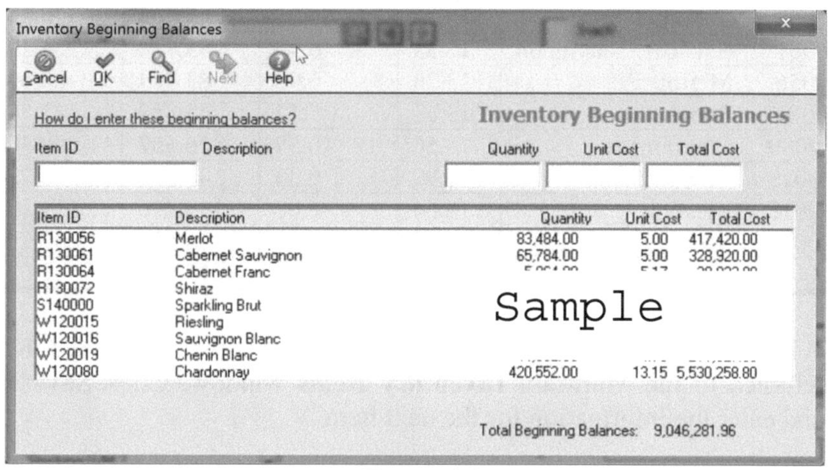

Figure 36

The following presents the inventory information for each Transaction Set. Be sure you choose the correct Transaction Set before you begin to enter the information.

Inventory Data

Transaction Set A

Inventory ID	Description	Price	Last Unit Cost	Quantity On Hand	Beginning Balance
R130064	Cabernet Franc	$10.91	$5.17	5,964	$ 26,838.00
R130061	Cabernet Sauvignon	9.55	5.00	65,784	276,292.80
R130056	Merlot	9.75	5.00	83,484	385,696.08
R130072	Shiraz	11.25	5.15	75,888	347,567.04
W120080	Chardonnay	13.15	9.58	420,552	1,909,306.08
W120019	Chenin Blanc	8.98	4.75	44,532	148,736.88
W120015	Riesling	9.85	5.55	118,596	339,184.56
W120016	Sauvignon Blanc	10.50	5.60	93,636	267,798.96
S140000	Sparkling Brut	15.99	10.52	47,064	342,625.91

Transaction Set B

Inventory ID	Description	Price	Last Unit Cost	Quantity On Hand	Beginning Balance
R130064	Cabernet Franc	$11.48	$5.74	5,964	$ 26,838.00
R130061	Cabernet Sauvignon	9.94	5.23	65,784	276,292.80
R130056	Merlot	10.08	5.17	83,484	385,696.08
R130072	Shiraz	11.71	5.36	75,888	347,567.04
W120080	Chardonnay	13.83	10.07	420,552	1,909,306.08
W120019	Chenin Blanc	9.51	5.03	44,532	148,736.88
W120015	Riesling	10.54	5.94	118,596	339,184.56
W120016	Sauvignon Blanc	11.27	6.01	93,636	267,798.96
S140000	Sparkling Brut	16.36	10.76	47,064	342,625.91

Transaction Set C

Inventory ID	Description	Price	Last Unit Cost	Quantity On Hand	Beginning Balance
R130064	Cabernet Franc	$13.76	$7.25	5,964	$ 26,838.00
R130061	Cabernet Sauvignon	12.33	6.49	65,784	276,292.80
R130056	Merlot	13.26	6.98	83,484	385,696.08
R130072	Shiraz	13.63	7.17	75,888	347,567.04
W120080	Chardonnay	18.50	10.57	420,552	1,909,306.08
W120019	Chenin Blanc	10.90	6.23	44,532	148,736.88
W120015	Riesling	10.64	6.08	118,596	339,184.56
W120016	Sauvignon Blanc	15.82	9.04	93,636	267,798.96
S140000	Sparkling Brut	21.94	11.25	47,064	342,625.91

6. When you finish entering the information for one item and click **OK**, you are returned to the **Maintain Inventory Items** window. Click **Save** and **New** and enter the information for the next item.

   When you are finished entering all of the inventory items, click **Close**.

SETTING UP PAYROLL

Requirements

1. Open the Chateau Americana file. Click on **the Employees & Payroll** tab.

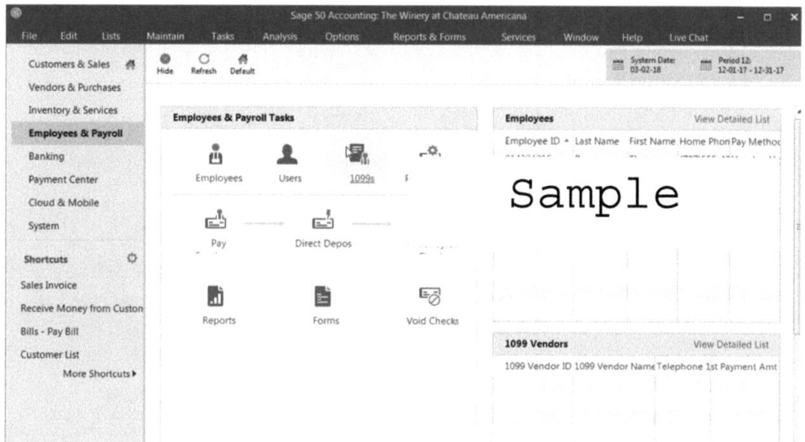

Figure 37

2. Click on the **Employees** icon. Set up the initial payroll fields by clicking on **Set Up Employee Defaults**. A window pops up asking if you would like to open the Payroll Setup Wizard. Click **Yes**.

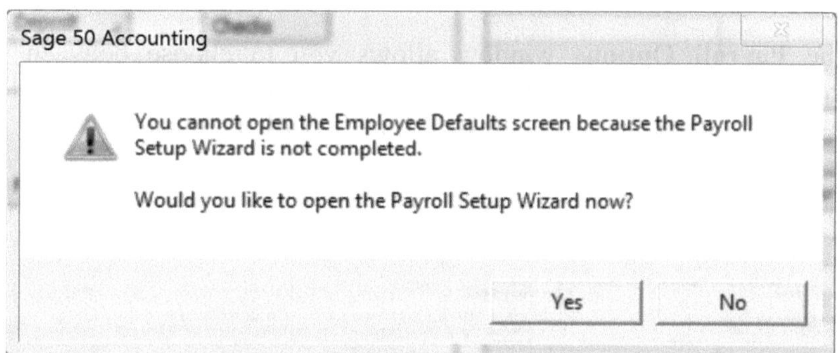

Figure 38

3. The first screen describes the various steps in the Payroll Setup Wizard. Click **Next**.

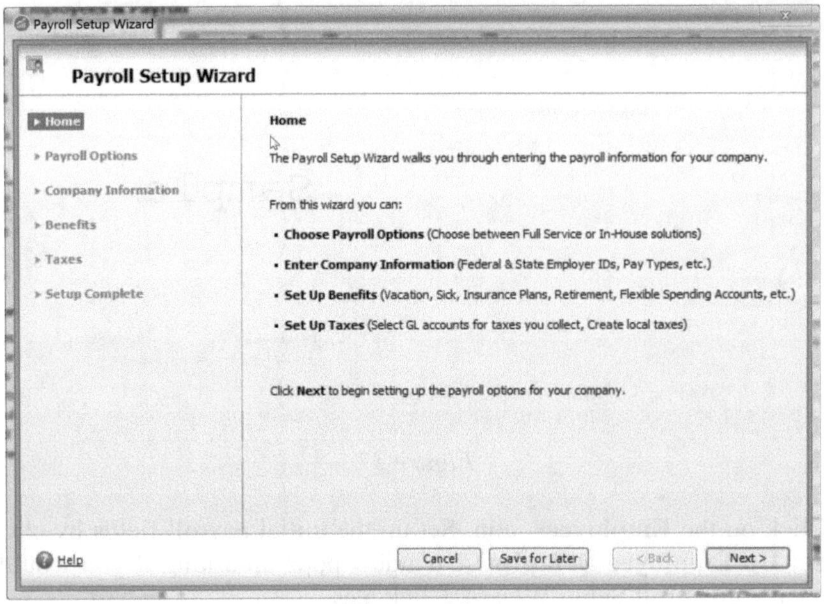

Figure 39

2. The **Payroll Options** window allows you to choose between allowing *Sage 50* to handle your payroll and allowing the company to handle payroll in-house. Leave the setting on **Desktop Payroll** and click **Next**.

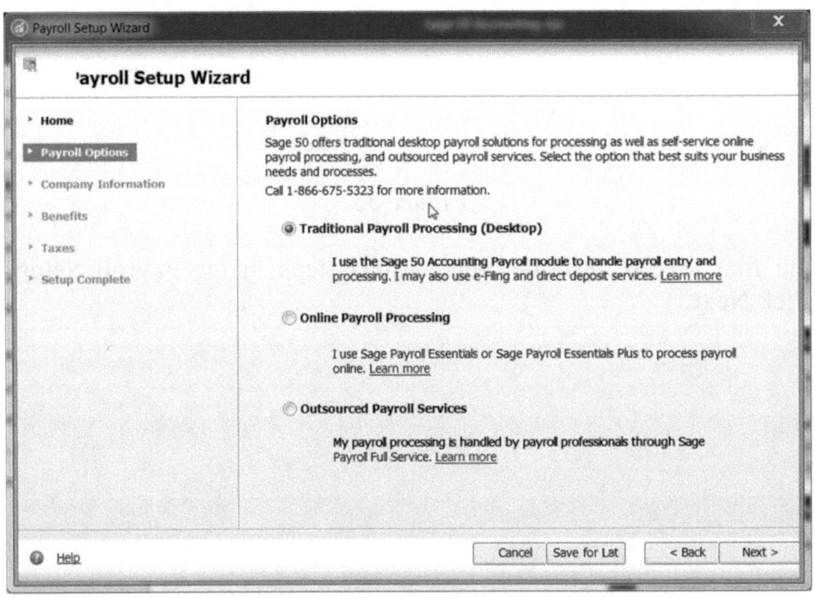

Figure 40

3. The following window informs you that you need to update your subscription in order to run payroll. Your corporation would typically want this service so that the administrator and/or accounting clerk would not have the burden of entering all of the tax formulas. However, in order to determine how these formulas actually work, we are going to create them ourselves. Click on **OK**.

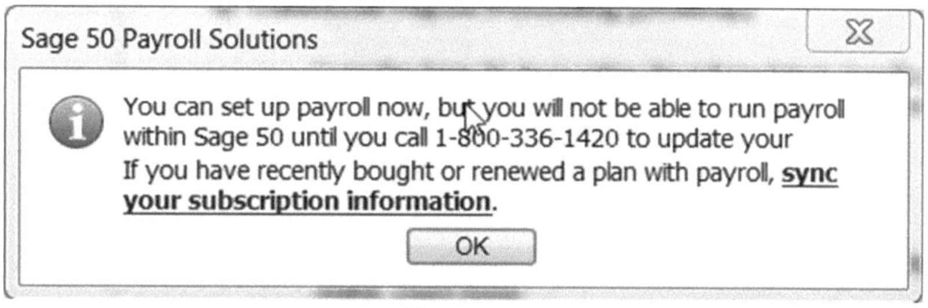

Figure 41

4. The next window provides additional Payroll options that *Sage 50* offers. We are not interested in any of these for this assignment so click **Next**.

5. In the next screen, we will leave the Federal Employer ID, State Employer ID and State Unemployment ID blank. Assume the unemployment tax rate is 6.0%. Do not record meals and tips. Click on **Next**.

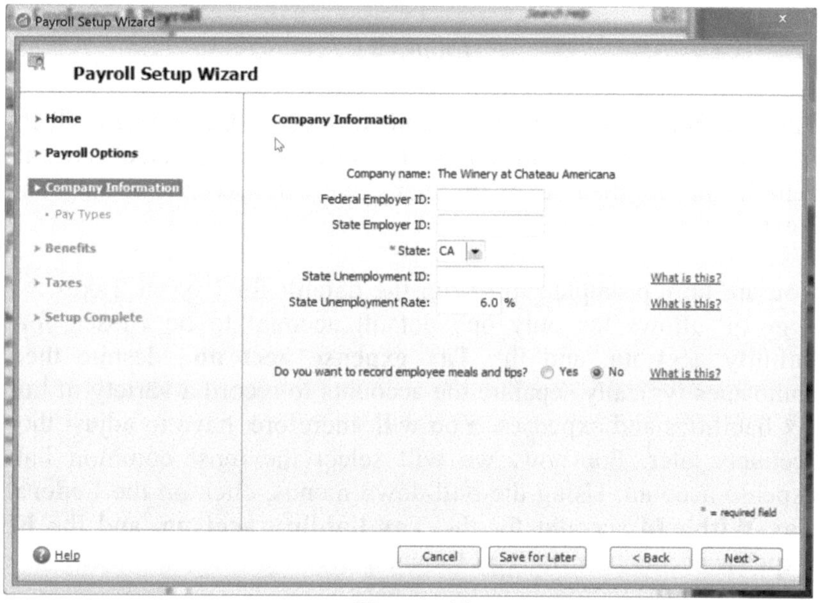

Figure 42

6. You are now prompted to enter the Gross Pay accounts for both Hourly and Salary employees. Chateau Americana has only one expense account for wages and salary. Select the **Wages and Salaries Expense** account for the default Gross Pay account. Be sure to include both the **Regular** and **Overtime Pay Type** for **Hourly** employees. Click **Next**.

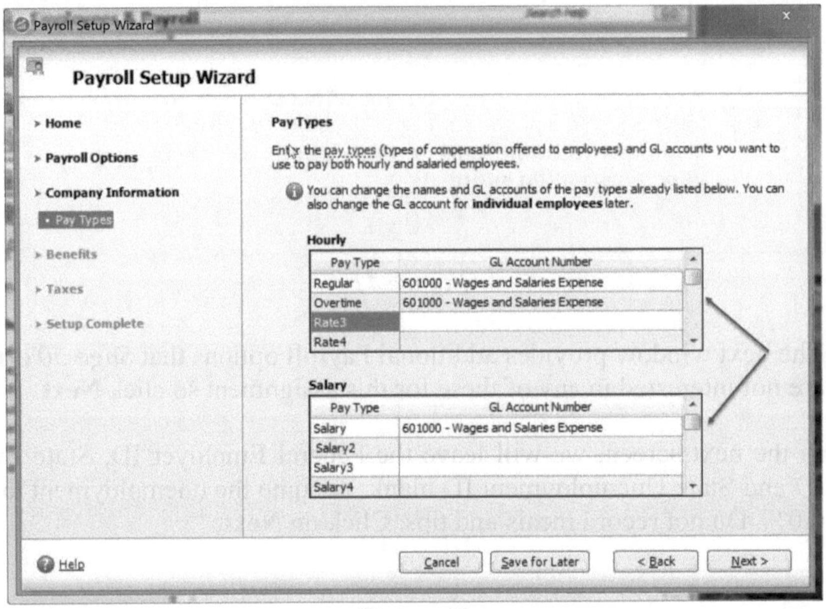

Figure 43

7. The following window asks you to select the benefits that Chateau Americana offers. Obviously, you would typically select several of these benefits but, for the sake of simplicity, we will leave these blank and click on **Next**.

8. You are now prompted to set up the default for Payroll Taxes. Notice that *Sage 50* allows for only one default account to be chosen for the **Tax liability acct no.** and the **Tax expense acct no.**, despite the fact that companies typically separate the accounts to record a variety of both payroll tax liabilities and expenses. You will, therefore, have to adjust these default accounts later. For now, we will select the most common liability and expense account. Using the pull-down menus, click on the **Federal Income Tax Withheld** account for the **Tax liability acct no.** and the **FICA Tax Expense** account for the **Tax Expense acct no.** Click on **Next**.

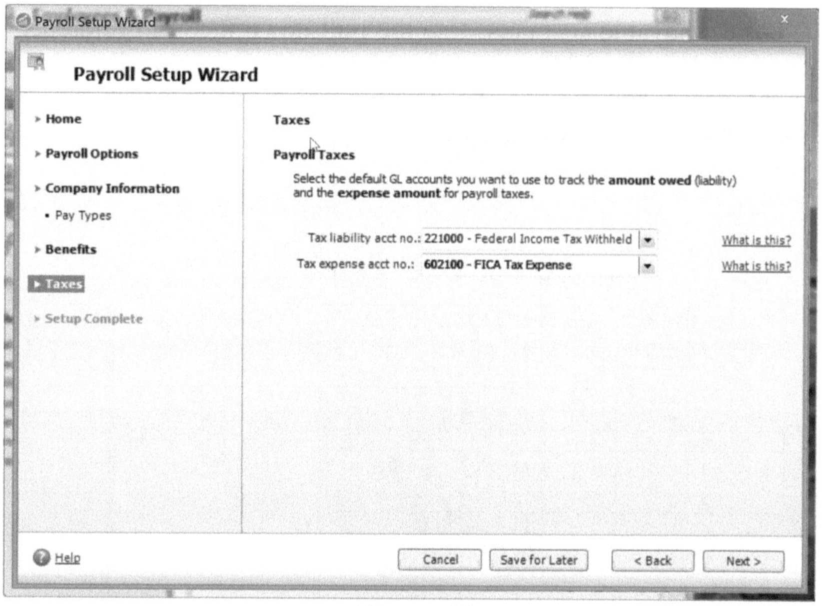

Figure 44

9. Click **Finish** in the following window. We now need to adjust the **Employee Defaults**. Click on **Employees** and click on **Set Up Employee Defaults**. Click on the **Employee Fields** tab. When we were in the Payroll Wizard, we set up the G/L Account for the Tax Liability as the Federal Income Tax Withheld account. We now need to adjust the FICA Withheld account and the Medicare Withheld account. In addition, there are two accounts that *Sage 50* is going to try to use that our company does not need. We will remove those accounts. Use the pull-down menu and enter the proper **G/L Account** code for FICA Withheld (Soc_Sec) and Medicare Withheld (MEDICARE). Remove the checkmarks from the remaining two fields (the fields not being used).

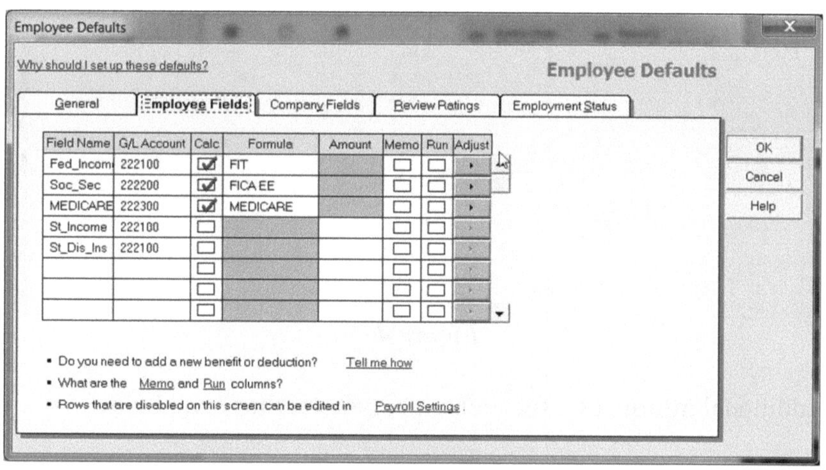

Figure 45

10. Enter the Company payroll information by clicking on the **Company Fields** tab. You will again have to select the proper GL accounts for the employee's portion of FICA and Medicare or the amounts will not be properly posted to

the correct payable accounts. Use the pull-down menu to reference Chateau Americana's general ledger to select the appropriate payroll accounts for the expense accounts and for the payable accounts. Uncheck any remaining fields not being used. Click **OK**.

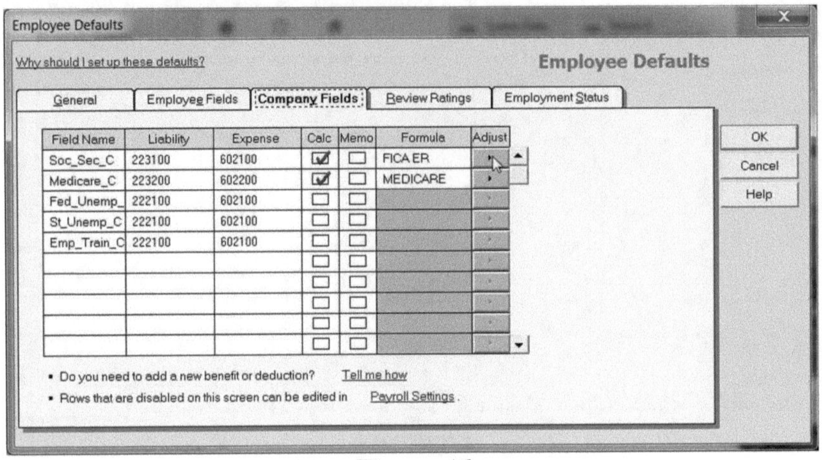

Figure 46

11. Click on **Employees** and click on **New Employee** to enter the individual employee's payroll information. Enter the employee's social security number without hyphens as the "Employee ID."

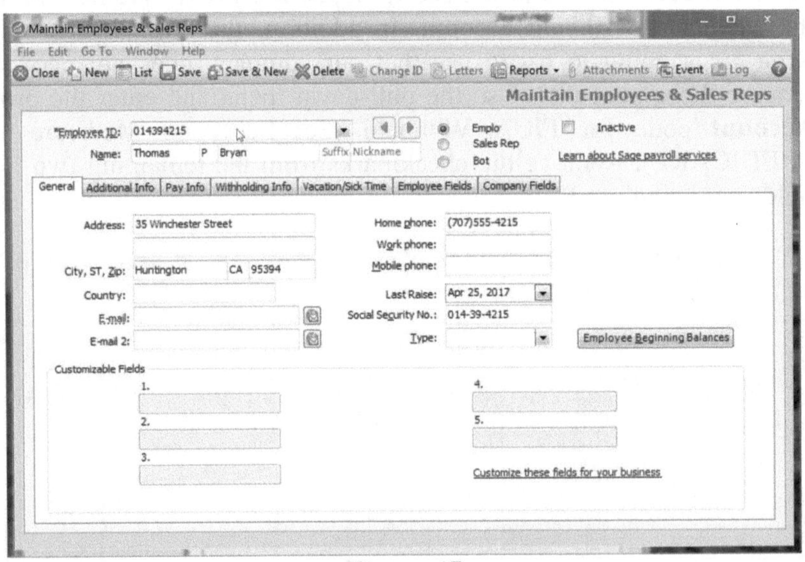

Figure 47

Additional information for each employee can be found below:

Name: Thomas P. Bryan			
Social Security No:	014-39-4215	**Pay rate:**	$17.50
Address:	35 Winchester Street, Huntington, CA 95394	**Pay type:**	Hourly
Phone:	(707) 555-1495	**Position:**	Presses
Date of Birth:	6/14/85	**Filing Status:**	Single
Date of Employment:	4/25/05	**Withholding Allowances**	1
Date of Last Raise:	4/25/XX		
Name: Robert T. Hissom			
Social Security No:	349-43-6417	**Pay rate:**	$15.75
Address:	3187 Heckert Way, Apt. 4A, Huntington, CA 95394	**Pay type:**	Hourly
Phone:	(707) 555-1219	**Position:**	Receiving
Date of Birth:	11/9/87	**Filing Status:**	Single
Date of Employment:	1/4/08	**Withholding Allowances**	0
Date of Last Raise:	1/4/XX		
Name: Anna C. Johnson			
Social Security No:	296-49-3438	**Pay rate:**	$1,800
Address:	175 Bunker Hill Lane, Huntington, CA 95394	**Pay type:**	Salary
Phone:	(707) 555-3856	**Position:**	Acct Sup
Date of Birth:	9/7/78	**Filing Status:**	Married
Date of Employment:	2/14/01	**Withholding Allowances**	3
Date of Last Raise:	2/16/XX		
Name: José G. Rodriquez			
Social Security No:	124-11-7755	**Pay rate:**	$3,500
Address:	2953 Whistler Hill Lane, Huntington, CA 95394	**Pay type:**	Salary
Phone:	(707) 555-2024	**Position:**	Supervisor
Date of Birth:	7/7/71	**Filing Status:**	Married
Date of Employment:	11/3/93	**Withholding Allowances**	4
Date of Last Raise:	1/1/XX		

12. Click on the **Pay Info** tab to enter the employee type and pay rate information. The **Pay Method** for the hourly employees is "**Hourly - Time Ticket Hours**" and for salaried employees is "Salary." You will need to enter the Regular Hourly Rate and the Overtime Hourly Rate (1.5 times the regular hourly rate) for hourly employees. All employees are paid on the 15th and the last day of each month. Leave the **Hours Per Pay Period** at 88. This can be adjusted later.

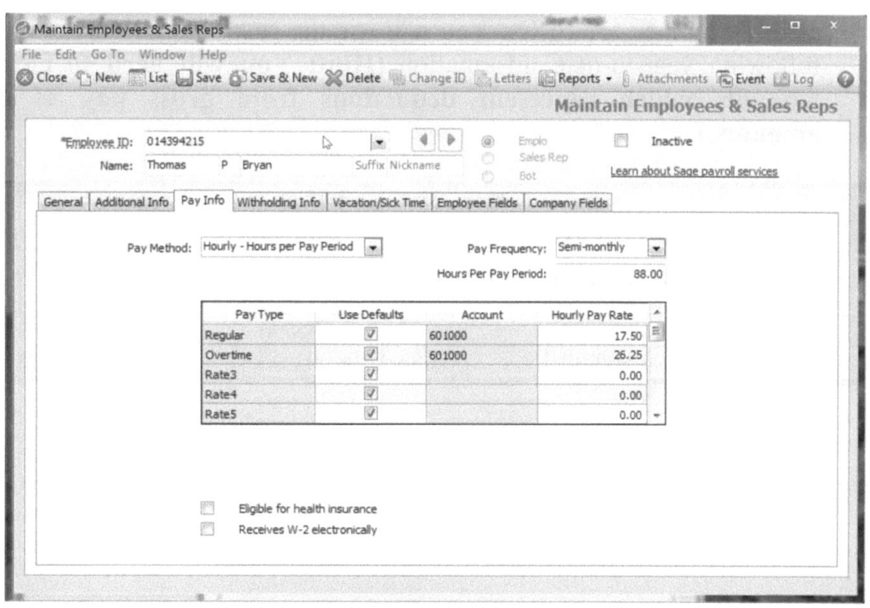

Figure 48

13. Enter the withholding information on the **Withholding Info** tab. Make sure you save each employee as they are entered. Note that you only need to enter the Federal withholding information since state withholdings have not been considered in this exercise.

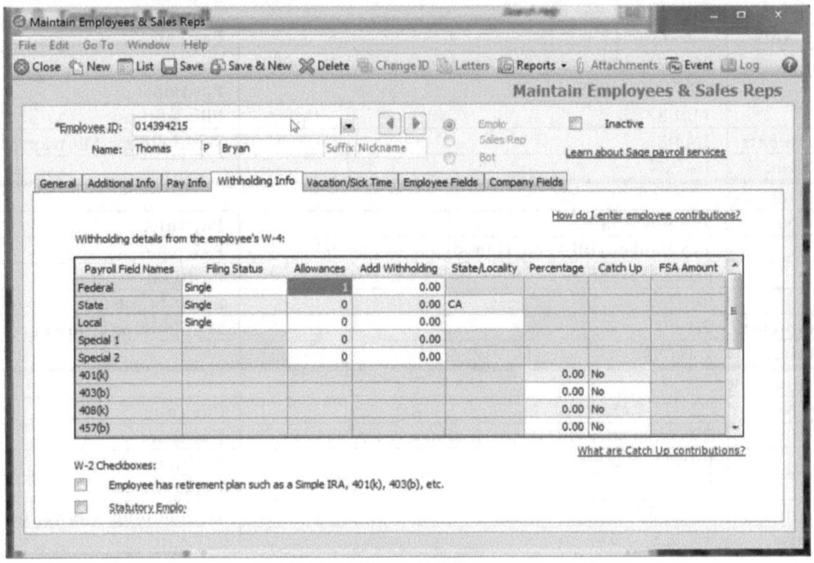

Figure 49

14. Be sure that all fields that are not being used, remain unchecked under the **Employee Fields** and **Company Fields** tabs.

15. When you are finished entering the employee data, go back to the **General** tab, click on **Employee Beginning Balance** (be sure to click Save) and, using the pull-down menu, access each employee to enter the **Employee Beginning Balances** screen. Enter the payroll information for each employee as of December 15, 20XX. You will use the first column only and enter the following year-to-date information (**Hint: You will need to enter those amounts which represent deductions from gross pay as negative amounts.**)

Name	Gross Pay	Federal Income Tax	FICA Withheld	Medicare Withheld	Net Pay
Bryan, T	38,269.37	4,380.66	2,372.70	554.91	30,961.10
Hissom, R	35,093.32	4,486.61	2,175.79	508.85	27,922.07
Johnson, A	40,950.00	2,258.72	2,538.90	593.78	35,558.60
Rodriquez, J	80,500.00	7,608.86	4,991.00	1,167.25	66,732.89

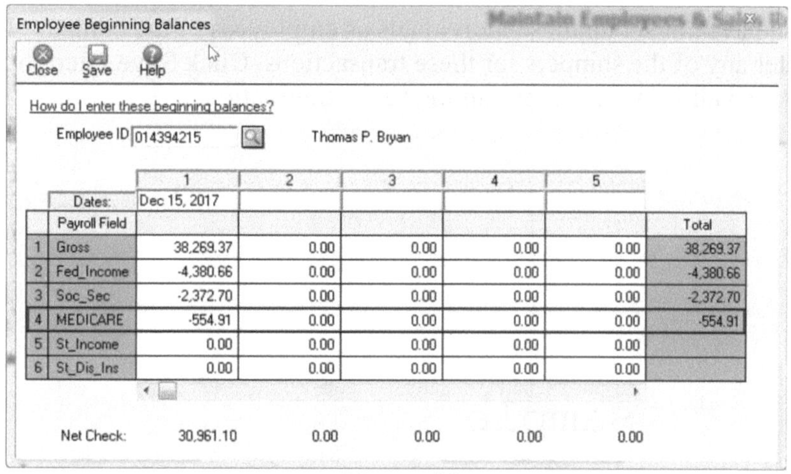

Figure 50

Click **Save** and click on the **Employee ID** view icon to choose the next employee. After entering the beginning balances for all employees, click **Close** and return to the **Employee & Payroll Tasks** screen.

ENTERING TRANSACTIONS

Requirements

1. Open the Chateau Americana file. There are two ways in which you can enter transactions. The first way is to click on **Tasks** and select the appropriate task. For example, you would click on **Sales/Invoicing** to enter credit sales. The second is to click on the Navigation Bar on the left side to open the appropriate window. For example, you would click on **Customers & Sales** to enter credit sales and then click on **New Sales Invoice**. This is the way we will follow in these instructions.

2. The listings of the transaction sets begin on page 99. The following, however, provides some detailed instructions and hints on entering those transactions. Using the Transaction Set assigned by your instructor, examine the first transaction for December 16. The documents supporting the transactions are provided behind each Transaction Set. (**Note: The amounts in the figures that follow do not necessarily agree with those in the Transaction Set assigned to you!!**)

3. The first transaction is a sale to California Premium Beverage. Enter this transaction in *Sage 50* by clicking on **Customers & Sales**. Click on the **Sales Invoices** icon and select **New Sales Invoice**.

4. Using the **View** button next to the **Customer ID** field, select the customer name. Notice that the Customer ID number appears next to the **View** button and the customer name and address appear in the **Bill To:** and **Ship To:** areas. Enter the transaction **Date** and **Invoice No.** and complete the remainder of the form. Do not enter the sales account representative since

you have not set up these individuals as employees of the company. Do not enter any of the shippers for these transactions. Click **Save** after you have entered all information pertaining to the transaction.

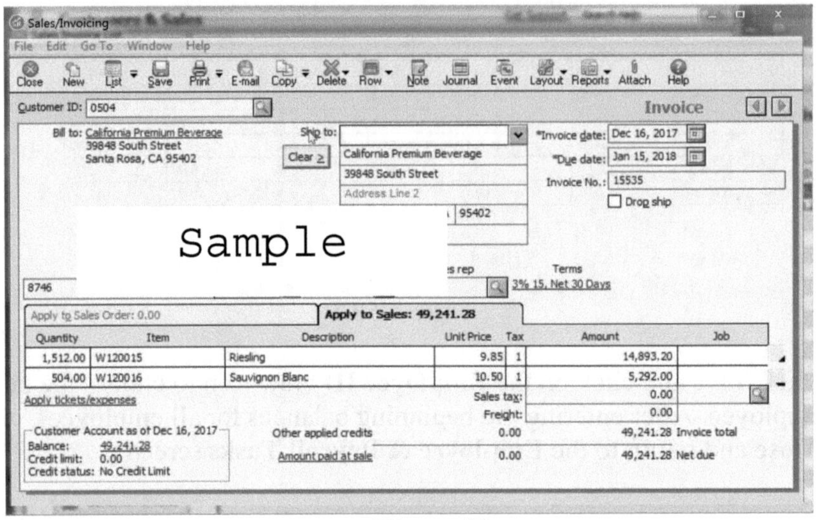

Figure 51

5. Create the **Purchase Order** for the second transaction. Note that when you enter the Item number the field flashes. In addition, you have to manually enter the unit price. When you click on **Save**, an **Invalid ID** window pops up asking if you want to set up the inventory item. Click on **Set Up**.

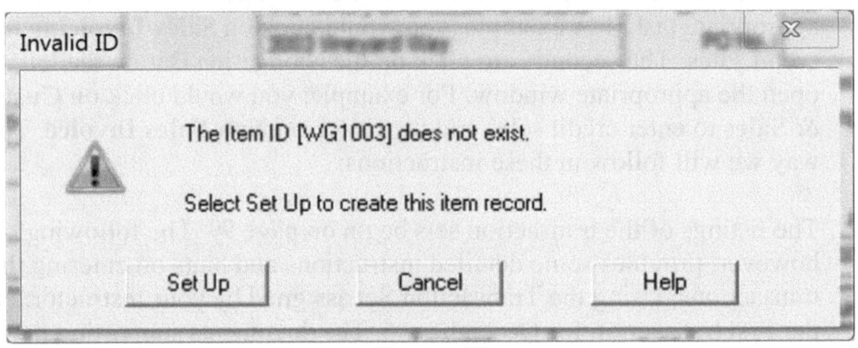

Figure 52

6. Enter the appropriate information. Note that you will need to change the **GL Inventory Acct** to **Inventory – Production**. There is no beginning balance. Click on **Save** and close the window.

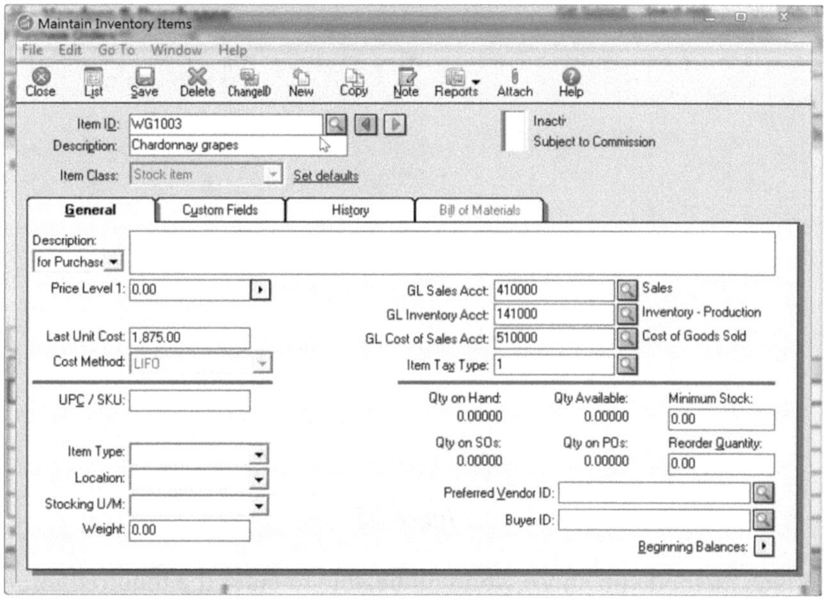

Figure 53

7. Before you **Save** the **Purchase Order**, make sure that all the appropriate information has been entered.

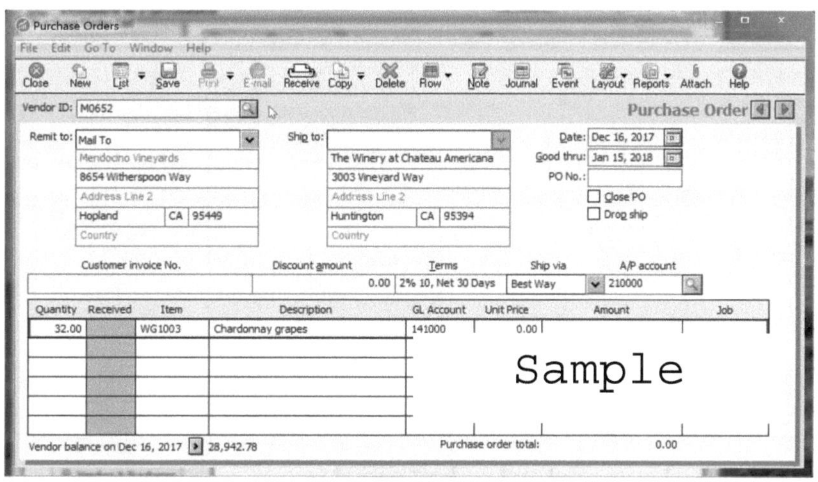

Figure 54

Close the window.

8. The third transaction on December 16th requires you to record the purchase of a truck. When you click on the **Banking** tab, you will notice that there are two ways in which cash disbursements can be handled. You can click on either **Write Checks** or **Bills** and then **Pay Bills** in the **Tasks** menu. Alternatively, you can click on **Banking** in the Navigation window on the left hand side of your screen and select either of the above from the **Banking Tasks** window.

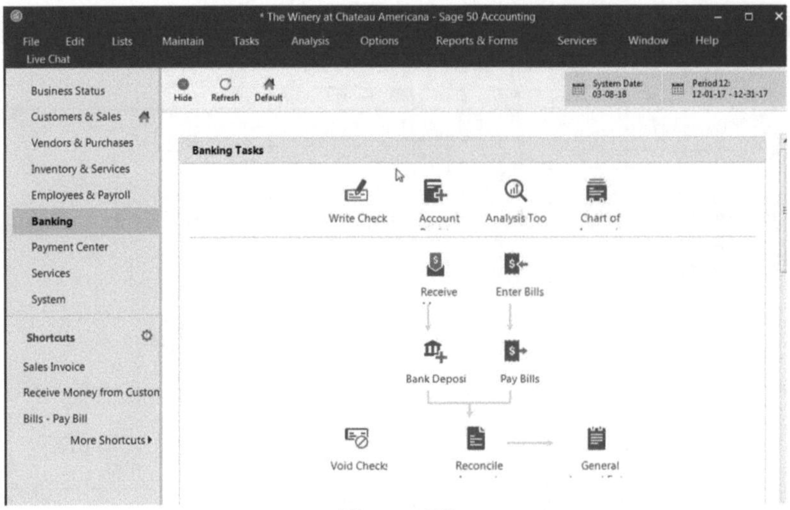

Figure 55

Which method you chose, you will be able to enter the required information for this transaction. If, however, you click on **Pay Bills**, you will notice that the lower part of the window has space to enter a description, along with the ability to change the **GL Account**.

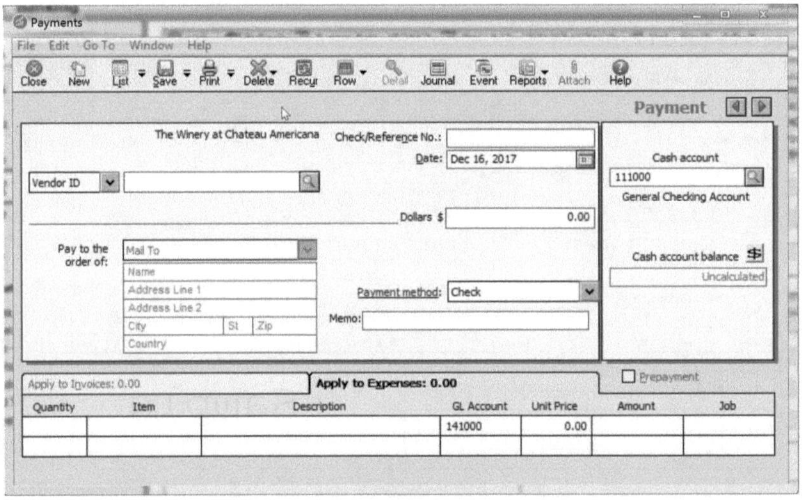

Figure 56

Notice, however, that **Write Checks** does not have any obvious place in which to enter multiple accounts.

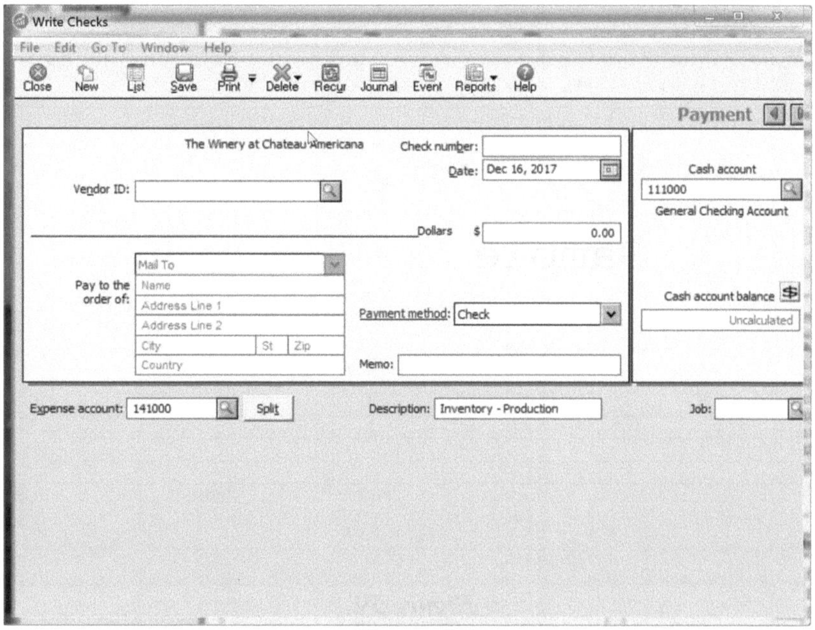

Figure 57

If you choose this option, first fill in all of the appropriate information on the face of the check. Note that there is no Vendor ID for this transaction. You can skip to the vendor Name field. You can then click on the **Split** button  next to the **Expense account** field to enter all of the accounts involved in this transaction.

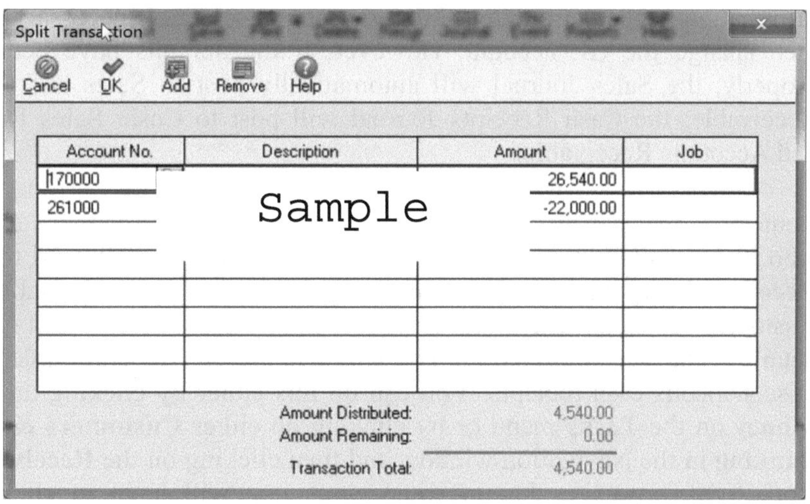

Figure 58

9. For the fourth entry on December 16th, the Board of Directors has declared a cash dividend. This transaction represents a General Journal entry. General Journal entries are recorded by clicking on the **Tasks** button in the main menu and then clicking on **General Journal Entry**. Each General Journal entry should be given its own **Reference** number.

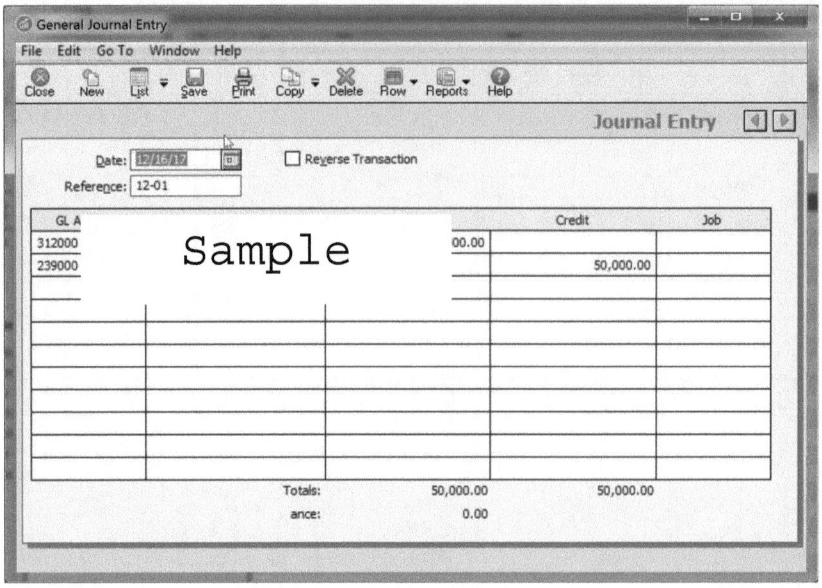

Figure 59

10. Continue working through the transactions from December 17th through the first transaction on December 31st transactions listed below, selecting **Customers & Sales**, **Inventory & Services**, **Employees & Payroll**, or **Banking** as appropriate. Be sure the default accounts being used by the *Sage 50* Journals are the appropriate accounts for the particular transaction you are entering. You can check the accounts being debited and credited by each transaction by clicking on the **Journal** icon once you have entered the information needed at the top of the transaction screen. If necessary, you can then change the GL account. However, if the defaults have been set up properly, the Sales Journal will automatically post to Sales and Accounts Receivable; the Cash Receipts Journal will post to Cash, Sales Discounts, and Accounts Receivable.

    Remember that not all customers receive credit terms. For those customers who have remitted a check along with their order, you will need to use the **Receive Money** task. If a customer number is not available, tab past the Customer ID field, enter the customer name and address, and enter the details of the sales transaction. You will also use the **Receipts** task for other miscellaneous cash receipts. You can do this either by clicking on **Receive Money** on the **Tasks** menu or by clicking on either **Customers & Sales** or **Banking** in the Navigation window and then clicking on the **Receive Money** icon. Note, however, that in some cases you will have to click on the **Journal** icon and change the account being credited.

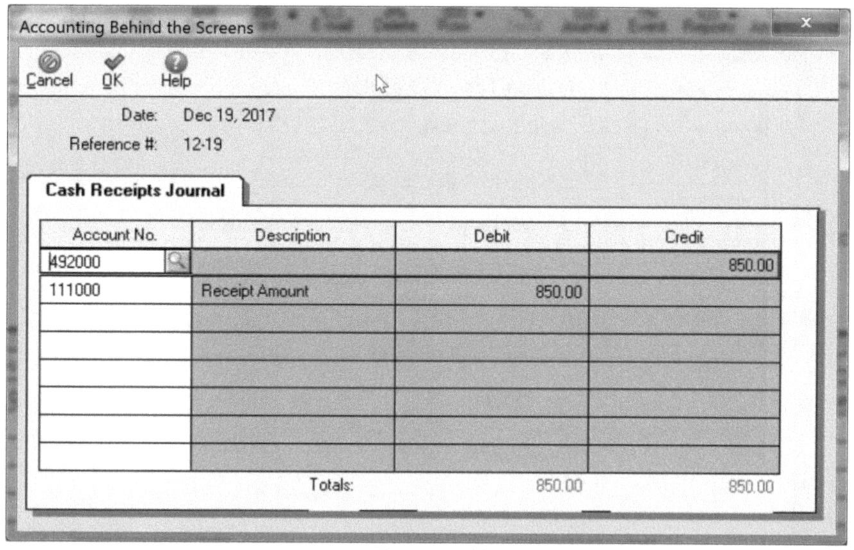

Figure 60

11. When inventory is received, you will need to access the purchase order that it relates to and click on the Receive icon. Enter the necessary information from the invoice to the form. This will add the purchase order amount to Accounts Payable and allow you to pay it as required. If a purchase order has not previously been prepared, click on **Purchases/Receive Inventory** to enter the information. When this bill is paid, you will need to access this item again and click on **Pay Now** to mark it as Paid. You will then be able to complete the payment.

12. For the payroll transactions on December 31, click on **Pay Employees** and then select on **Enter Payroll for Multiple Employees**. Be sure that the **Pay End Date** is set at December 31st and that the on box checked under **Include Pay Frequencies** is Semi-Monthly.

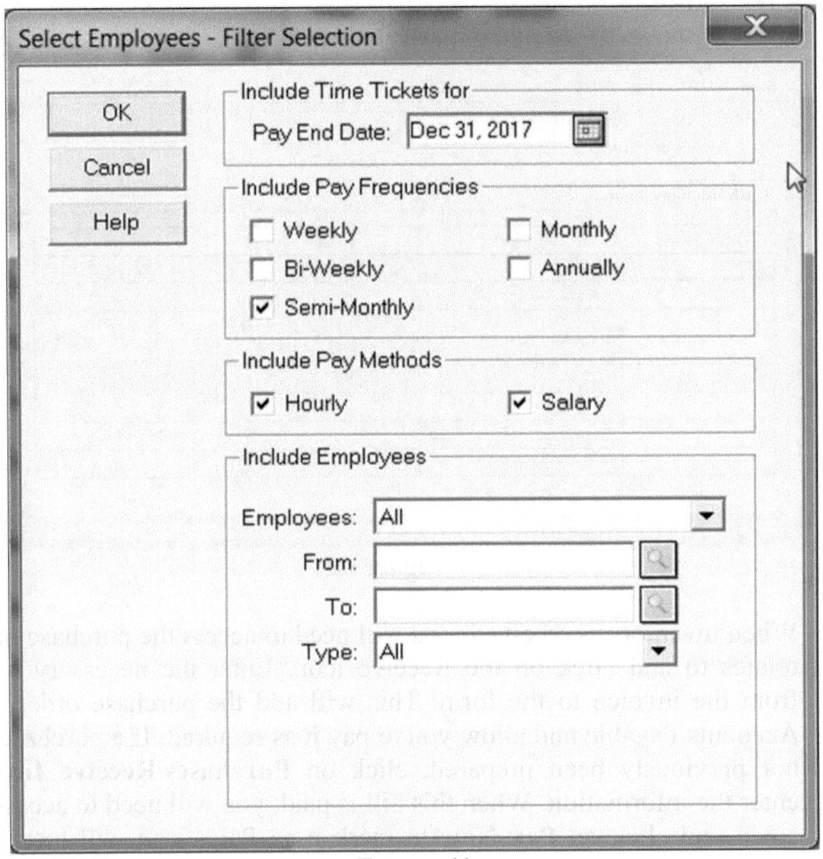

Figure 61

13. In addition, refer to the payroll cards for the hourly employees to be sure you enter the appropriate hours for these employees. Finally, think about the Cash Account from which the payroll checks are written. You will need to print a report or the checks in order to record the payroll.

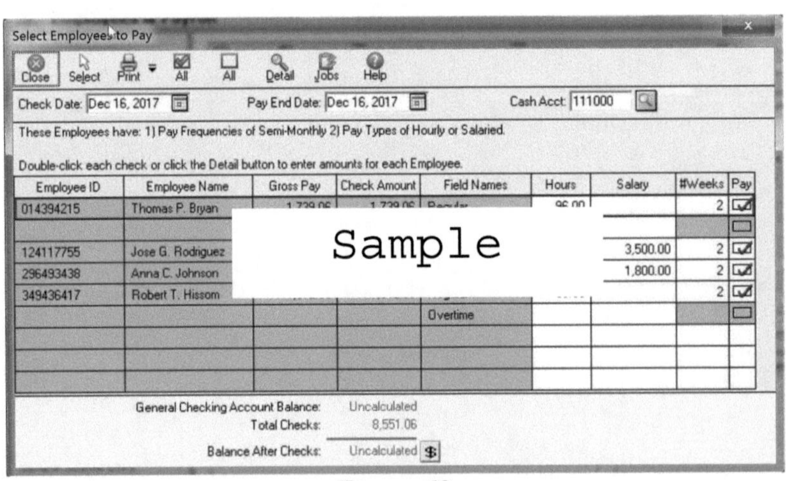

Figure 62

Note that when you enter the payroll data the net pay may be slightly different from the net pay you calculated if you prepared the payroll checks in the *CAST Manual AIS Module*. This is because the formulas contained in

Sage 50 are for the current year and this may not coincide with those you used in the *CAST Manual AIS Module.*

TRANSACTION SET A

December	Transaction
16	Receive a purchase order from California Premium Beverage (page 102). Fill and ship the order. Complete Invoice No. 15535.
16	Order 32 tons of Chardonnay grapes at $1,875.00 per ton from Mendocino Vineyards. The item number for the white grapes is WG1003. Add the item to inventory when prompted. Be sure to change the Inventory account. Complete Purchase Order No. 9682.
16	Purchase a 20XW Ford truck for $26,540.00. The terms include a $4,540.00 down payment and a 3-year, 6% promissory note to Ford Credit for the remaining $22,000.00. Principal and interest on the note are due monthly beginning January 4, 20XY. The company expects the truck to have a useful life of 5 years and no salvage value. Prepare Check No. 19257 payable to Potter Valley Ford for the down payment.
16	The Board of Directors of Chateau Americana authorized a $50,000 cash dividend payable on January 20th to the stockholders of record on January 15th. Record the transaction.
17	Receive a phone complaint from Seaside Distributors about a case of Chenin Blanc that was damaged in shipment. The case was part of Invoice No. 15175, dated November 5, 20XX, in the amount of $20,438.40. Seaside paid the invoice on November 19, 20XX and took advantage of the discount (terms 3/15, net 30). Prepare Check No. 19286 to reimburse Seaside for the damaged inventory that was *not* returned to the company.
19	Receive $850 refund from California Wine & Cheese Monthly for overpayment of advertising costs (page 103). The reference number is 12-19.
19	Receive payment in full from Pacific Distribution Co. on Invoice No. 15243 dated November 13, 20XX, in the amount of $19,576.80 (page 104). Record the cash receipt.

December	Transaction
19	Receive a purchase order (page 105) with payment (page 106) from Sonoma Distributors. Fill and ship the order. Record the sale.
22	Receive 19 tons of cabernet sauvignon grapes at $2,279.00 per ton from Mendocino Vineyards (inventory number CS1250). Also received Invoice No. M7634 from Mendocino Vineyards with the shipment (page 107). Terms on the invoice are 2/10, net 30. Record the receipt of the inventory.
26	Receive utility bill from Pacific Gas and Electric in the amount of $18,887.62 (page 108). Prepare Check No. 19402.
30	Receive Brokerage Advice from Edwards Jones for purchase of 500 shares of Microsoft at $65.73 per share plus $400 broker's commission (page 109). Prepare Check No. 19468.
30	Prepare Check No. 19473 payable to Mendocino Vineyards for the shipment received on December 22.
31	Receive payment in full for the December 16 purchase from California Premium Beverage (page 110). Record the cash receipt.
31	Prepare Payroll Checks (Nos. 7111-7114) for Anna Johnson, José Rodriguez, Tom Bryan, and Bob Hissom. Time cards for Tom and Bob are on pages 111-112. (You will be asked if you want to print the checks. You can elect to print them in PDF format to save paper unless your professor wants you to turn them in.) Prepare Check No. 19474 to transfer cash from the general cash account to the payroll account. Record the payroll transactions. If you have set up payroll correctly, the accruals should be automatically posted. Also note that if you have completed the *CAST Manual AIS Module*, the payroll amounts might differ from those calculated in *Sage 50*. Your version of *Sage 50* should be using the current year and your professor may have chosen a different year in the Manual Module.
31	Prepare Check No. 19475 to repay $50,000 of the principal on long-term debt to Bank of Huntington.

MONTH-END PROCEDURES

There are two methods by which you can access the General Journal in *Sage 50*. You can use the menu: **Tasks > General Journal Entry** or you can go through the Navigation window and click on **Banking**. Either method will pull up the **General Journal** window.

1. Calculate monthly accrued interest expense for the installment note to Ford Credit (based on 365 days per year and interest starting to accrue on December 17, 20XX). Make the appropriate adjusting entry. The payable is posted to Other Accrued Expenses Payable.

2. For your convenience, depreciation in the amount of $105,341.50 has been calculated on all assets for the month of December **except** for the Ford Pickup. Calculate the depreciation for the truck and add that amount to the

$105,341.50 to determine the total depreciation expense for December. Record the appropriate adjusting entry in the General Journal.

3. The monthly bank statement indicates bank charges of $30, a returned check from Alota Wine Distributors in the amount of $19,475.26, and a check printing fee of $60. Record this in the General Journal.

4. If you have completed the *CAST Manual AIS Module*, your account balances can be verified at this time by clicking on **Reports & Forms**, then on **General Ledger** and finally on **Working Trial Balance**. Remember that your net payroll might be slightly different due to differences in Federal Tax Withheld.

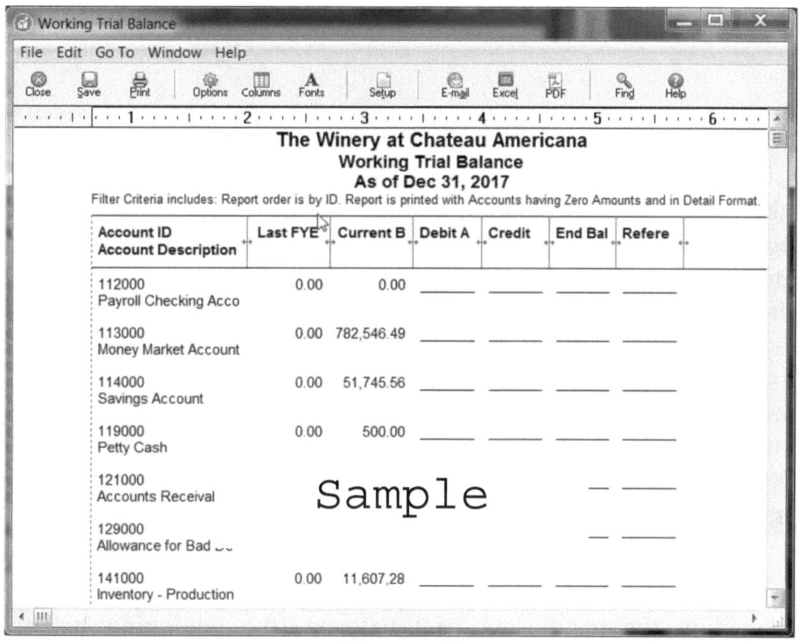

The Winery at Chateau Americana
Working Trial Balance
As of Dec 31, 2017
Filter Criteria includes: Report order is by ID. Report is printed with Accounts having Zero Amounts and in Detail Format.

Account ID Account Description	Last FYE	Current B	Debit A	Credit	End Bal	Refere
112000 Payroll Checking Acco	0.00	0.00				
113000 Money Market Account	0.00	782,546.49				
114000 Savings Account	0.00	51,745.56				
119000 Petty Cash	0.00	500.00				
121000 Accounts Receival						
129000 Allowance for Bad						
141000 Inventory - Production	0.00	11,607.28				

Figure 63

5. The transactions for the Payroll Journal, Accounts Receivable, and Accounts Payable can also be verified through the **Reports** menu under each of the transaction tabs.

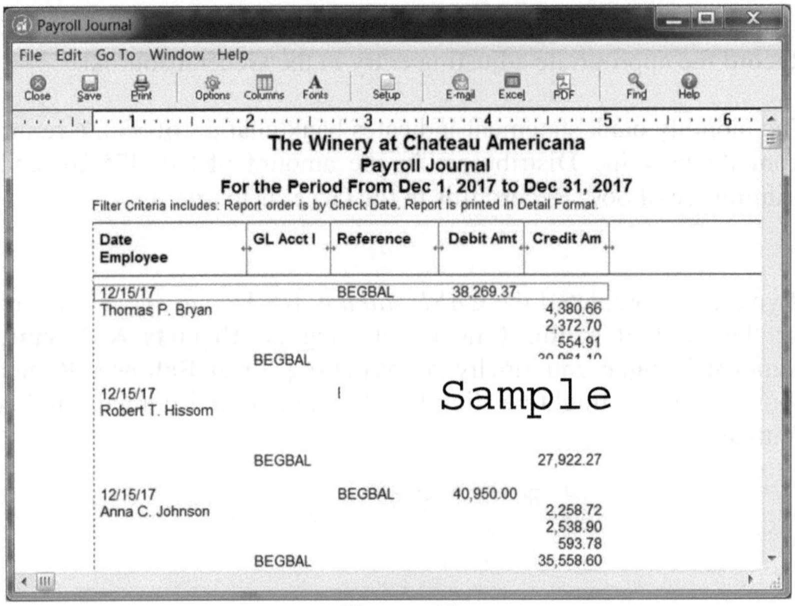

Figure 64

6. Take some time and examine some of the journals provided for you in *Sage 50*. If you completed the *CAST Manual AIS Module*, think about the similarities and differences of these journals to those you prepared manually. For example, compare and contrast the processes required to create and post a sales entry in *Sage 50* to those required in the *CAST Manual AIS Module*. You should observe that the defaults you created during set-up have simplified the posting process, but also have obscured part of the double-entry process.

YEAR-END PROCEDURES

1. Year-end adjusting entries should be recorded in the general journal after reconciling the unadjusted trial balance (the beginning balances in the working trial balance). You **DO NOT** need to close the books for the end of the year. Prepare the following year-end adjusting journal entries:

    a. Calculate the allowance for bad debts using the net sales method. Experience indicates that 0.05% of net sales should be set aside for bad debts. Record the appropriate adjusting entry.

    b. The calculation of federal income tax expense is a year-end adjusting entry but it cannot be made until all other entries have been made and *net income before taxes* has been determined. Therefore, you must first calculate net income before taxes. Then calculate federal income tax expense and record the adjusting entry. **HINT:** The rates can be found in the instructions to Schedule J of Form 1120 (the Federal corporate income tax return) or in a tax textbook that contains corporate tax information.

Adjusting entries should be verified through the working trial balance as was done previously.

2. Print, and prepare to submit, the financial statements (including the **Balance Sheet**, the **Income Statement**, and the **Statement of Cash Flows**), the **Aged Receivables Report,** the **Aged Payables Report,** and the **Payroll Checks, Register** or **Report** and any other reports or statements that your instructor requests.

PURCHASE ORDER

California Premium Beverage

39848 South Street
Santa Rosa, CA 95402
Phone (707) 555-7451 Fax (707) 555-7452

To:
Chateau Americana
3003 Vineyard Way
Huntington, CA 95394

Ship To:
California Premium Beverage
39848 South Street
Santa Rosa, CA 95402

ABC Permit #: A59782

P.O. DATE	P.O. NUMBER	SHIPPED VIA	F.O.B. POINT	TERMS
12/13/XX	8746	CA Express	Destination	3/15, net 30

ITEM NO	QTY	SIZE	DESCRIPTION	UNIT PRICE	TOTAL
W120015	1512	0.750	Riesling	9.85	14,893.20
W120016	504	0.750	Sauvignon Blanc	10.50	5,292.00
W120019	336	0.750	Chenin Blanc	8.98	3,017.28
R130061	1176	0.750	Cabernet Sauvignon	9.55	11,230.80
R130056	672	0.750	Merlot	9.75	6,552.00
S140000	240	0.750	Sparkling Brut	15.99	3,837.60
W120080	336	0.750	Chardonnay	13.15	4,418.40
				TOTAL	49,241.28

Jorge Gonzalez — *12/13/XX*

Authorized by — Date

California Wine and Cheese Monthly | Lone Star Bank | **23545**
573 Parkins Ave. | Dallas, TX 27540
Ukiah, CA 95482

Date 12/15/XX

PAY Eight Hundred Fifty and 00/100 Dollars -- $ 850.00

To the order of
Chateau Americana
3003 Vineyard Way
Huntington, CA 95394

- SAMPLE, DO NOT CASH -

⑆000000⑆ ⑈000000000⑈ 23545

California Wine and Cheese Monthly **23545**

Reference	Amount
Overpayment of monthly advertising	$850.00

Pacific Distribution Company
10034 Westborough Boulevard
San Francisco, CA 94080

Bank of America
San Francisco, CA 94104

69712

Date 12/16/XX

PAY Nineteen Thousand Five Hundred Seventy Six and 80/100 Dollars ------------------ $ 19,576.80

To The Order Of
Chateau Americana
3003 Vineyard Way
Huntington, CA 95394

- SAMPLE, DO NOT CASH -

⑆000000⑆ ⑈000000000⑈ 69712

Pacific Distribution Company **69712**

Reference	Net Amount
Invoice #15243, customer # 0505	$19,576.80

PURCHASE ORDER

PO Number: 4376
Date: 12/19/XX

To:
Chateau Americana
3003 Vineyard Way
Huntington, CA 95394

Ship To:
SONOMA DISTRIBUTORS
3224 Greenlawn Street
Ukiah, CA 95482
Phone (707) 555-1705 Fax (707) 555-1706

SHIPPED VIA	ABC #	F.O.B. POINT	TERMS
United Express	A557912	Huntington	Cash

ITEM NO	QTY	SIZE	DESCRIPTION	UNIT PRICE	TOTAL
W120015	480	0.750	Riesling	9.85	4,728.00
W120080	468	0.750	Chardonnay	13.15	6,154.20
W120019	300	0.750	Chenin Blanc	8.98	2,694.00
R130072	780	0.750	Shiraz	11.25	8,775.00
R130056	672	0.750	Merlot	9.75	6,552.00
				TOTAL	28,903.20

Chrystal Harrington 12/19/XX
Authorized by Date

Sonoma Distributors **17003**
3224 Greenlawn Street
Ukiah, CA 95482

Humboldt Bank
Ukiah, CA 95482

Date 12/19/XX

PAY Twenty-eight Thousand Nine Hundred Three and 20/100 Dollars --------------- $ 28,903.20

To the order of
Chateau Americana
3003 Vineyard Way
Huntington, CA 95394

- SAMPLE, DO NOT CASH -

¦:000000¦: :000000000: 17003

Sonoma Distributors **17003**

Reference	Discount	Net Amount
Payment for PO 4376		$28,903.20

CUSTOMER INVOICE

Mendocino Vineyards
8654 Witherspoon Way
Hopland, CA 95449
Phone: (707) 555-1890

Invoice Number M7634

Invoice Date 12/20/20XX

Sold To:
Chateau Americana, Inc.
3003 Vineyard Way
Huntington, CA 95394

Credit Terms: 2/10, Net 30

Ship To:
Chateau Americana, Inc.
3003 Vineyard Way
Huntington, CA 95394

Customer I.D	Customer P.O. Number
CHATAM	9660

Description	Product Number	Quantity	Cost	Extended
Cabernet Sauvignon Grapes	CS1250	19 tons	$2,279.00	$43,301.00

Total Cost: $43,301.00

Comments:

Distribution: Copy 1 — Accounting; Copy 2 – Shipping; Copy 3 – Customer

Payment Coupon

Bill Date: 12/23/20XX

Please Pay by 01/17/20XX
$18,887.62

Amount Enclosed

Account No. 21790-1879

Chateau Americana, Inc.
3003 Vineyard Way
Huntington, CA 95394

Send Payment to:

Pacific Gas and Electric
P.O. Box 2575
San Francisco, CA 94103

Retain bottom portion for your records, detach and return stub with payment.

Service	Chateau Americana, Inc.	Your Account Number	Rate Class	Billing Date
For:	3003 Vineyard Way Huntington, CA 95394	**21790-1879**	**Commercial**	**12/23/20XX**

Meter Number	Service Period	Days	Type of Reading	Multiplier	Units	Meter Readings Current	Meter Readings Past	Usage
68869800	**11/23/XX – 12/23/XX**	**31**	**Actual**	**1**	**KWH**	**1098412**	**1001301**	**97111**
Previous Balance								16,895.53
Payment								16,895.53
Balance Forward								0.00
Current Charges								18,887.62
						Due Date		**Total Due**
						01/17/20XX		18,887.62

Pacific Gas and Electric

1000 Energy Drive, San Francisco, CA 94103, (415) 973-8943

Edward Jones Financial Services

100 Market Street
San Francisco, CA 94109
(415)504-9000

Customer
Chateau Americana, Inc.
3003 Vineyard Way
Huntington, CA 95394

Account Number
02334-85763

Tax Identification #
23-7788954

SAVE THIS STATEMENT FOR TAX PURPOSES

Date	Description	Symbol	Fees and/or Commissions($)	Net Dollar Amount ($)	Share Price ($)	Transaction Shares
12/30/03	Microsoft Corporation Common Shares	MSFT	400.00	33,265.00	65.73	500.0000

California Premium Beverage
39848 South Street
Santa Rosa, CA 95402

Bay View Bank
Santa Rosa, CA 95407

21803

Date 12/29/XX

PAY Forty-Seven Thousand Seven Hundred Sixty-Four and 04/100 Dollars ------------------ $ 47,764.04

To The Order Of
Chateau Americana
3003 Vineyard Way
Huntington, CA 95394

- SAMPLE, DO NOT CASH -

⑆000000⑆ ⑈000000000⑈ 21803

California Premium Beverage **21803**

Reference	Discount	Net Amount
# 0504 Invoice 15535	$1,477.24	$47,764.04

Period Ending	December 19, 20XX
Employee Name	Thomas P. Bryan
Signature	*Tom Bryan*
Approved	*PJB*

Out		7th Day	
In			
Out			
In			
Out	*4*	6th Day	**04:00 PM**
In			**12:01 PM**
Out	*4*		**11:30 AM**
In			**07:29 AM**
Out	*4*	5th Day	**04:01 PM**
In			**12:00 PM**
Out	*4*		**11:30 AM**
In			**07:31 AM**
Out	*4*	4th Day	**04:02 PM**
In			**11:58 AM**
Out	*4*		**11:30 AM**
In			**07:30 AM**
Out	*4*	3rd Day	**04:03 PM**
In			**11:59 AM**
Out	*4*		**11:30 AM**
In			**07:31 AM**
Out		2nd Day	
In			
Out			
In			
Out		1st Day	
In			
Out			
In			

Period Ending	December 26, 20XX
Employee Name	Thomas P. Bryan
Signature	*Tom Bryan*
Approved	*PJB*

Out		7th Day	
In			
Out			
In			
Out	*4*	6th Day	
In			
Out	*4*		
In			*Holiday*
Out	*4*	5th Day	
In			
Out	*4*		
In			*Holiday*
Out	*4*	4th Day	**04:00 PM**
In			**12:02 PM**
Out	*4*		**11:30 AM**
In			**07:29 AM**
Out	*4*	3rd Day	**04:00 PM**
In			**12:01 PM**
Out	*4*		**11:33 AM**
In			**07:30 AM**
Out	*4*	2nd Day	**04:04 PM**
In			**12:02 PM**
Out	*4*		**11:31 AM**
In			**07:28 AM**
Out		1st Day	
In			
Out			
In			

Period Ending	December 31, 20XX
Employee Name	Thomas P. Bryan
Signature	*Tom Bryan*
Approved	*PJB*

Out		7th Day	
In			
Out			
In			
Out		6th Day	
In			
Out			
In			
Out		5th Day	
In			
Out			
In			
Out	*4*	4th Day	**04:02 PM**
In			**11:58 AM**
Out	*4.75*		**11:30 AM**
In			**06:45 AM**
Out	*4.5*	3rd Day	**04:33 PM**
In			**11:59 AM**
Out	*4*		**11:30 AM**
In			**07:31 AM**
Out	*5*	2nd Day	**05:00 PM**
In			**12:01 PM**
Out	*4*		**11:30 AM**
In			**07:29 AM**
Out		1st Day	
In			
Out			
In			

Period Ending	December 19, 20XX
Employee Name	Robert T. Hissom
Signature	Bob Hissom
Approved	PJB

Day		Hours	Time
7th Day	Out		
	In		
	Out		
	In		
6th Day	Out	4	04:02 PM
	In		12:01 PM
	Out	4	11:30 AM
	In		07:29 AM
5th Day	Out	4	03:59 PM
	In		12:02 PM
	Out	4	11:30 AM
	In		07:27 AM
4th Day	Out	4	04:00 PM
	In		11:59 AM
	Out	4	11:30 AM
	In		07:31 AM
3rd Day	Out	4	04:03 PM
	In		12:02PM
	Out	4	11:34 AM
	In		07:30 AM
2nd Day	Out		
	In		
	Out		
	In		
1st Day	Out		
	In		
	Out		
	In		

Period Ending	December 26, 20XX
Employee Name	Robert T. Hissom
Signature	Bob Hissom
Approved	PJB

Day		Hours	Time
7th Day	Out		
	In		
	Out		
	In		
6th Day	Out	4	
	In		
	Out	4	
	In		Holiday
5th Day	Out	4	
	In		
	Out	4	
	In		Holiday
4th Day	Out	4	04:03 PM
	In		12:04 PM
	Out	4	11:30 AM
	In		07:29 AM
3rd Day	Out	4	04:00 PM
	In		12:00 PM
	Out	4	11:33 AM
	In		07:30 AM
2nd Day	Out	4	04:03 PM
	In		12:01 PM
	Out	4	11:31 AM
	In		07:31 AM
1st Day	Out		
	In		
	Out		
	In		

Period Ending	December 31, 20XX
Employee Name	Robert T. Hissom
Signature	Bob Hissom
Approved	PJB

Day		Hours	Time
7th Day	Out		
	In		
	Out		
	In		
6th Day	Out		
	In		
	Out		
	In		
5th Day	Out		
	In		
	Out		
	In		
4th Day	Out	4	04:00 PM
	In		11:58 AM
	Out	4	11:32 AM
	In		07:32 AM
3rd Day	Out	4	04:01 PM
	In		11:59 AM
	Out	4	11:30 AM
	In		07:30 AM
2nd Day	Out	4	03:57PM
	In		11:55 AM
	Out	4	11:30 AM
	In		07:26 AM
1st Day	Out		
	In		
	Out		
	In		

TRANSACTION SET B

December	Transaction
16	Receive a purchase order from California Premium Beverage (page 115). Fill and ship the order. Complete Invoice No. 15535.
16	Order 31 tons white grapes at $1,925.11 per ton from Mendocino Vineyards. The item number for the white grapes is WG1003. Add the item to inventory when prompted. Be sure to change the Inventory account. Complete Purchase Order No. 9682.
16	Purchase a 20XX Ford truck for $31,250.00. The terms include a $6,250.00 down payment and a 3-year, 6% promissory note to Ford Credit for the remaining $25,000.00. Principal and interest on the note are due monthly beginning January 4, 20XY. The company expects the truck to have a useful life of 5 years and no salvage value. Prepare Check No. 19257 payable to Potter Valley Ford for the down payment.
16	The Board of Directors of Chateau Americana authorized a $60,000 cash dividend payable on December 31st to the stockholders of record on December 26th. Use Check No. 19476 when paid.
17	Receive a phone complaint from Seaside Distributors about a case of Chenin Blanc that was damaged in shipment. The case was part of Invoice No. 15175, dated November 5, 20XX, in the amount of $20,438.40. Seaside paid the invoice on November 19, 20XX and took advantage of the discount (terms 3/15, net 30). Prepare Check No. 19286 to reimburse Seaside for the damaged inventory that was *not* returned to the company.
19	Receive notification of $850 interest income that was deposited directly into the checking account from a certificate of deposit from State Employees' Credit Union. Record the cash receipt.
19	Receive payment in full from Pacific Distribution Co. on Invoice No. 15243 dated November 13, 20XX, in the amount of $19,576.80 (page 104). Record the cash receipt.

December	Transaction
19	Receive a purchase order (page 116) with payment (page 117) from Sonoma Distributors. Fill and ship the order. Record the sale.
22	Receive 18 tons red grapes at $2,437.40 per ton from Mendocino Vineyards (inventory number CS1250). Also received Invoice No. M7634 from Mendocino Vineyards with the shipment (page 118). Terms on the invoice are 2/10, net 30. Record receipt of the inventory.
26	Receive utility bill from Pacific Gas and Electric in the amount of $18,887.62 (page 108). Prepare Check No. 19402.
30	Receive Brokerage Advice from Edwards Jones for purchase of 500 shares of Microsoft at $74.26 per share plus $400 broker's commission (page 119). Prepare Check No. 19468.
31	Receive payment in full for the December 16 purchase from California Premium Beverage (page 120). Record the cash receipt.
31	Prepare Check No. 19473 payable to Mendocino Vineyards for the shipment received on December 22.
31	Prepare Payroll Checks (Nos. 7111-7114) for Anna Johnson, José Rodriguez, Tom Bryan, and Bob Hissom. Time cards for Tom and Bob are on pages 111-112. Prepare Check No. 19474 to transfer cash from the general cash account to the payroll account. Record the payroll transactions.
31	Prepare Check No. 19475 to repay $75,000 of the principal on long-term debt to Bank of Huntington.

Refer to pages 98-101 for the Month-End and Year-End procedures.

PURCHASE ORDER

California Premium Beverage

39848 South Street
Santa Rosa, CA 95402
Phone (707) 555-7451 Fax (707) 555-7452

To:
Chateau Americana
3003 Vineyard Way
Huntington, CA 95394

Ship To:
California Premium Beverage
39848 South Street
Santa Rosa, CA 95402

ABC Permit #: A59782

P.O. DATE	P.O. NUMBER	SHIPPED VIA	F.O.B. POINT	TERMS
12/13/XX	8746	CA Express	Destination	3/15, net 30

ITEM NO	QTY	SIZE	DESCRIPTION	UNIT PRICE	TOTAL
W120015	1512	0.750	Riesling	10.54	15,936.48
W120016	504	0.750	Sauvignon Blanc	11.27	5,680.08
W120019	336	0.750	Chenin Blanc	9.51	3,195.36
R130061	1176	0.750	Cabernet Sauvignon	9.94	11,689.44
R130056	672	0.750	Merlot	10.08	6,773.76
S140000	240	0.750	Sparkling Brut	16.36	3,926.40
W120080	336	0.750	Chardonnay	13.83	4,646.88
				TOTAL	51,848.40

Jorge Gonzalez — Authorized by

12/13/XX — Date

PURCHASE ORDER

PO Number: 4376
Date: 12/19/XX

To:
Chateau Americana
3003 Vineyard Way
Huntington, CA 95394

Ship To:
SONOMA DISTRIBUTORS
3224 Greenlawn Street
Ukiah, CA 95482
Phone (707) 555-1705 Fax (707) 555-1706

SHIPPED VIA	ABC #	F.O.B. POINT	TERMS
United Express	A557912	Huntington	Cash

ITEM NO	QTY	SIZE	DESCRIPTION	UNIT PRICE	TOTAL
W120015	480	0.750	Riesling	10.54	5,059.20
W120080	468	0.750	Chardonnay	13.83	6,472.44
W120019	300	0.750	Chenin Blanc	9.51	2,853.00
R130072	780	0.750	Shiraz	11.71	9,133.80
R130056	672	0.750	Merlot	10.08	6,773.76
				TOTAL	30,292.20

Chrystal Harrington   12/19/XX
Authorized by   Date

Sonoma Distributors
3224 Greenlawn Street
Ukiah, CA 95482

Humboldt Bank
Ukiah, CA 95482

17003

Date 12/19/XX

PAY Thirty Thousand Two Hundred Ninety-Two and 20/100 Dollars ---------------- $ 30,292.20

To the order of
Chateau Americana
3003 Vineyard Way
Huntington, CA 95394

- SAMPLE, DO NOT CASH -

⁝000000⁝ ⁝000000000⁝ 17003

Sonoma Distributors **17003**

Reference	Discount	Net Amount
Payment for PO 4376		$30,292.20

CUSTOMER INVOICE

Invoice Number **M7634**

Invoice Date 12/20/20XX

Mendocino Vineyards
8654 Witherspoon Way
Hopland, CA 95449
Phone: (707) 555-1890

Sold To:
Chateau Americana, Inc.
3003 Vineyard Way
Huntington, CA 95394

Credit Terms: 2/10, Net 30

Ship To:
Chateau Americana, Inc.
3003 Vineyard Way
Huntington, CA 95394

Customer I.D	Customer P.O. Number
CHATAM	9660

Description	Product Number	Quantity	Cost	Extended
Cabernet Sauvignon Grapes	CS1250	18 tons	$2,437.40	$43,873.20

Total Cost: $43,301.00

Comments:

Distribution: Copy 1 — Accounting; Copy 2 – Shipping; Copy 3 – Customer

Edward Jones Financial Services

100 Market Street
San Francisco, CA 94109
(415)504-9000

Customer
Chateau Americana, Inc.
3003 Vineyard Way
Huntington, CA 95394

Account Number
02334-85763

Tax Identification #
23-7788954

SAVE THIS STATEMENT FOR TAX PURPOSES

Date	Description	Symbol	Fees and/or Commissions($)	Net Dollar Amount ($)	Share Price ($)	Transaction Shares
12/30/03	Microsoft Corporation Common Shares	MSFT	400.00	37,130.00	74.26	500.0000

California Premium Beverage **21803**
39848 South Street
Santa Rosa, CA 95402

Bay View Bank
Santa Rosa, CA 95407

Date 12/29/XX

PAY Fifty Thousand Two Hundred Ninety-Two and 95/100 Dollars ------------------ $ 50,292.95

To The Order Of
Chateau Americana
3003 Vineyard Way
Huntington, CA 95394

- SAMPLE, DO NOT CASH -

¦:000000¦: :000000000: 21803

California Premium Beverage **21803**

Reference	Discount	Net Amount
# 0504 Invoice 15535	1,555.45	$50,292.95

TRANSACTION SET C

December	Transaction
16	Receive a purchase order from California Premium Beverage (page 123). Fill and ship the order. Complete Invoice No. 15535.
16	Order 31 tons white grapes at $1,936.78 per ton from Mendocino Vineyards. The item number for the white grapes is WG1003. Add the item to inventory when prompted. Be sure to change the Inventory account. Complete Purchase Order No. 9682.
16	Purchase a 20XX Ford truck for $36,750.00. The terms include a $5,250.00 down payment and a 3-year, 6% promissory note to Ford Credit for the remaining $31,500.00. Principal and interest on the note are due monthly beginning January 4, 20XY. The company expects the truck to have a useful life of 5 years and no salvage value. Prepare Check No. 19257 payable to Potter Valley Ford for the down payment.
16	Receive Check No. 10375 in the amount of $19,250.00 (see page 124) from Castle Vineyards for the sale of the fork Lift that was purchased on December 23, 20XW. The Fork Lift originally cost $18,881.00 and was being depreciated over 10 years. To record this transaction, you will need to calculate the depreciation that was taken on the Fork Lift. Depreciation for December was calculated and included in the total depreciation given to you in the Month-End entries before the sale took place and depreciation for the year needs to be adjusted. Record the transaction.
17	Receive a phone complaint from Seaside Distributors about a case of Chenin Blanc that was damaged in shipment. The case was part of Invoice No. 15175, dated November 5, 20XX, in the amount of $20,438.40. Seaside paid the invoice on November 19, 20XX and took advantage of the discount (terms 3/15, net 30). Prepare Check No. 19286 to reimburse Seaside for the damaged inventory that was *not* returned to the company.

December	Transaction
19	Receive notification of $850 interest income that was deposited directly into the checking account from a certificate of deposit from State Employees' Credit Union. Record the cash receipt.
19	Receive payment in full from Pacific Distribution Co. on Invoice No. 15243 dated November 13, 20XX, in the amount of $20,164.30 (page 125). Record the cash receipt.
19	Receive a purchase order (page 126) with payment (page 127) from Sonoma Distributors. Fill and ship the order. Record the sale.
22	Receive 23 tons cabernet sauvignon grapes at $2,489.21 per ton from Mendocino Vineyards (inventory number CS1250). Also received Invoice No. M7634 from Mendocino Vineyards with the shipment (page 128). Terms on the invoice are 2/10, net 30. Record receipt of the inventory.
26	Receive utility bill from Pacific Gas and Electric in the amount of $19,271.12 (page 129). Prepare Check No. 19402.
30	Receive Brokerage Advice from Edwards Jones for purchase of 500 shares of Microsoft at $74.26 per share plus $400 broker's commission (page 130). Prepare Check No. 19468.
31	Receive payment in full for the December 16 purchase from California Premium Beverage (page 131). Record the cash receipt.
31	Prepare Check No. 19473 payable to Mendocino Vineyards for the shipment received on December 22.
31	Prepare Payroll Checks (Nos. 7111-7114) for Anna Johnson, José Rodriguez, Tom Bryan, and Bob Hissom. Time cards for Tom and Bob are on pages 111-112. Prepare Check No. 19474 to transfer cash from the general cash account to the payroll account. Record the payroll transactions.
31	Prepare Check No. 19475 to repay $90,000 of the principal on long-term debt to Bank of Huntington.

Refer to pages 98-101 for the Month-End and Year-End procedures.

PURCHASE ORDER

California Premium Beverage

39848 South Street
Santa Rosa, CA 95402
Phone (707) 555-7451 Fax (707) 555-7452

To:
Chateau Americana
3003 Vineyard Way
Huntington, CA 95394

Ship To:
California Premium Beverage
39848 South Street
Santa Rosa, CA 95402

ABC Permit #: A59782

P.O. DATE	P.O. NUMBER	SHIPPED VIA	F.O.B. POINT	TERMS
12/13/06	8746	CA Express	Destination	3/15, net 30

ITEM NO	QTY	SIZE	DESCRIPTION	UNIT PRICE	TOTAL
W120015	1512	0.750	Riesling	10.64	16,087.68
W120016	504	0.750	Sauvignon Blanc	15.82	7,973.28
W120019	336	0.750	Chenin Blanc	10.90	3,662.40
R130061	1176	0.750	Cabernet Sauvignon	12.33	14,500.08
R130056	672	0.750	Merlot	13.26	8,910.72
S140000	240	0.750	Sparkling Brut	21.94	5,265.60
W120080	336	0.750	Chardonnay	18.50	6,216.00
				TOTAL	62,615.76

Jorge Gonzalez *12/13/XX*

Authorized by Date

Castle Vineyards
3224 Castle Way
Ukiah, CA 95482

Humboldt Bank
Ukiah, CA 95482

17003

Date 12/16/XX

PAY Nineteen Thousand Two Hundred Fifty and 00/100 Dollars ----------------- $ 19,250.00

To the order of
Chateau Americana
3003 Vineyard Way
Huntington, CA 95394

- SAMPLE, DO NOT CASH -

⑆000000⑆: :000000000: 17003

Sonoma Distributors **17003**

Reference	Discount	Net Amount
Payment for Fork Lift		$19,250.00

Pacific Distribution Company
10034 Westborough Boulevard
San Francisco, CA 94080

Bank of America
San Francisco, CA 94104

69712

Date 12/16/XX

PAY Twenty Thousand One Hundred Sixty Four and 30/100 Dollars ----------------- $ 20,164.30

To The Order Of
Chateau Americana
3003 Vineyard Way
Huntington, CA 95394

- SAMPLE, DO NOT CASH -

⁝000000⁝ ⁝000000000⁝ 69712

Pacific Distribution Company **69712**

Reference	Net Amount
Invoice #15243, customer # 0505	$20,164.30

PURCHASE ORDER

PO Number: 4376
Date: 12/19/XX

To:
Chateau Americana
3003 Vineyard Way
Huntington, CA 95394

Ship To:
SONOMA DISTRIBUTORS
3224 Greenlawn Street
Ukiah, CA 95482
Phone (707) 555-1705 Fax (707) 555-1706

SHIPPED VIA	ABC #	F.O.B. POINT	TERMS
United Express	A557912	Huntington	Cash

ITEM NO	QTY	SIZE	DESCRIPTION	UNIT PRICE	TOTAL
W120015	480	0.750	Riesling	10.64	5,107.20
W120080	468	0.750	Chardonnay	18.50	8,658.00
W120019	300	0.750	Chenin Blanc	10.90	3,270.00
R130072	780	0.750	Shiraz	13.63	10,631.40
R130056	672	0.750	Merlot	13.26	8,910.72
				TOTAL	36,577.32

Chrystal Harrington *12/19/XX*
Authorized by Date

Sonoma Distributors
3224 Greenlawn Street
Ukiah, CA 95482

Humboldt Bank
Ukiah, CA 95482

17003

Date 12/19/XX

PAY Thirty-six Thousand Five Hundred Seventy-seven and 32/100 Dollars -------------- $ 36,577.32

To the order of
Chateau Americana
3003 Vineyard Way
Huntington, CA 95394

- SAMPLE, DO NOT CASH -

⑆000000⑆ ⑈000000000⑈ 17003

Sonoma Distributors **17003**

Reference	Discount	Net Amount
Payment for PO 4376		$36,577.32

CUSTOMER INVOICE

Mendocino Vineyards
8654 Witherspoon Way
Hopland, CA 95449
Phone: (707) 555-1890

Invoice Number **M7634**

Invoice Date 12/20/20XX

Sold To:
Chateau Americana, Inc.
3003 Vineyard Way
Huntington, CA 95394

Credit Terms: 2/10, Net 30

Ship To:
Chateau Americana, Inc.
3003 Vineyard Way
Huntington, CA 95394

Customer I.D	Customer P.O. Number
CHATAM	9660

Description	Product Number	Quantity	Cost	Extended
Cabernet Sauvignon Grapes	CS1250	23 tons	$2,489.21	$57,251.83

Total Cost: $57,251.83

Comments:

Distribution: Copy 1 — Accounting; Copy 2 – Shipping; Copy 3 – Customer

Payment Coupon

Bill Date: 12/23/20XX

Please Pay by 01/17/20XX
$18,851.58

Amount Enclosed

Account No. 21790-1879

Chateau Americana, Inc.
3003 Vineyard Way
Huntington, CA 95394

Send Payment to:

Pacific Gas and Electric
P.O. Box 2575
San Francisco, CA 94103

Retain bottom portion for your records, detach and return stub with payment.

Service	Chateau Americana, Inc.	Your Account Number	Rate Class	Billing Date
For:	3003 Vineyard Way Huntington, CA 95394	**21790-1879**	**Commercial**	**12/23/20XX**

Meter Number	Service Period	Days	Type of Reading	Multiplier	Units	Meter Readings Current	Past	Usage
68869800	**11/23/XX – 12/23/XX**	**31**	**Actual**	**1**	**KWH**	**1098412**	**1001301**	**97111**

Previous Balance	16,895.53
Payment	16,895.53
Balance Forward	0.00
Current Charges	19,271.12

Due Date	**Total Due**
01/17/20XX	19,271.12

Pacific Gas and Electric

1000 Energy Drive, San Francisco, CA 94103, (415) 973-8943

Edward Jones Financial Services

100 Market Street
San Francisco, CA 94109
(415)504-9000

Customer
Chateau Americana, Inc.
3003 Vineyard Way
Huntington, CA 95394

Account Number
02334-85763

Tax Identification #
23-7788954

SAVE THIS STATEMENT FOR TAX PURPOSES

Date	Description	Symbol	Fees and/or Commissions($)	Net Dollar Amount ($)	Share Price ($)	Transaction Shares
12/30/03	Microsoft Corporation Common Shares	MSFT	400.00	37,130.00	74.26	500.0000

California Premium Beverage
39848 South Street
Santa Rosa, CA 95402

Bay View Bank
Santa Rosa, CA 95407

21803

Date 12/29/XX

PAY Sixty Thousand Seven Hundred Thirty-seven and 29/100 Dollars ----------------- $ 60,737.29

To The Order Of
Chateau Americana
3003 Vineyard Way
Huntington, CA 95394

- SAMPLE, DO NOT CASH -

⑆000000⑆ ⑈000000000⑈ 21803

California Premium Beverage **21803**

Reference	Discount	Net Amount
# 0504 Invoice 15535	1,878.47	$60,737.29

DATABASE APPLICATIONS USING MICROSOFT® ACCESS 2016: The Winery at Chateau Americana

LEARNING OBJECTIVES

After completing and discussing this material, you should be able to:

- Recognize and explain the purpose of the elements of a relational database
- Build selected elements of a database management system
- Recognize and evaluate the strengths and weaknesses of the controls embedded in a database management system
- Compare and contrast a database package with a general ledger package and with a manual accounting information system

BACKGROUND

Before you begin the database assignments, it is important to understand a little about a database management system and its terminology and to understand the scope of these assignments. A database management system (DBMS) is based on a logical data model. The majority of DBMSs in existence today (*Access*, *MySQL*, *Oracle*, *FoxPro*, etc.) are based on the relational data model. A relational database (which will be the only type of database to which we refer) represents all of the data about the entity in a collection of tables. The following exercises are specific to *Microsoft® Access 2016*, but the theory discussed herein applies to any relational database.

The structures and methods used to manage the data are called objects. There are seven types of objects in *Access*. They are tables, queries, forms, reports, pages, macros, and modules.

Tables are the fundamental storage entity of a relational database. Therefore, all database data is stored in one or more tables comprised of rows and columns. A row, or **record**, contains all the data about a specific instance, or item, in the table.

A column, or **field**, in a table represents characteristics or attributes of the data. Most tables will contain one field that represents the **primary key** (i.e., a value that uniquely identifies each record). In *Figure 1* below, CustomerNo is the primary key. Each field can contain only one data type. Data types constrain the type of data that can be entered into a field (e.g., text, number, counter, currency, date/time).

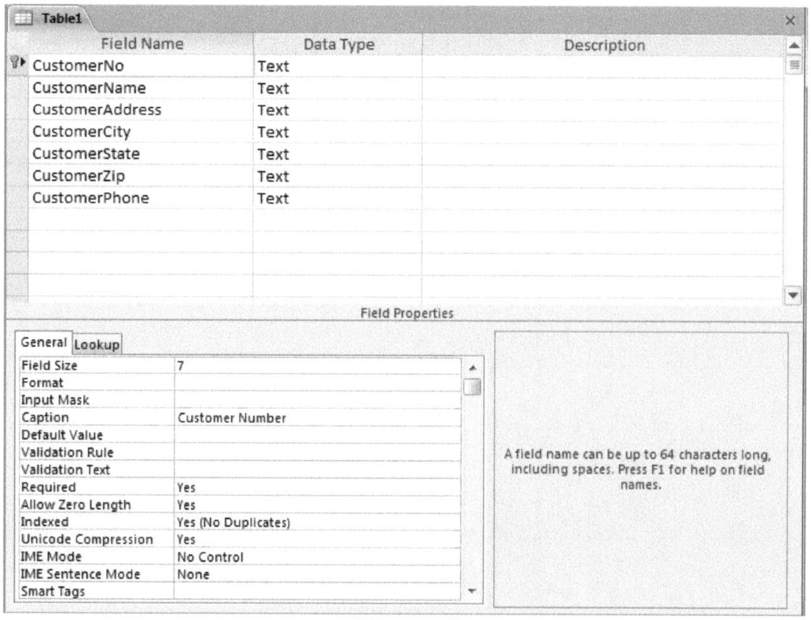

Figure 1

A record's fields contain individual values for each attribute that characterizes that particular record, as shown in *Table 1*.

CustomerNo	CustomerName	CustomerAddress	CustomerCity
WD564	Wine Distributors, Inc.	1285 Napa Ave.	Mendocino

Table 1

Queries are used for asking questions about the data in one or more tables in a database. Queries can be used to locate and display a subset of the records of a table (the **select query**), or modify data (using one of four types of **action queries**) such as combining information from several tables into a single result (the **append query**), changing the values in one or more records (the **update query**), selecting one or more records and creating a new table for them (the **make-table query**), or deleting one or more records (the **delete query**).

Queries can be created in *Access* using SQL (structured query language), a text-based query language. Syntax is very important and very specific in creating SQL statements. The SQL in *Figure 2* uses a field (SupplierNo) common to two tables that might exist in an organization's database (i.e., a Purchase Order table and a Supplier table) to present several fields from the two tables in one form.

Figure 2

Queries can also be created in *Access* using QBE (query by example), a graphical database query interface in which the user selects one or more tables to query and then selects the columns which should be included in the query response. Since it is a graphical interface, QBE is typically the technique of choice because it is easier to use. QBE allows the user to place values or expressions, called selection criteria, below particular field names, thereby limiting the records that are retrieved. Thus, queries are used to reduce the amount of displayed information, summarizing it, and giving it meaning. *Figure 3* presents the same query using the QBE technique as was described in *Figure 2*.

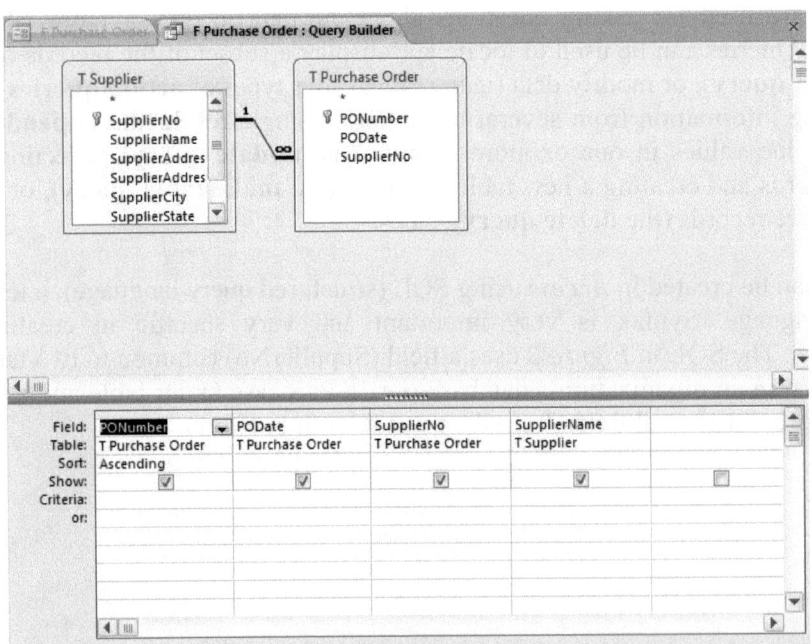

Figure 3

Forms allow the user to see data from tables in a more convenient and attractive format. Forms can be customized so that they precisely match an existing paper form, making it easier to move from hard copy to soft copy. Therefore, with the use of forms, the user can easily view or change the information that is contained in a table.

Forms contain **labels** and **controls**. **Controls** display data, perform actions, or make forms easier to read. Text boxes are examples of bound controls. A bound control is one that obtains its data from a field in an underlying table or query. An unbound control is not connected to a field. Lines, shapes, and instructions regarding the use of a form are examples of unbound controls. **Labels** can be attached to controls, in which case they are pre-specified by the **Caption**, or they can be stand-alone, in which case they are created using the **Label** icon in the Menu. (Both of these will be discussed later). Forms can also include other forms, or subforms, to allow data entry into more than one table at a time.

Embedded aids and prompts are other useful tools that aid in the creation of forms. Some of these can be created by the database designer and some of them are provided by the program itself. For example, **Form Navigation** buttons, located at the bottom of the screen, enable the user to move to another record by moving up or down one record at a time, selecting a particular record number, or moving to the first or last record in the table.

Reports utilize data from one table or several tables linked together to provide the user with meaningful information. Reports allow the user to decide where that information should appear on a printed page. In other words, the user can specify how information will be grouped, sorted and formatted for the printer. Reports can be used to sort, group, and summarize data in almost limitless ways. As a result, reports can appear as invoices, purchase orders, sales summaries, or financial statements. However, whereas the user can enter, edit, and interact with the data in a **Form**, he or she cannot interact with the data in a **Report**.

Macros are more advanced *Access* objects. Macros are mini-programs that contain sets of instructions that automate frequently performed tasks, such as opening a form, printing a report, or processing an order. They can also be used to automate custom tasks and are a relatively easy way to achieve custom results in a database without having programming knowledge. Finally, they can also assist in the creation of turnkey applications that anyone can use, whether or not they have experience with *Access*.

Modules are even more advanced *Access* objects than macros. They are similar to macros in that they allow for automation and customization. However, these tools require knowledge of *Visual Basic* programming and give the user more precise control over the actions taken.

REQUIREMENTS

These assignments will be limited to familiarizing you with tables, queries, forms, and reports. We leave the development of macros and modules for more advanced database design classes. The objective of this assignment is ***not*** to provide you with expertise in the development of a database, but to provide you with an initiation to and an appreciation of both the complexity and the power of a database when used to create an accounting information system.

Good programming procedures require a certain amount of structure or standardization. For example, when saving tables, queries, forms, and reports created in a database, it is often useful to use a naming convention (i.e., a method which names the objects in a way that will let the user know to which classification the object belongs). This assists the designer and the user alike in navigating throughout the database. Therefore, the naming convention indicated in *Table 2* will be used throughout this assignment:

Table	T *tablename*
Queries	Q *queryname*
Forms	F *formname*
Reports	R *reportname*

Table 2

Please read the following sections carefully. They are intended to be tutorial in nature as well as providing you with the information necessary to complete your *Access* assignments. In some instances, the assignment provides you with explicit instructions about creating the necessary tables, forms, queries and reports. However, in other instances, the assignment allows you to make choices about design considerations such as form style, size, font size, etc. Therefore, it is imperative to follow the directions carefully **AND** to critique the forms and reports you create from a user's perspective.

Finally, as always, it is important to **back your work up frequently**!

CREATING A NEW DATABASE AND NEW TABLE

Requirements

1. Create a new database by launching *Access*. Click on the **Blank Database** icon. A **Blank Database** screen pops up indicating that the **File Name** for the database is **Database1.accdb**. Check with your instructor to determine his or her required file naming convention for the assignment and change the name accordingly. Now click on **Create** under **Blank Database**.

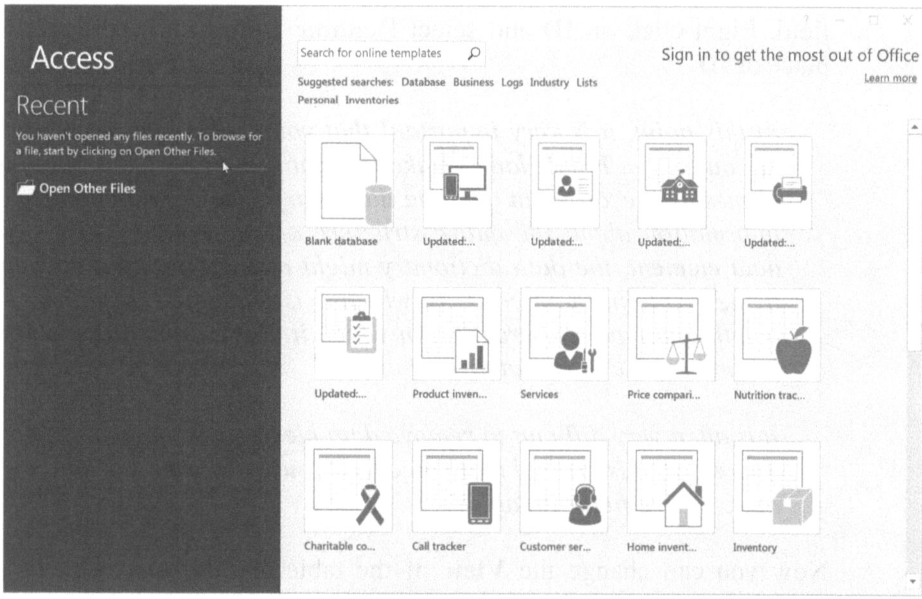

Figure 4

You are now ready to design the database. As discussed previously, tables are the fundamental storage entity of a relational database so we will begin there.

2. When your newly created database opens, it automatically creates a table for you. See *Figure 5*.

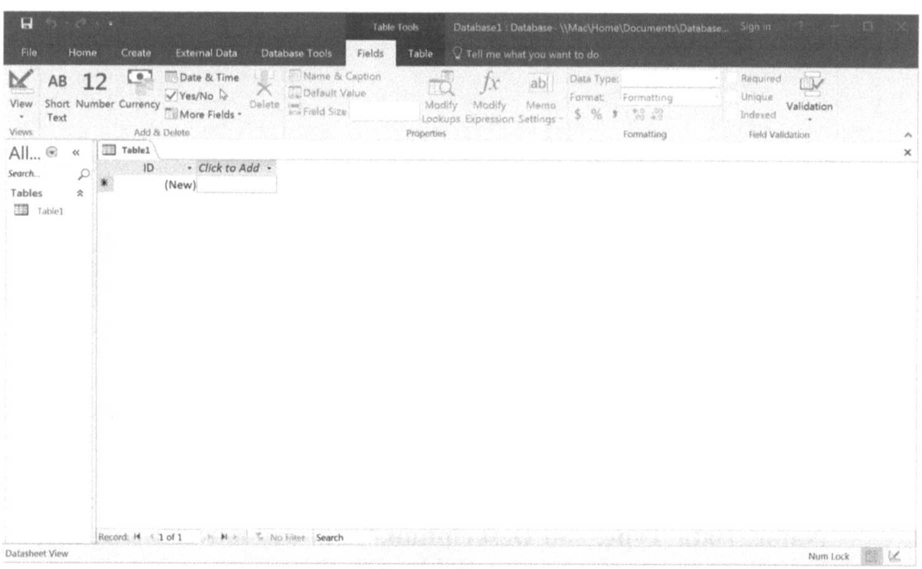

Figure 5

We will make some adjustments to this table. Notice that the table has one field whose field name is "ID." This field name is very generic and would not be specific to any table that you would create as many tables might have a field entitled "ID". Therefore, we would like to make this field more descriptive, i.e., specific to this table. Therefore, begin by renaming this field. Right-click on **ID** and select **Rename Column**. Type **SupplierNo** in place of **ID**.

> *At this point, it is very important that you check your work. Before you tab out of the Field Name, make it a habit to check your spelling. Field Names are recorded in the* ***data dictionary****. The data dictionary contains information about the entire structure of the database. Thus, for each data element, the data dictionary might include the data element name, its description, the records in which it is contained, its source, its field length and type, the program in which it is used, the outputs in which it is contained, and its authorized users.*
>
> *It is often very difficult to remove data elements from the data dictionary. Therefore, it is critical that you check your work very carefully when you are creating fields in tables.*

Now you can change the **View** of the table. To do this, click on **View >** **Design View** in the **Views** section 

of the **Fields** tab. *Access* prompts you to save the table and ask for the table name. Save the table as **T Supplier**. Notice the changes in the **Design View** (*Figure 6*).

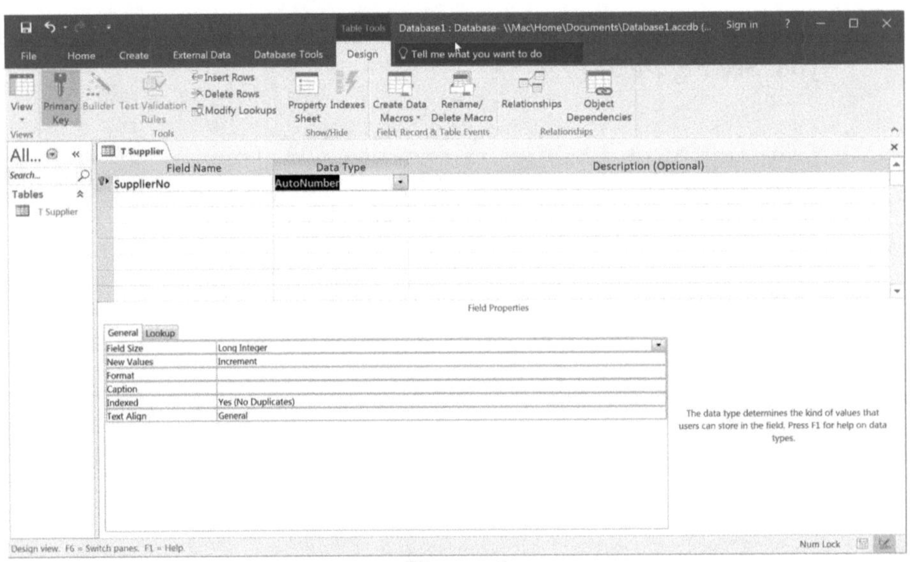

Figure 6

The **Table** window that is displayed now contains three columns: **Field Name, Data Type,** and **Description**. You may move among these columns by either clicking in various fields with the mouse or by clicking in a field and then using the **Tab** key.

Field Names can be up to 64 characters long and can include almost any combination of letters, numbers, spaces, and special characters. **Field Names** may not include a period, an exclamation point, a backquote character, or brackets. In addition, a **Field Name** cannot contain leading spaces.

When the cursor is in the **Data Type** column, you will see a button to pull down a menu. This button allows you to select the **Data Type** for the given **Field Name**. Take some time to explore the various data types. The **Description** property is optional and is used to provide useful information about the table or query and its fields. Check with your instructor to determine whether you are to complete the description field for this assignment.

3. Notice that *Access* has automatically made **SupplierNo** the primary key. You can tell this because the field has the **Primary Key** icon next to it now.

   As we discussed earlier, a primary key is a value that uniquely identifies each record. By defining a primary key, Access does three things:
   a. It insures that no two records in that table will have the same value in the primary key field.
   b. It keeps records sorted according to the primary key field.
   c. It speeds up processing.

4. Notice that *Access* has also automatically set the **Data Type** for **SupplierNo** to **AutoNumber**. If we leave the **Data Type** for this field as an **AutoNumber**, *Access* will begin to number the items consecutively from "1". This is not what you want since Chateau Americana uses a combination of letters and numbers to identify their suppliers. Change the **Data Type** to **Short Text** using the pull-down menu
   You can move to the **Field Properties** pane by moving your mouse to the desired field. This pane allows the user to specify the properties for the chosen field and type. *Table 3* describes some of the most important field properties.

Field Property	**Description**
Field Size	Sets the maximum size for data stored in a Text, Number or AutoNumber field. In a text field, the size may range from 1 to 255. The default is 255 and, therefore, should be set to something reasonable to fit the field. In Number fields, the default is set to Long Integer.
Format	Specifies how data is to be displayed in a field. It is particularly useful in specifying the format for numbers, currency, dates, and times.
Decimal Places	Specifies the number of digits to the right of the decimal point. "**Auto**" allows the Format property to determine the number of decimal places automatically.
Input Mask	Makes data entry easier by adjusting the data entered so that it conforms to the standard set in the Input Mask. It is also used to control the values users can enter.
Caption	Specifies the text for labels attached to controls created by dragging a field from the field list and serves as the heading for the field when the table or query is in Datasheet view.

Default Value	Specifies a default value for a field (e.g., Napa can be set as the Default Value for a City field; the user then has the option of accepting the Default Value or inputting different data).
Validation Rule	Specifies the requirements for data entry. For example, you can create a rule that specifies that all entries must contain five numeric characters as might be the case with zip codes.
Validation Text	Text input in the Validation Text property specifies the message to be displayed to the user when the Validation Rule is violated. For example, when a record is added for a new employee, you can create a Validate Rule requiring that the entry in the **Start Date** field fall between the company's founding date and the current date. If the date entered is not in this range, you can enter text into the Validation Text property so that it will display a message such as, "**Start date is incorrect**."

Field Property	Description
Allow Zero Length	Indicates whether an empty string (i.e., a string containing no characters) is a valid entry. If **Yes**, the field will accept an empty string even when the Required property is set to **Yes**.
Indexed	Sets a single-field index (i.e., a feature which speeds the sorting and searching of a table). The primary key is always indexed. When a record is indexed, it is also necessary to specify whether duplicates will be allowed. For example, when creating a purchase order table, the primary key might be "PO #" and you would not want to allow duplicates. However, when creating a table to add the inventory purchased on a particular purchase order, you might still want to be able to sort and search based upon the PO # (which would require that field to be indexed), but you would expect that a particular purchase order might have several items of inventory. Therefore, duplicates would be allowed.

Table 3

5. Press **F6** to switch to the **Field Properties** pane of the **Table** window and establish the following properties for **SupplierNo** (no entries are required for any other properties for **SupplierNo.**):

Field Size	**5**
Caption	**Supplier Number**
Validation Rule	**Like "?####"** (Note: Include quotation marks)
Validation Text	**Invalid entry. The Supplier Number must consist of one letter and four numbers.**
Required	**Yes**
Indexed	**Yes (No duplicates)**

Table 4

6. All Data Types for all subsequent fields in this table should be set to **Text**. The second Field Name should be **SupplierName**, the Field Size is **35**, and the Caption should be **Supplier Name**. The third Field Name should be **SupplierAddress1**, the Field Size is **35**, and the Caption should be **Supplier Address**. The fourth Field Name should be **SupplierAddress2** and the field size is **35**. There is no caption for this field. The fifth Field Name should be **SupplierCity** with a Field Size of **25** and an appropriate Caption.

7. The sixth Field Name should be **SupplierState**. The Field Size is **2**. Set the Input Mask property for the **SupplierState** field by typing **>LL** and use an appropriate Caption. The > symbol will cause all characters that follow to be converted to uppercase. The two L's mean that the input requires two letters. No other characters are allowed and there must be two letters.

8. The seventh Field Name should be **SupplierZip**. Set the Field Size to **10.** Activate the **Input Mask Wizard** (the button with three small dots located in the Input Mask Property) to aid in making a template for the Zip Code. You will have to save the table before proceeding. Select **Zip Code** from the menu (see *Figure 7*).

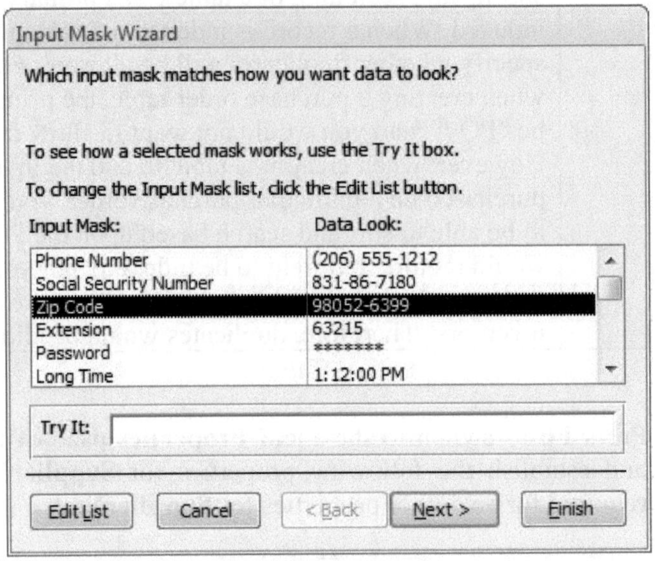

Figure 7

9. Click **Next** twice, and choose to store the Zip Code with the hyphen. Click on **Finish.** Select an appropriate Caption.

10. The last field name is **SupplierTelephone**. Set the Field Size to **14**. Use the Input Mask Wizard to set the Input Mask property to the pre-defined Phone Number setting. Use an appropriate Caption.

11. You are now finished with the table.

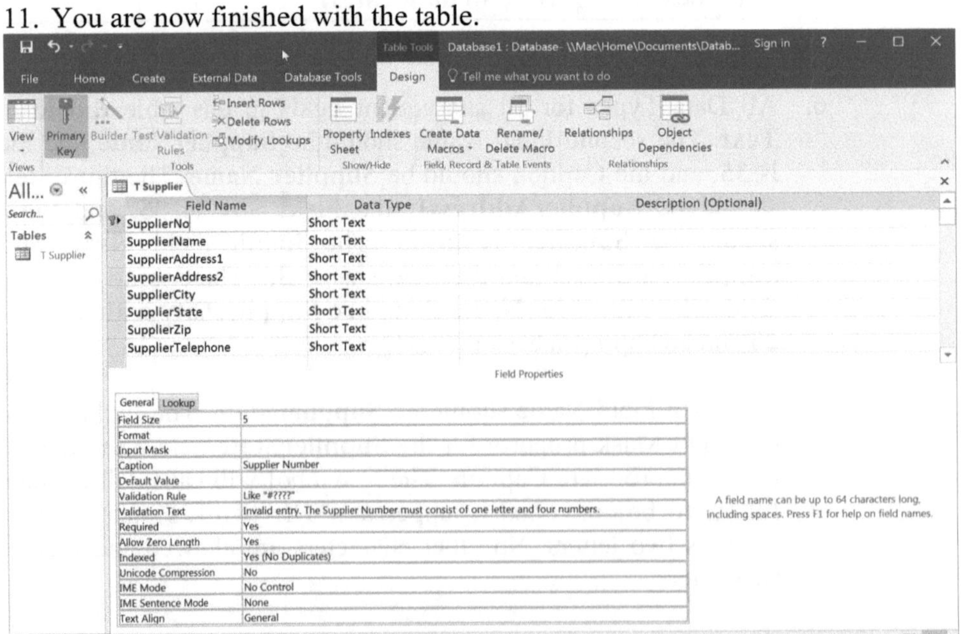

Figure 8

12. When you close this object and all objects in the future, use the **X** in the upper right-hand corner of the row containing the **Object** names to save and close the object. By doing this, you will avoid having to provide names to queries that are underlying the database that should not appear in the Query window, thus limiting the possibility that users may gain unauthorized access.

13. If you wish to quit *Access* at this time, simply close the program and your database will be saved with the name you used to create it.

CREATING A FORM

Although data can be entered from the **Datasheet** view of a table, this would be similar to entering data in a spreadsheet. It is not very easy to do this if the spreadsheet is large, with many columns and many rows. The utilization of forms makes data entry easier and the database more user friendly. A form can display data in almost any format. A very simple form can be designed to display one record at a time. More complex forms can be created as 'fill-in-the-blanks' forms that resemble paper documents used within a company.

Requirements

1. Open your database. You will now enter relevant data into the Supplier Table (i.e., T Supplier) after you create a form utilizing the **Form Wizard**.

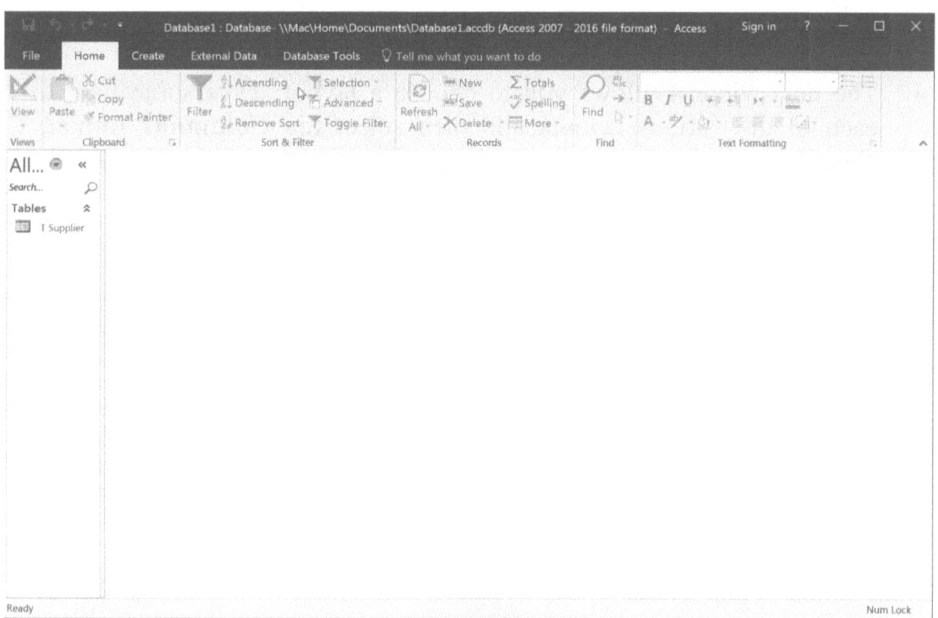

Figure 9

2. Select the **Create** tab in your **Database** window and click on the **Form Wizard**  icon. Be sure that **T Supplier** appears in the **Tables/Queries** box.

3. Select all the fields you created in the table for inclusion in the new form by clicking on the >> button in the middle of the window and click on **Next**. See *Figure 10*.

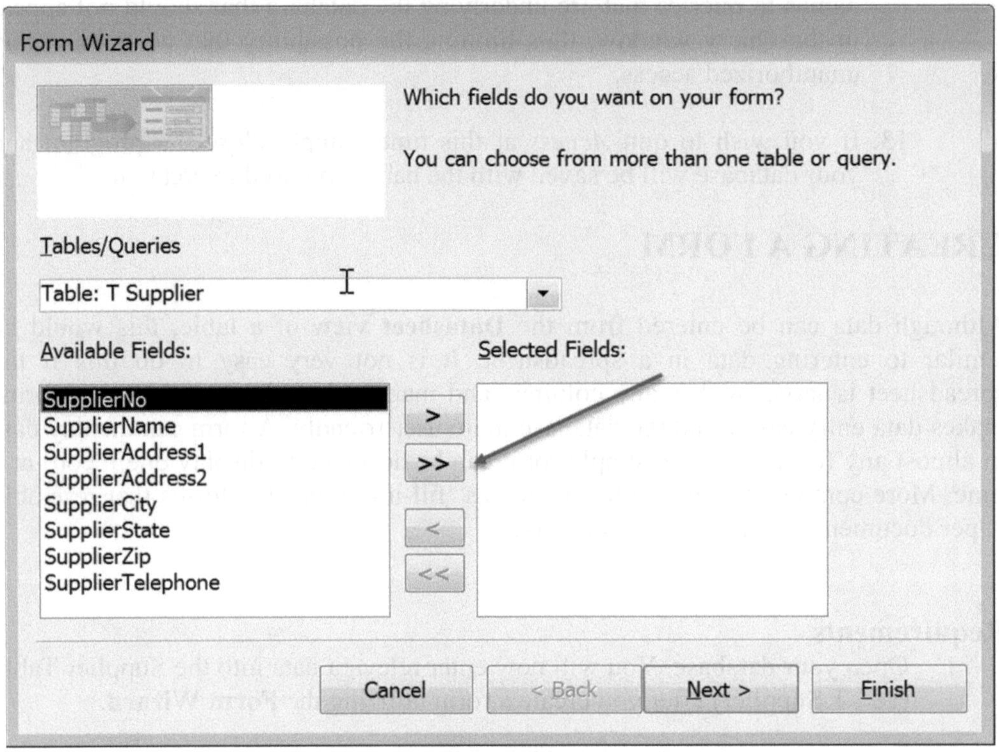

Figure 10

4. The next window allows you to choose a layout. Take some time to view each of the various layouts and then select the **Columnar** format. Click **Next**.

5. Recalling the naming convention discussed earlier, entitle the form **F Supplier**. Select **Modify the form's design**. Click **Finish**.

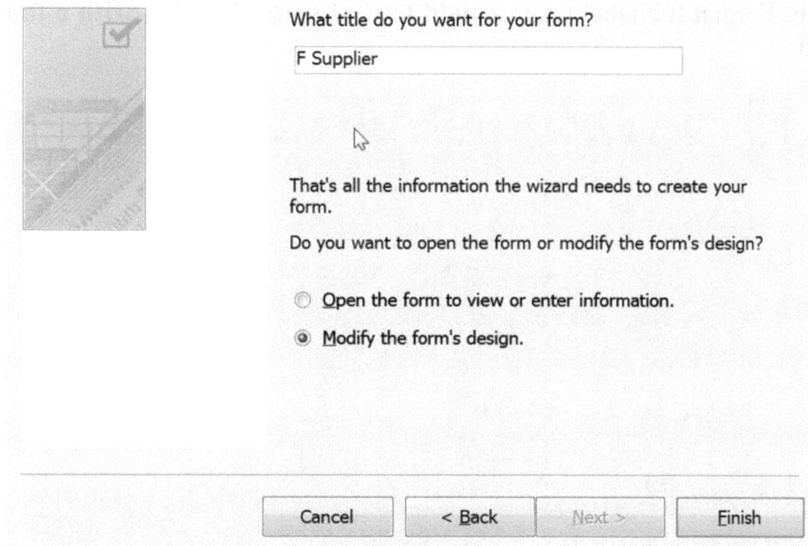

Figure 11

6. First, notice that when the form is created, the fields are different sizes. This relates to the varying sizes that we specified when we created the table. This format is the default format for the Form Wizard in Access 2016. We will still want to make some adjustments to the field sizes, however, as well as to the form in general.

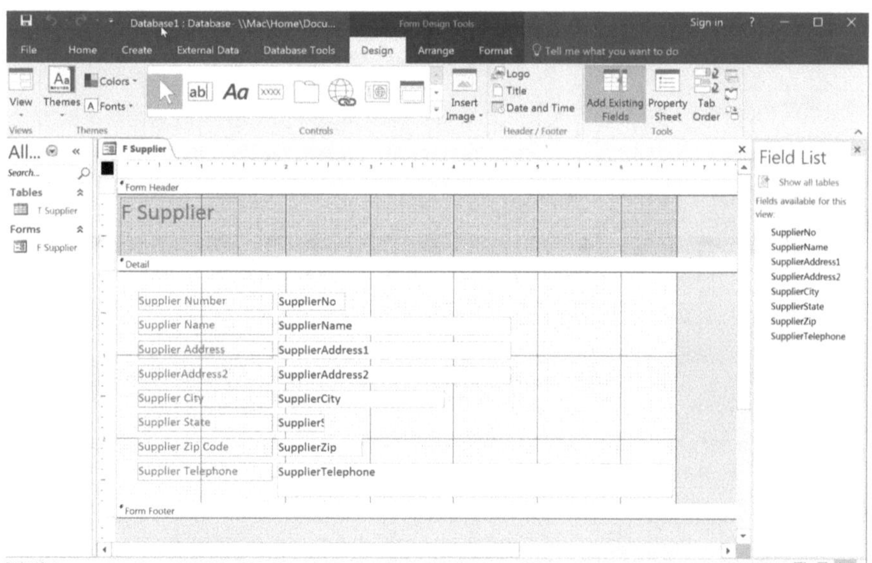

Figure 12

7. Click on the Design tab. Click on the box that contains the label "**F Supplier**" in the **Form Header** section and change this to "**Supplier Form**." Be sure to stretch the length of the box out so that the words appear on one line. You can do this by clicking outside the label lines and then clicking on the edge of the label box once again. Drag the right edge of the box to the right to increase the width. While the box is highlighted, click on the **Home**

tab. Format the label using a **bold font of your choosing with a font size of 20**.

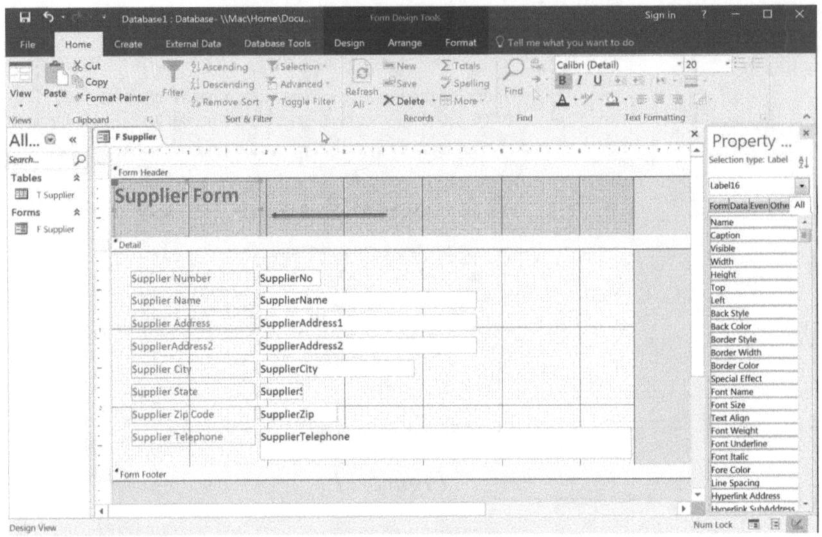

Figure 13

8. Shrink the height and length of the **Supplier Address** field, if necessary. Move the remaining fields up to maintain the proper spacing between the fields.

9. Shrink the **Supplier State** field.

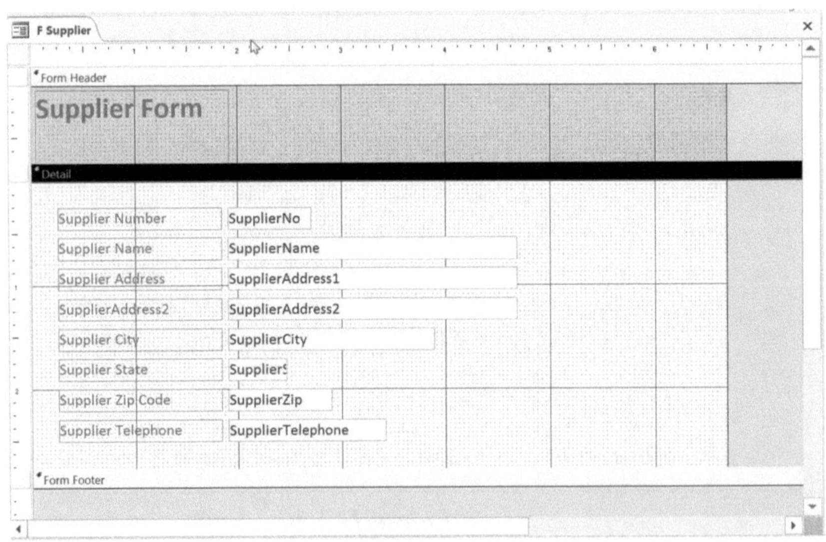

Figure 14

10. Close the form and select **Yes** to save it.

11. Now you are ready to begin entering data using your newly created Supplier form. Open the Supplier Form by double clicking on **F Supplier** in the **Database** window. Enter data for each of Chateau Americana's suppliers listed below:

Supplier Name	Supplier Number	Supplier Address	Supplier Phone
Delicio Vineyards	D2538	12701 South Fernwood Livermore, CA 94550	(925)555-2967
Mendocino Vineyards	M0652	8654 Witherspoon Way Hopland, CA 95449	(707)555-1890

As you enter the supplier information, pay attention to the size of the fields. You can adjust the size by toggling back to the **Design View**. Click on **Views** 

icon (at the upper left-hand side of the Home section of the toolbar) and stretch or shrink the desired field and then toggle back to the **Form View** by clicking on the **Views** 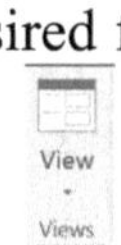

icon again. After you have entered the first supplier's information press the **Enter** key to input the next supplier's information.

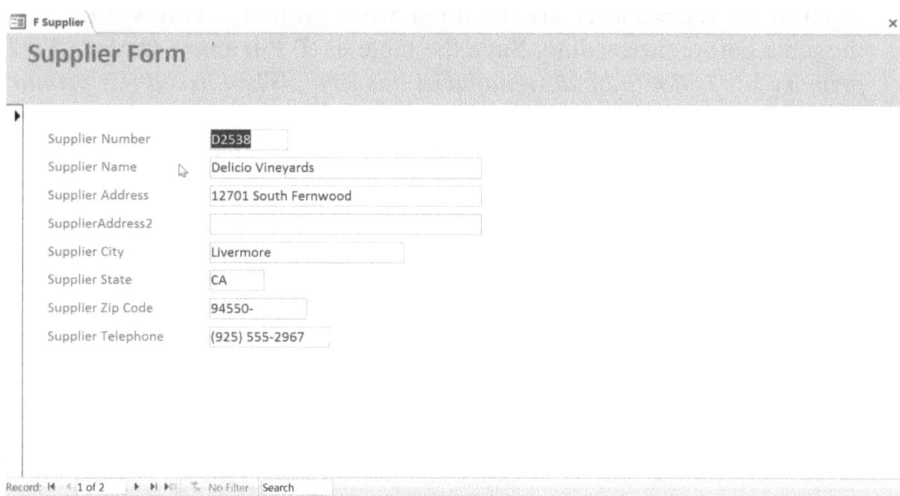

Figure 15

12. Close the form by clicking on the **X** in the upper right hand corner of the form.

13. If you wish to quit *Access* at this time, simply close the program and your database will be saved with the name you used to create it.

ENSURING SEQUENTIAL INTEGRITY

Completeness is an important aspect of internal control. Completeness suggests not only that all data in a transaction are captured, but also that all transactions **are** recorded. Therefore, it is important to ensure that no documents are lost or misplaced. One way to accomplish this is to pre-number documents and verify the sequential integrity of the completed documents.

Requirements

1. Open your *Access* database used for the previous assignments and create a new table by clicking on the **Create** tab and then clicking on the **Table Design** icon.

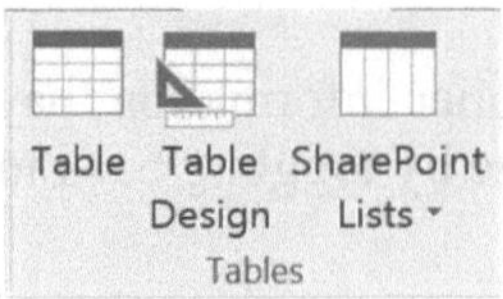

Figure 16

2. The first Field Name in this new table is **PONumber**. Choose **AutoNumber** as the Data Type and enter **PO #** as the Caption. Do not change any other default values for this or other Field Names in the **Field Properties** pane unless instructed to do so.

3. The second Field Name is **PODate**. The Data type is **Date/Time**. Use the Input Mask Wizard to create the Input Mask property. You will have to save the table before proceeding. Save the table as **T Purchase Order**. ***NOTE:*** *A primary key is not to be designated at this time. When asked if a primary key should be created, click* ***NO****. If a primary key was created automatically, remove it. You will have another chance to set the primary key later.*

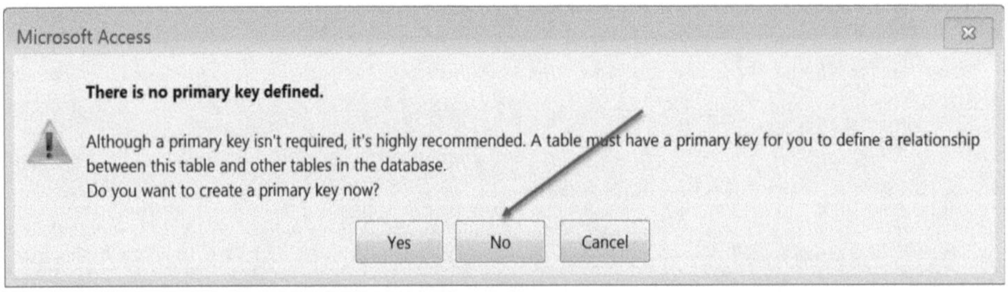

Figure 17

Choose **Short Date** for the Input Mask. Click on **Next** twice and then click **Finish**. The Caption should be **PO Date**.

4. The third Field Name is **SupplierNo**. The Data Type should be set to **Text**. Set the Field Size to **5** and enter the Caption as **Supplier Number**. Close the **T Purchase Order** table.

*Notice that you have already used the Field Name "****SupplierNo.****" It was the primary key in the T Supplier table. When a field name appears in one table that is a primary key in another table, it is called a* ***Foreign Key****. Foreign keys are used to link tables together.*

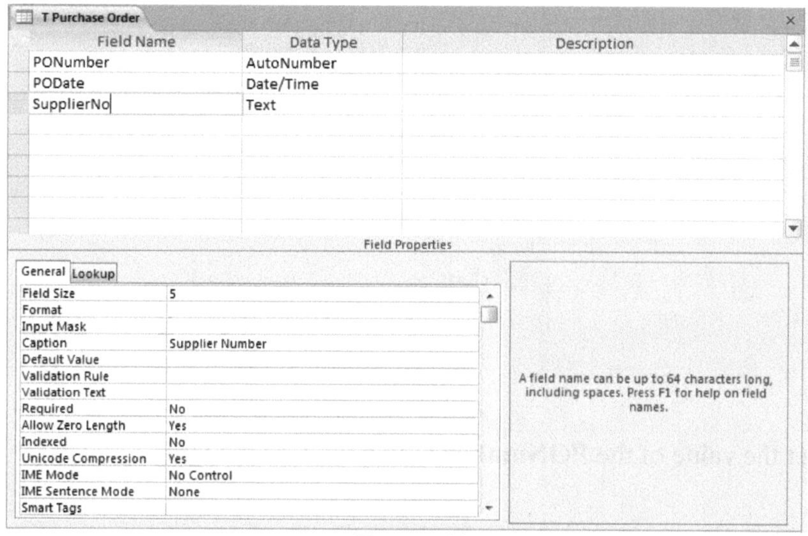

Figure 18

5. Create another new table using the **Table Design** icon.

6. The only field in this table is **PONumber**. The Data Type should be **Number** and the Field Size property should be set to **Long Integer**.

7. Save the table as **T TempPONo**. When asked if a primary key should be created, click **NO**.

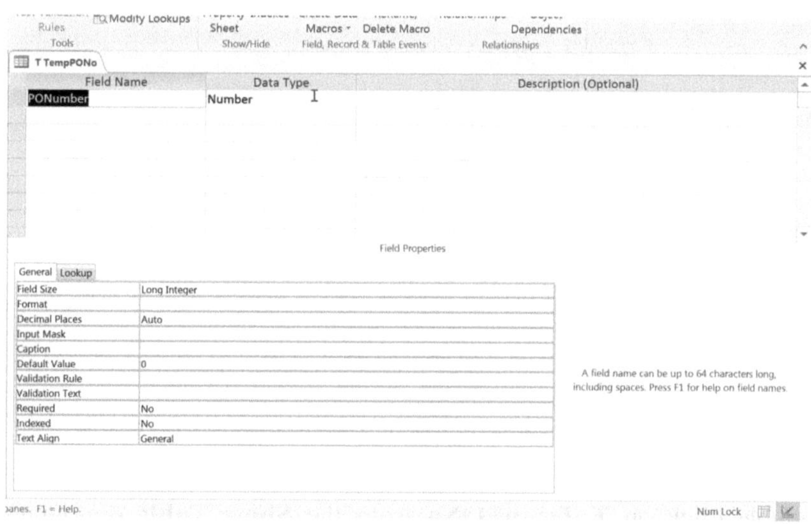

Figure 19

8. Open **T TempPONo** in **Datasheet View** by double clicking the table name in the **All Access Objects** window.

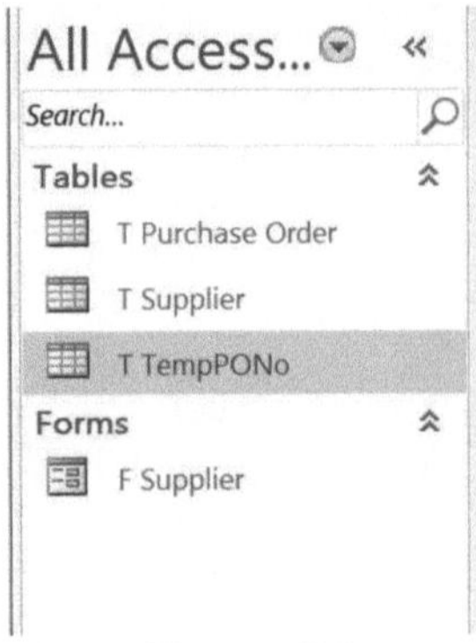

Figure 20

9. Set the value of the **PONumber** to **9681**. Close the table.

Figure 21

10. Click on the **Create** tab and click **Query Design** in the **Queries** section.

Figure 22

11. Double click on **T TempPONo** from the **Show Table** dialogue window, click ADD and close the dialogue window.

Figure 23

12. Click on the **Append** icon in the **Query Type** section. The **Append Query** copies some or all of the records from one table (e.g., the **T TempPONo**) to another table (e.g., the **T Purchase Order**).

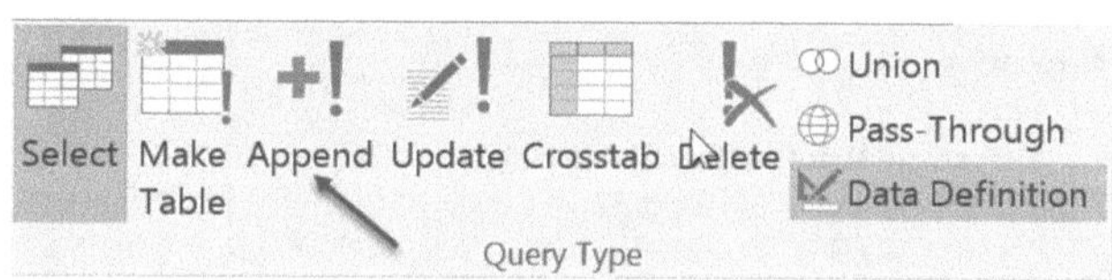

Figure 24

To begin the prenumbering of the purchase orders with 9682, the number you just entered in the **T TempPONo** table (**PONo 9681**) must be appended (added) to the **T Purchase Order** table. To do this, select **T Purchase Order** in the **Table Name** pull-down menu in the **Append** window. Be sure that **Current Database** is selected and click **OK**.

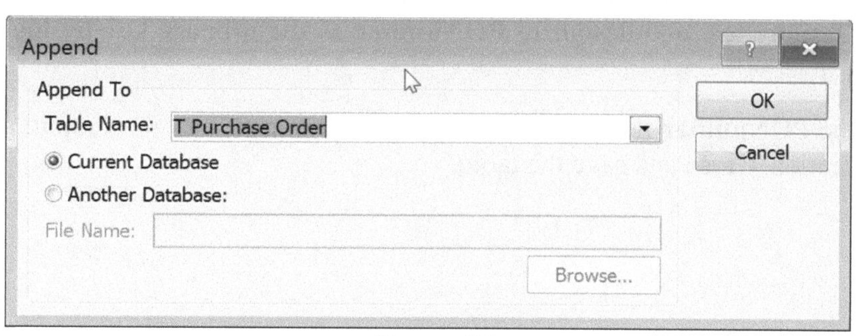

Figure 25

13. Click on **PONumber** in the **T TempPONo** window and drag it to the Append To: field in the Design Grid in the lower half of the window.

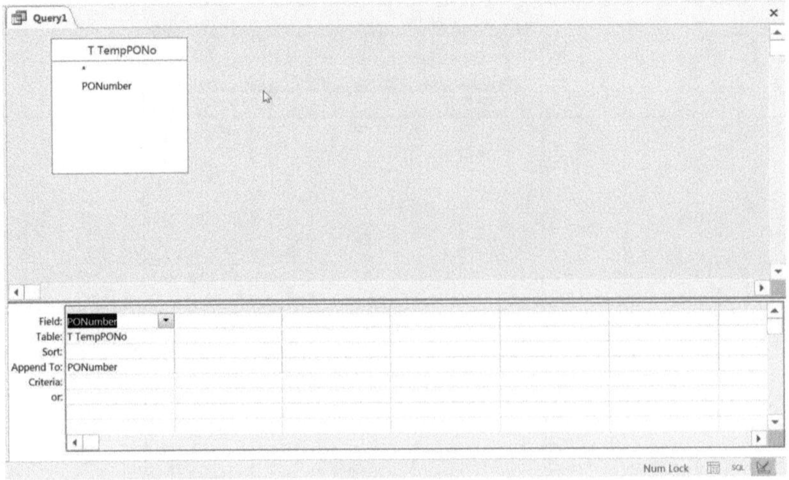

Figure 26

14. Now, click on the **Run** 

icon in the **Results** section. A dialog window will then appear stating "You are about to append 1 row(s). Click on **Yes** to append the row of data from the T TempPONo table to the T Purchase Order table. Save it as **Q TempPONo**.

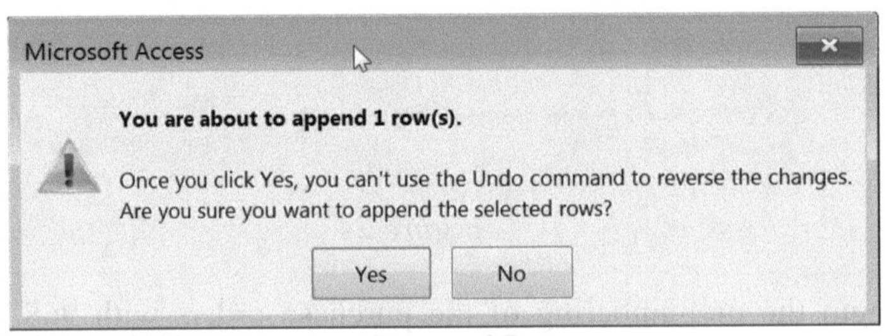

Figure 27

15. Double-click on the **T Purchase Order** table. You will notice that the first PO # in this table is now 9681. Therefore, when you begin to enter data the next purchase order entered will be PO # 9682. Change the view to the **Design** view and designate **PONumber** as the primary key by highlighting the **PONumber** field and clicking on the Primary Key 

icon in the **Tools** section. Close and save the table.

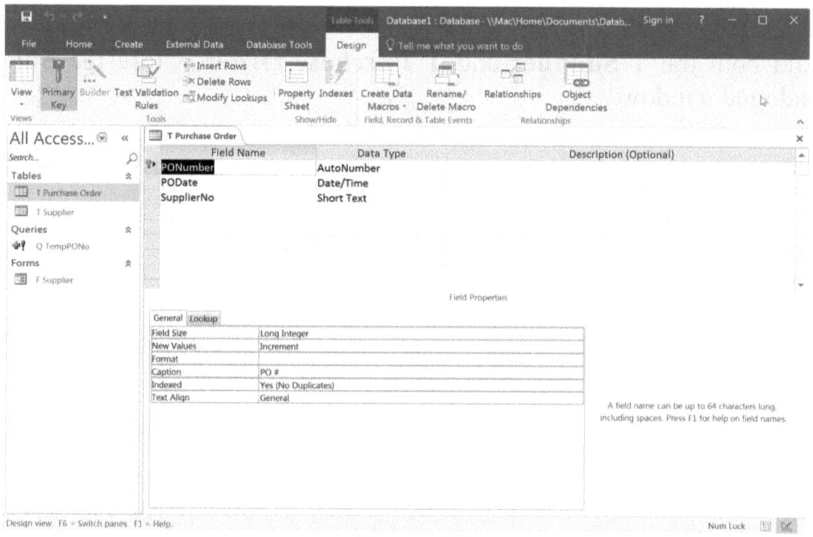

Figure 28

16. Finally, delete **T TempPONo**.

17. If you wish to quit *Access* at this time, simply close the program and your database will be saved with the name you used to create it.

CREATING RELATIONS

As stated previously, *Access* is a relational database. This implies that associations or relationships are created between common fields (i.e., columns) in two tables to link the data from one table to another. For example, one-to-one (1:1) relationships occur when a record (i.e., row) in a table relates to a record in another table once and only once. One-to-many (1:N) relationships occur when a record in a table relates to several records in another table. Many-to-many (N:N) relationships occur when several records in a table relate to several records in another table.

For example, there should be a one-to-many relationship established between the **Supplier** table and the **Purchase Order** table so that data regarding suppliers does not have to be duplicated on the purchase orders. In this section, you will set up these other tables for the expenditure cycle and create relations among them. The following instructions will aid in setting up a relationship linking the **Purchase Order** table to the **Supplier** table.

Requirements

1. Open your previously created database. Open the Relationships window by clicking on the **Relationships** icon in the **Database Tools** tab.

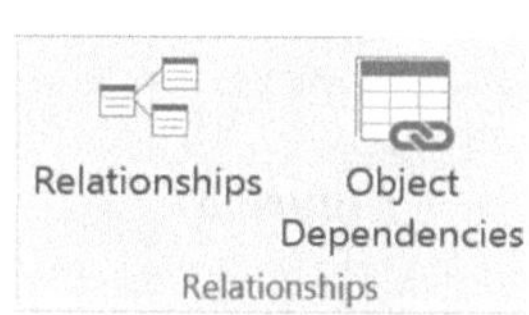

Figure 29

2. Add both the **T Supplier** and **T Purchase Order**. Close the **Show Table** dialogue window.

Figure 30

3. Click and drag the **SupplierNo** field in **T Supplier** to the **SupplierNo** field in the **T Purchase Order**.

4. Click the **Enforce Referential Integrity** check box. Referential integrity ensures that records referenced by a foreign key cannot be deleted unless the record containing the foreign key is first removed. Thus, in this case, a supplier cannot be deleted from the database if there is an outstanding purchase order for that supplier.

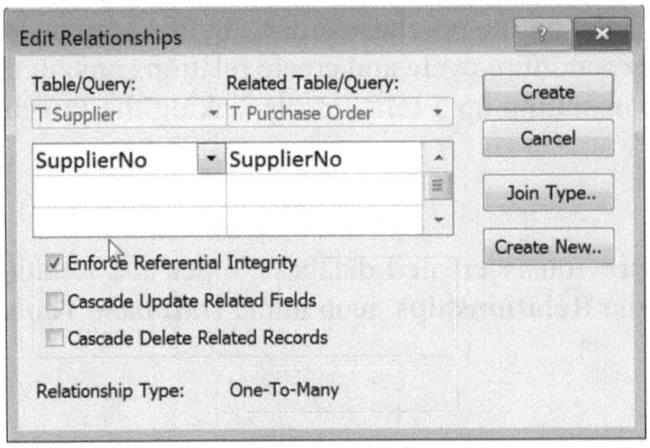

Figure 31

5. Click on the **Create** button.

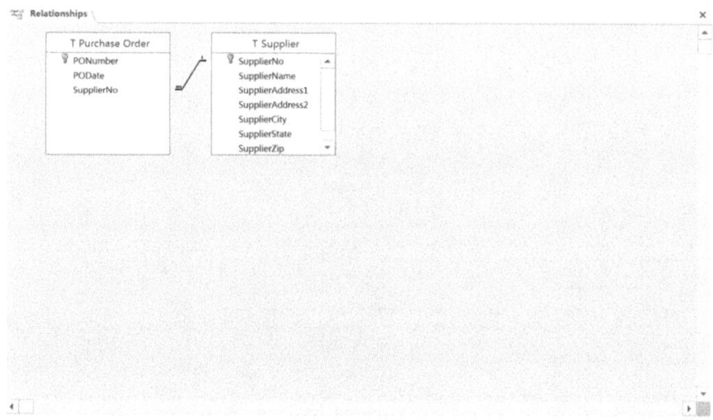

Figure 32

6. Save and close the relationship.

7. If you wish to quit *Access* at this time, simply close the program and your database will be saved with the name you used to create it.

INTEGRATING FORMS WITHIN FORMS

There are times when you may want to show data from tables that are linked with a one-to-many relationship. To do this, we can insert one form within another. That is, we can create a subform within the main form. For example, we might want to insert inventory data into a purchase order form. The following instructions will assist you in doing this.

Requirements

1. Open your *Access* database and create a new table.

2. The first Field Name is **InvCode**. Set the Data Type to **Text** and the Field Size to **7.** Enter the Caption as **Inventory Code**. Set this field as the table's primary key. Since this is the primary key, make sure that you make it a Required field. Other than that, do not change any other default values for this or other Field Names in the **Field Properties** pane unless instructed to do so.

3. The second Field Name is **InvDescription**. Set Data Type to **Text**, the Field Size to **35**, and enter the Caption as **Description**.

4. The third Field Name is **InvCost**. Set Data Type to **Currency** and enter the Caption as **Cost**.

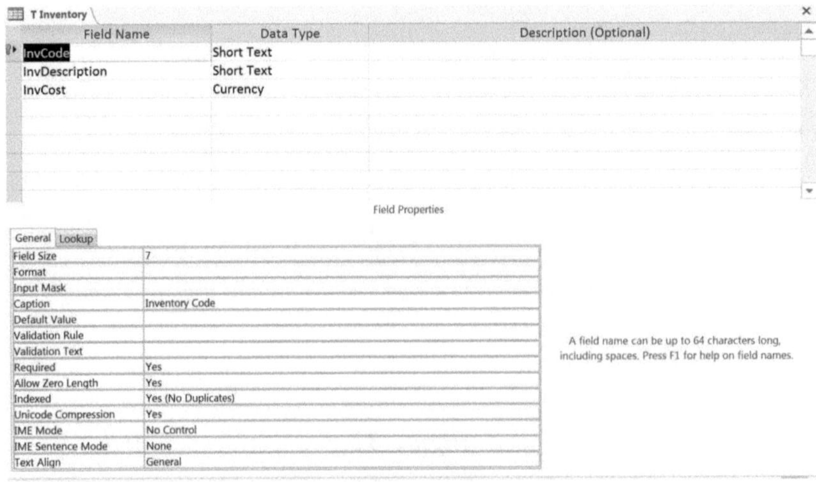

Figure 33

5. Save the table as **T Inventory** and close the table.

6. Select the **Create** tab in your **Database** window and click on the **Form Wizard** Form Wizard icon. Be sure that **T Inventory** is highlighted in the **Tables/Queries** box.

7. Select all of the available fields from **T Inventory** for inclusion in your new form using the >> icon. Click on **Next**. Choose a **Tabular** format and click on **Next**. Click on **Modify the form's design**. Change the form's title to be **F Inventory.** Be sure to select the radio button that allows you to modify the form design. Click on **Finish**.

8. Click on the Design tab. Click on the box that contains the label "F **Inventory**" and change this to "**Inventory.**" Click outside the label once and then click on the edge of the label box once again. Notice that the **Formatting** toolbar is enabled. Format the label using a **bold font of your choosing with a font size of 20**. Adjust the height of label text box as needed so that it does not overlap with the other labels in the **Form Header** section.

9. You now need to resize the remaining labels and controls as you did for the **Supplier Form.** Left align the label for **Cost**. Shrink the width of the label and the control box since these are more than wide enough for any potential entries.

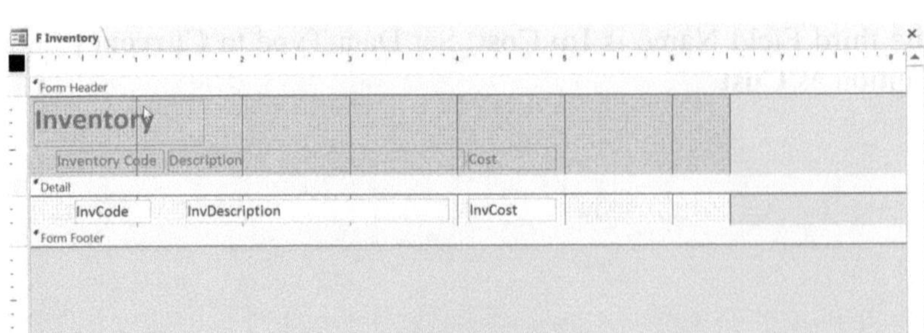

Figure 34

10. Review *Figure 34*. Notice that there is very little empty space below the control boxes in the **Detail** section and the **Form Footer**. This is because the **Detail** section represents one record. Therefore, any space that is left in the **Detail** section will be included as space between each record (i.e., space between each line of inventory in our Inventory form).

11. Close and save the form. Open the **Inventory** Form and enter all inventory data from Chateau Americana's Inventory Price List found below. Close the form after all data is entered.

Inventory Code	Description	Cost
CK30110	1 ¾ US Cork	0.25
CK30120	2 US Cork	0.34
CP30130	Crème Caps Wine	0.11
CP30140	Black Caps Wine	0.09
BT30010	750 Green Bottle	0.99
BT30020	750 Brown Bottle	0.60
LB30210	Crème Wine Bottle Labels	0.18
RM10005	Red Merlot Grapes	691.30
WC20004	White Chardonnay Grapes	732.50

12. Now you need to create the table that will store the inventory data so that it can be linked to the **Purchase Order** table and the **Inventory** table. Create a new table in **Design View**.

13. The first Field Name is **PONumber**. Set the field's Data Type to **Number**. Enter the Caption as **PO #**. Change the Required property to **Yes**. Set the Indexed property to **Yes (Duplicates OK)**. Do not set this field as the **Primary Key** at this time. Do not change any other default values for this or other Field Names in the **Field Properties** pane unless instructed to do so.

14. Enter **InvCode** in the next field and set the field's Data Type to **Text**. Set Field Size to **7** and enter the Caption as **Inventory Code**. Set the Required property to **Yes**. Set the Indexed property to **Yes (Duplicates OK)**.

15. While holding down the **Control** key, select the **PONumber** and **InvCode** fields by clicking on their row selectors (the grey area to the left of the **Field Name**.

16. Click on the **Primary Key** icon. This will allow both fields to be the primary key.

17. Enter **POInvQuantity** in the third field name and set its Data Type to **Number**. Set the Field Size property to **Long Integer** and the Decimal Places property to **0**. Set the Caption property to **Quantity**.

18. Enter **InvCost** in the last field name and set its Data Type to **Currency**. Set the Caption property to **Cost**.

19. Save the table as **T Purchase Order Sub** and close.

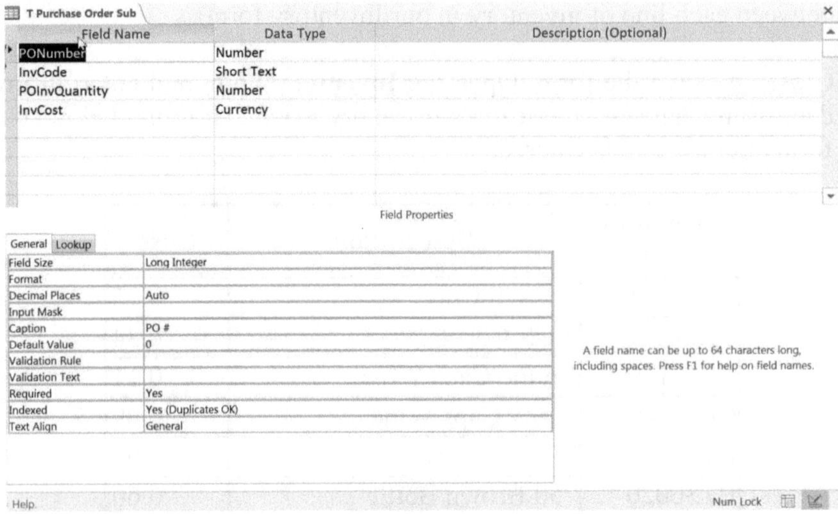

Figure 35

20. Click on the **Relationships** icon in the **Database Tools** tab again. Click on the **Show Table** icon 

. Add **T Inventory** and **T Purchase Order Sub**. Create a link between the two tables that is based on **InvCode**. Be sure to click the **Enforce Referential Integrity** check box. Also create a link between **T Purchase Order Sub** and **T Purchase Order** and click on **Enforce Referential Integrity**. Close the **Relationships** window and save the new relationships.

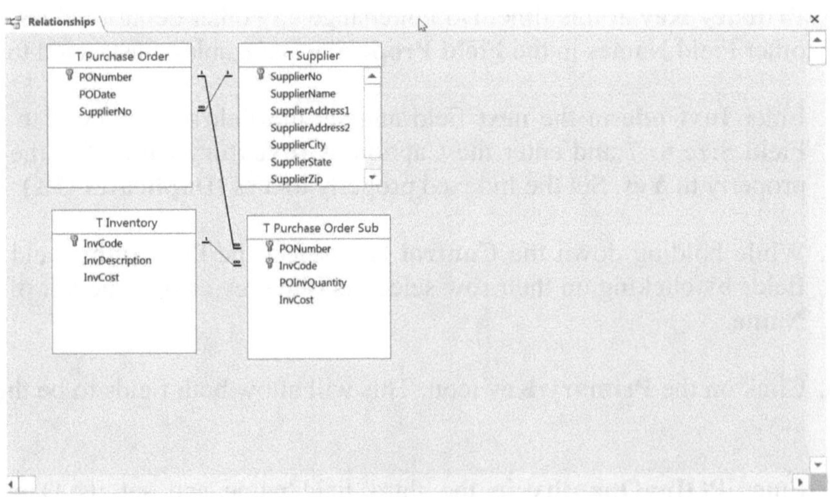

Figure 36

21. We will now create the **Purchase Order** form using the **Form Wizard** 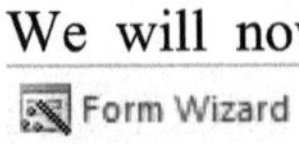

. Click on **T Purchase Order in the** Tables/Queries box and include all of the fields in the form. Then click on the **T Purchase Order Sub** table in the Tables/Queries box. Double click on **InvCode**, **POInvQuantity**, and **InvCost**. Click on **Next**. The **Form Wizard** should appear as shown in *Figure 37*.

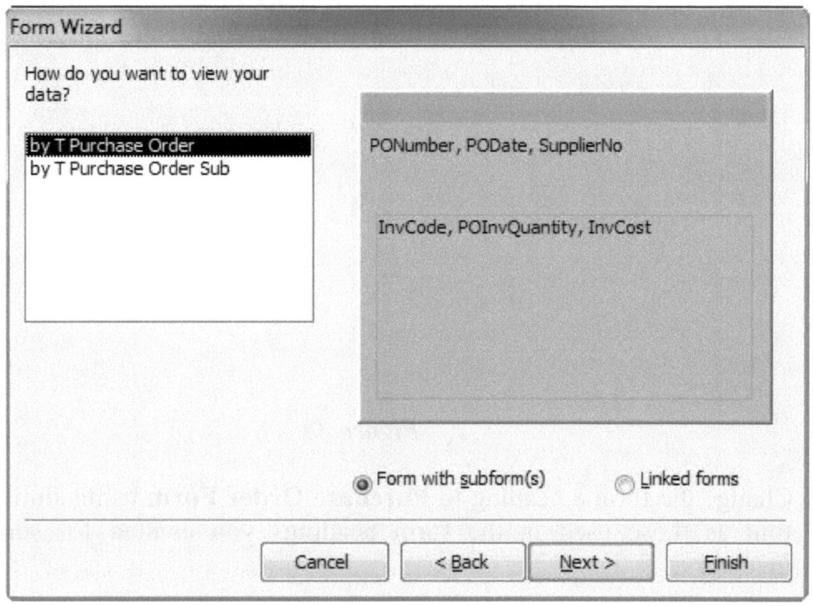

Figure 37

22. Note that the radial button next to **Form with subform(s)** is checked. Click **Next**. Accept **Datasheet for** the layout by clicking **Next** in the following screen. Change the form titles to **F Purchase Order and F Purchase Order Sub Subform**. Click the radio button that allows you to modify the form's design.

23. Highlight the **F Purchase Order Sub** label. Delete the label.

24. Slide the **F Purchase Order Sub Subform** to the left and expand the subform as shown in *Figure 38*.

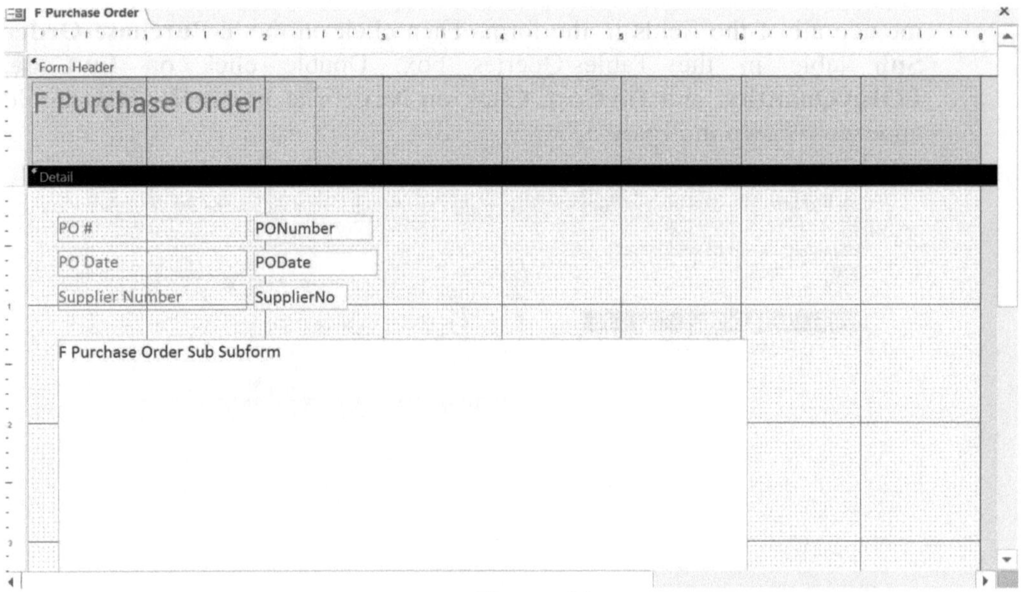

Figure 38

25. Change the form a heading to **Purchase Order Form** using similar size and font as those used in the form headings you created for suppliers and inventory.

26. Close the form and reopen it in Design View to obtain the design view of the subform. See *Figure 39.*

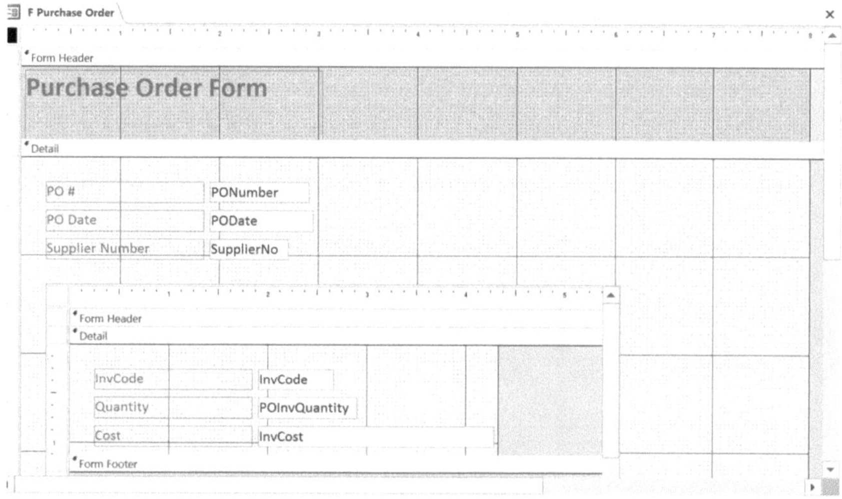

Figure 39

27. Highlight the **F Purchase Order Sub Subform**. Click on the **Design** tab and click on the **Property Sheet** icon  in the **Tools** section. Be sure there is a black box in the upper left corner of the subform (located to the left of the horizontal ruler and above the **Form Header** line. Locate the **Property Sheet** to the right of the form. Ensure that the **Record Source** under the **Data** tab on the is set to **T Purchase Order Sub**. The **Record Source** property specifies the source of the data for a form or a report. It can be a Table name, a Query name, or an SQL statement.

28. Click on the **Build** button  next to the **Record Source**. Click **Yes** in response to the question "Do you want to create a query based on the table?"

29. Click on the **Show Table** icon  under the **Query Setup** section and add the **T Inventory** table. Close the **Show Table** window.

30. Click and drag the **PONumber** field from **T Purchase Order Sub** to the first field cell in the design grid, then set its Sort order to **Ascending**.

31. Click and drag the **POInvQuantity** field from **T Purchase Order Sub** to the second field cell in the QBE grid. Click and drag the **InvCode** and the **InvCost** fields from **T Purchase Order Sub** to the third and fourth field cells, respectively.

32. Click and drag the **asterisk** row from **T Inventory** to the fifth field cell in the QBE grid. Note that **T Inventory*** appears in the cell. Selecting the **asterisk** captures all fields from that table. See *Figure 40*.

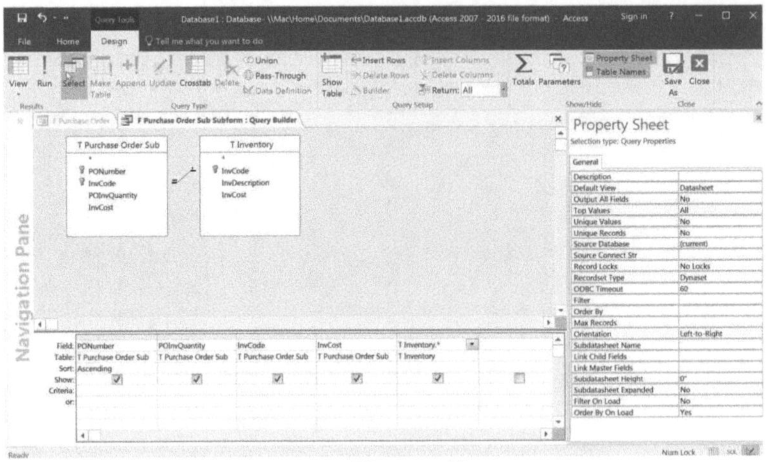

Figure 40

33. Click **Run** Run under the **Results** section of the **Design** tab of the menu bar. Close the **Query Builder** window by clicking on the **X** in the upper right-hand corner and **Yes** in response to the question as to whether you want to save the changes made and return to the design view. Notice that this query does not appear in the **All Access Objects** list to the left of the form.

34. Right click on the **InvCode** control box in the **Detail** section and select **Properties** from the pull-down menu. Make sure the **Control Source** property (**Data** tab) is not set to **T Inventory.InvCode**. If it is, use the **Control Source** pull-down menu and change it so that it is bound to **T Purchase Order Sub.InvCode**. The **Control Source** property specifies what data is to appear in the control. As stated before, a control can be bound to a table, query, or SQL statement. It can also be the result of an expression (i.e., a combination of field names, controls, constants, functions, operators, etc.). Now think about how these principles apply to the **Inventory Cost** field.

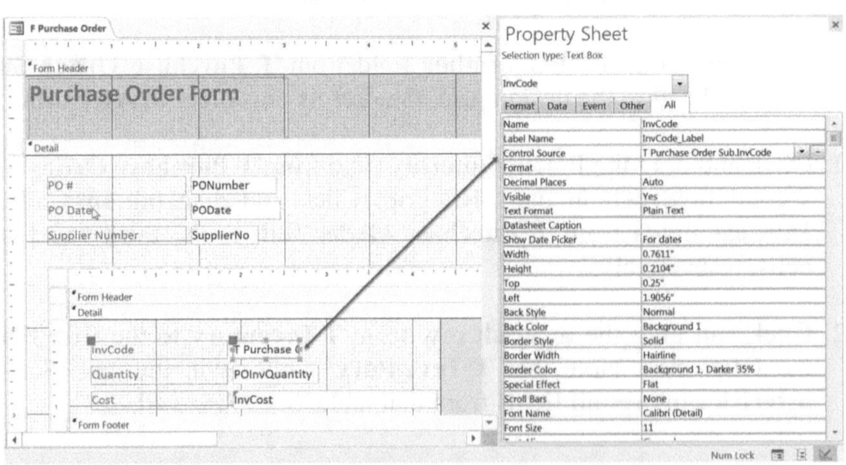

Figure 41

35. Shrink the size of the labels and move the controls over so that they are still close to the labels.

36. Drag down the **Form Footer.** Drag down both the label and the control for the **InvCost** field.

37. Click on the **Add Existing Fields** 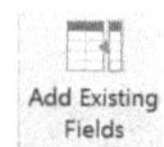

icon in the **Design** tab. Drag **InvDescription** to the space created between **POInvQuantity** and **InvCost**. Align the label and control so that they are in line with the other labels and controls. Lengthen the width of the **InvDescription** control. See *Figure 42*.

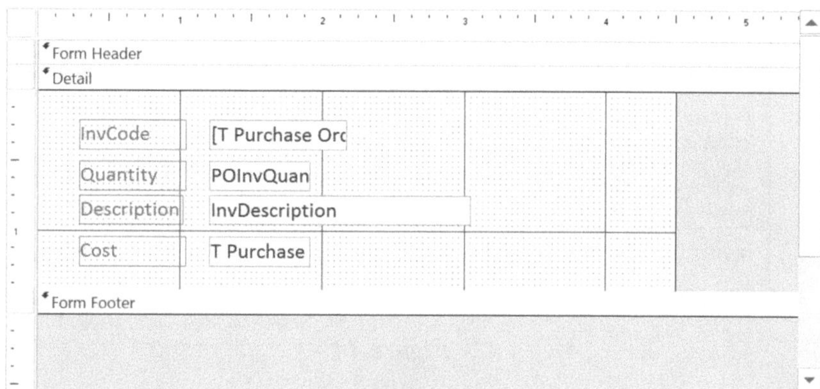

Figure 42

38. Click on the **Form View** to see how the form will appear to users. Notice that the **Cost** field appears before the **Description** field. In addition, the labels for the fields are truncated.

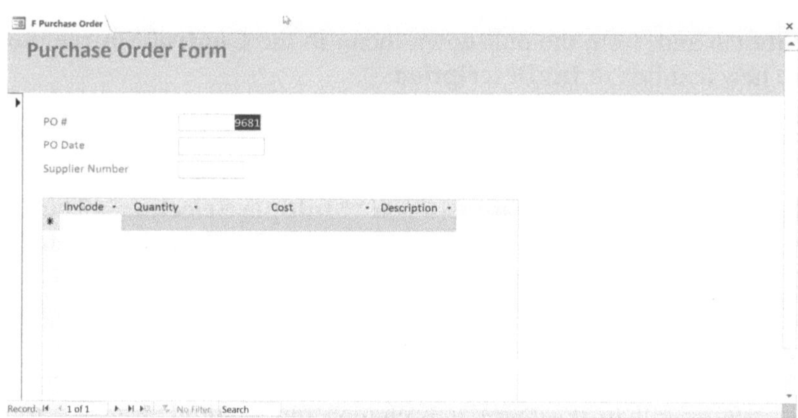

Figure 43

39. Click back on the **Design View**. Be sure you have selected **F Purchase Order Subform**. Click on the **Tab Order** icon 

to move the **Description** field above the **Cost** field. Close the **Tab Order** window.

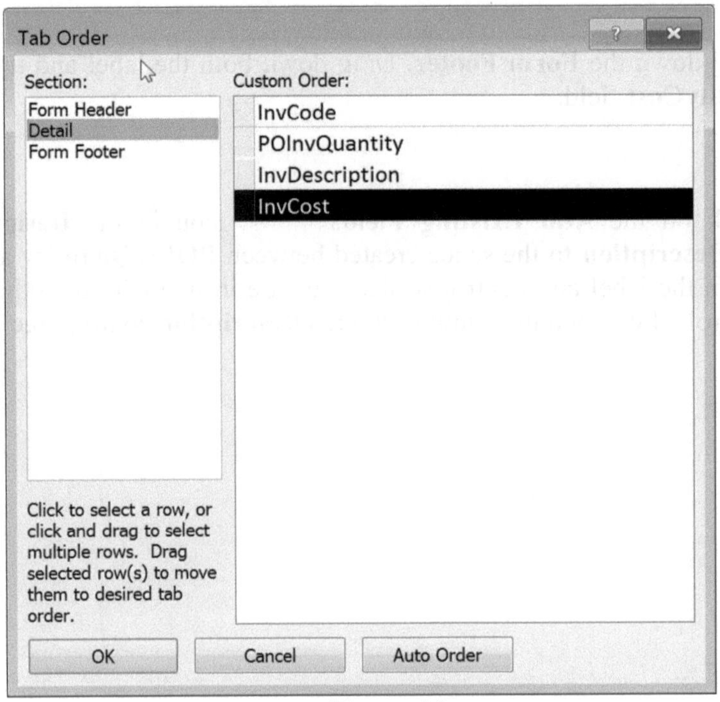

Figure 44

40. Drag the width of the fields in the **F Purchase Order Sub Subform** so that you can clearly see all of the labels and so there will be enough room for the inventory description.

41. In the **Design View**, click on the **Design** tab. Right click on the **Description** control box and select **Properties** from the pull down menu. Click on the **Data** tab and, from the pull-down menu in the **Control Source** property, set the new text box to **InvDescription**.

42. Highlight both the **InvDescription** and **InvCost** control boxes. Click on the **Property Sheet** icon. Note that the Selection type in the **Property Sheet** window now indicates that there is a "**Multiple Selection**". Thus, when you make changes, you are doing so for both **InvDescription** and **InvCost**. Change the controls as follows:

    - Click on the **Data** tab and change the **Enabled** property to **No**. The Enabled property specifies whether the field can receive user input.
    - While still in the **Data** tab, change the **Locked** property to **Yes**. The Locked property specifies whether the field can be edited by the user in the Form view.

    Note that setting these two properties in this fashion embeds internal controls in the database. This prevents unauthorized editing of the data.

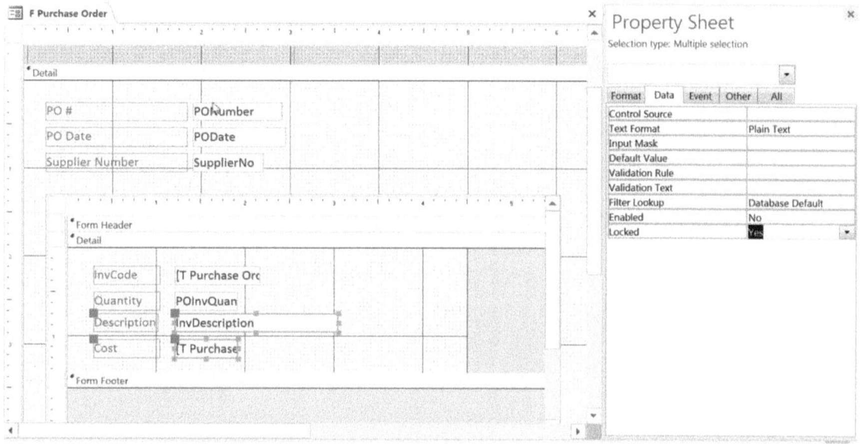

Figure 45

- Click on the **Other** tab and change the **Tab Stop** property to **No**. The Tab Stop specifies whether the cursor will stop in a particular field when the tab or enter key is hit.
- Click on the **Format** tab and change the **Back Color** property to "**Background Light**" (or choose gray from the color palette). The Back Color property specifies the color in the interior of a control box.
- While still in the the **Format** tab, change the **Border Style** property to **Transparent**. The Border Style property specifies the type of border surrounding a control box.

Note that setting these three properties in this fashion facilitates form design and user-friendliness. They signal to the user that no input is intended in these fields.

43. Now select the main **Purchase Order** form by right clicking on square between the two rulers on the **Purchase Order** form. The square will now have a black box in it.

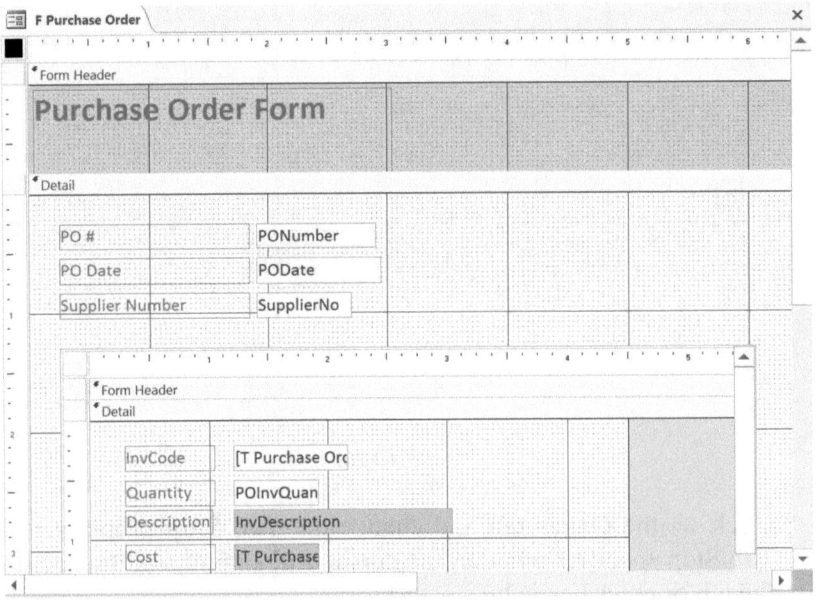

Figure 46

44. Right click on the black square and select **Properties** from the menu. Then select the **Record Source** property (**Data** tab) and click on the **Build** button . Click **Yes** in the dialogue box that appears to open the form's **Query Builder** window.

45. Click on the **Show Table** icon in the **Query Setup** section of the **Design** tab of the menu bar. Add **T Supplier** and close the **Show Table** window.

46. Click and drag the **PONumber** field from **T Purchase Order** to the first field cell in the QBE grid and then designate **Sort** as ascending.

47. Click and drag the remaining two fields from **T Purchase Order** to the second and third QBE grid field cells.

48. Click and drag the **SupplierName** field from the **T Supplier** to the fourth QBE grid field cell.

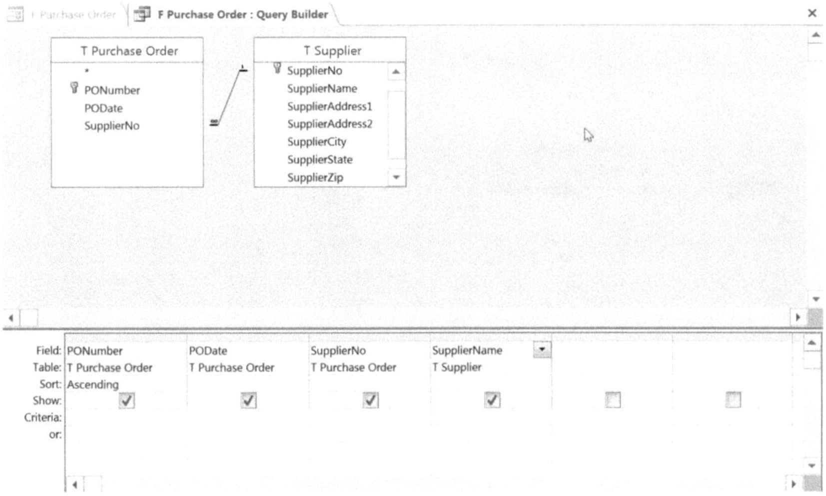

Figure 47

49. Now, select **Run**  under the **Results** section of the **Design** tab of the menu bar. Save and close the query to return to the form in the **Design View**. Close the form **Properties** window.

50. Click on the **Design** tab and click on the **Add Existing Fields** icon. Drag **SupplierName** next to **SupplierNumber** and delete the label. Right click on the control box and click on **Properties** to pull up the **Property Sheet**. Set the **Enabled** property (**Data** tab) to **No**, the **Locked** property (**Data** tab) to **Yes**, and the **Tab Stop** property (**Other** tab) to **No**. Set the **Font Size** (**Format** tab) to 10 and make the **Font Weight** property (**Format** tab) to bold. Use the build button next to the **Back Color** property (**Format** tab) to pull up the color palette and set the back color to grey. Close the color palette. Set the **Border Style** property (**Format** tab) to **Transparent**. Close the **Properties** window and save the form as **F Purchase Order**.

51. Open the **Purchase Order** form and create Purchase Order No. 9682 for the following transaction:

On December 16, 2018, Franz Bieler (CA Buyer) ordered 29 tons of white chardonnay grapes (inventory code: WC20004) at $732.50 per ton from Mendocino Vineyards (Supplier #: M0652).

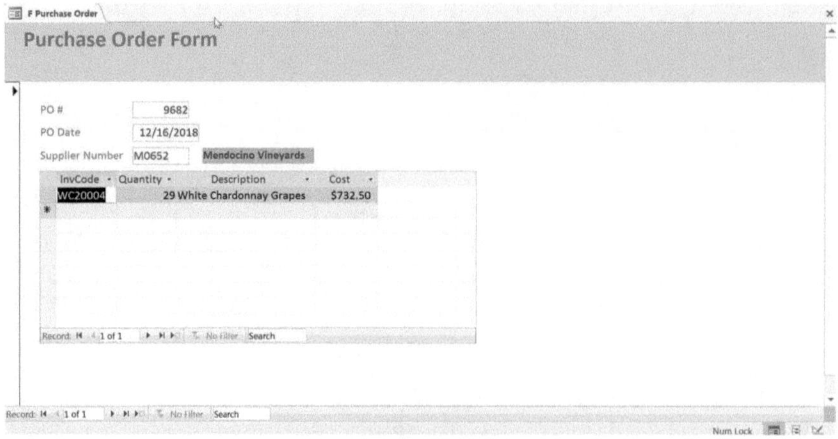

Figure 48

52. If you wish to quit *Access* at this time, simply close the program and your database will be saved with the name you used to create it.

CREATING A QUERY

Recall that queries can be used to ask questions about data or to perform actions on data. As you will now see, they can also be used as the basis for a report. You will need to create a purchase order to send to the supplier to order the inventory required by Chateau Americana. To do this, you will have to build a query that will obtain data from fields in several different tables. In this query, you will create a field that will calculate totals by extending unit prices and quantities ordered and a field that combines several address fields into a single address field.

Requirements

1. Open your *Access* database **Create** tab. Click on the **Query Design** icon 

 in the **Queries** section.

2. Highlight all four previously created tables (T Inventory, T Purchase Order, T Purchase Order Sub, and T Supplier) in the **Show Table** window by clicking on each while holding down the **Shift** key, and click on **Add**. Close the **Show Table** window.

3. Drag and click the fields from the tables listed below to the design grid Field cells:

T Purchase Order fields:

- **PONumber**
- **PODate**
- **SupplierNo**

T Inventory fields:

- **InvCode**
- **InvDescription**
- **InvCost**

T Supplier fields:

- **SupplierName**
- **SupplierAddress1**
- **SupplierAddress2**
- **SupplierCity**
- **SupplierState**
- **SupplierZip**

T Purchase Order Sub field:

- **POInvQuantity**

4. Set the **Sort** property for **PONumber** from **T Purchase Order** and **InvCode** from **T Inventory** to **Ascending**.

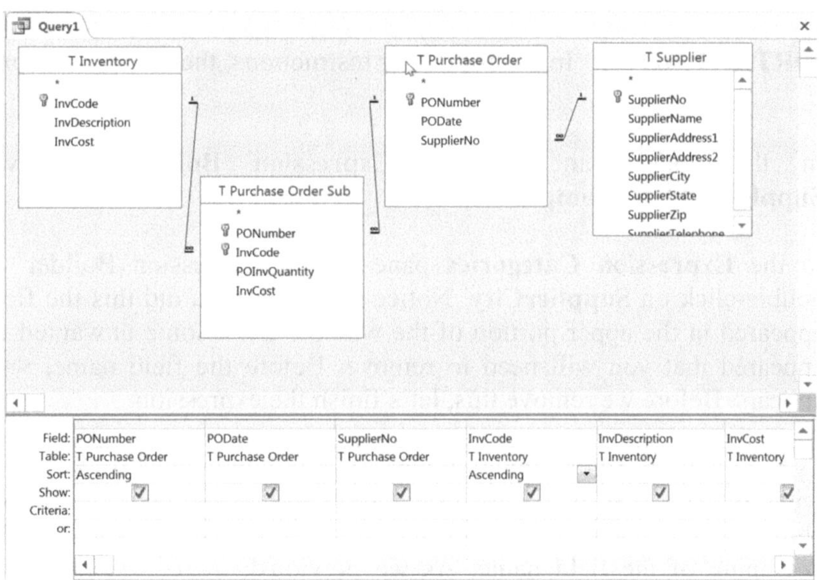

Figure 49

5. For mailing purposes, it is necessary to concatenate (i.e., link together) the city, state, and zip code fields. This is done by creating an additional field in the next open Field cell in the grid. Click on the next open Field cell and then click on the **Builder** 

icon in the **Query Setup** section under the **Design** tab to bring up the **Expression Builder** window. In the **Expression Elements** pane located in the lower left portion of the **Expression Builder** window, click on the + symbol next to the database file that refers to your database. Then click on **Tables** and click **T Supplier**. Note that the fields in the **T Supplier** table now appear in the **Expression Categories** pane located in the lower middle section of the **Expression Builder**.

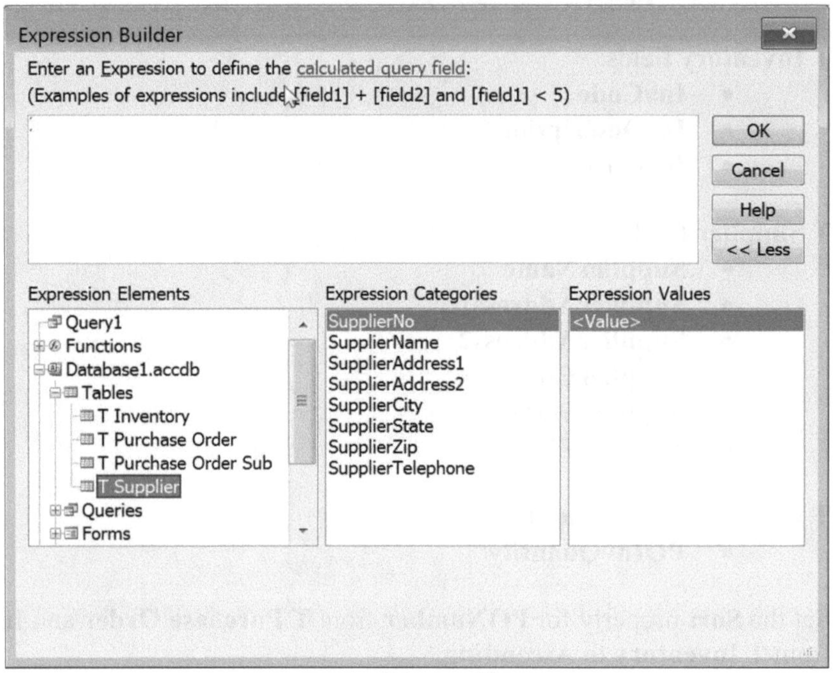

Figure 50

IMPORTANT NOTE: In the following instructions, the symbol ^ represents a space.

6. In the upper pane of the **Expression Builder** window, type **SupplierAddressComp:^**

7. In the **Expression Categories** pane of the Expression Builder window, double-click on **SupplierCity**. Notice that when you did this the field name appeared in the upper portion of the window **BUT** some unwanted text also appeared that you will need to remove. Before the field name, <<Expr>> appears. Before we remove this, let’s finish the expression.

8. Type **& “, ^” &** (with quotation marks) then double-click on **SupplierState**, type **& “ ^^^“ &** (with quotation marks) and double-click on **SupplierZip**. Now we will go back and remove the unwanted text. Scroll back to the beginning of the field name. As we previously noted, when you double-clicked on **SupplierCity**, *Access* inserted “«Expr»” into the expression just after the field name **SupplierAddressComp**. Highlight this and hit the **Delete** key so that your syntax will be correct. Next click **OK.**

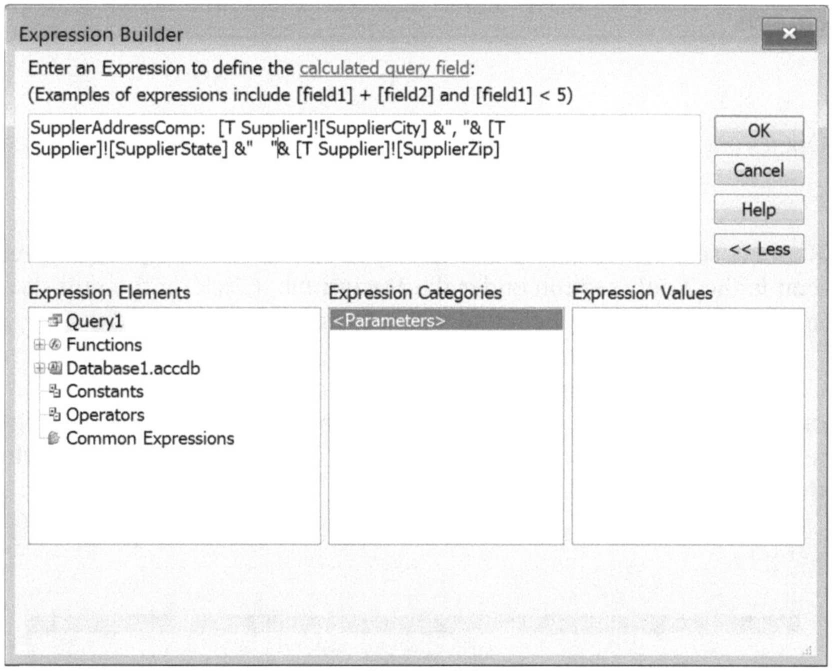

Figure 51

9. The next open grid Field cell will be used to calculate the extension for the cost times the quantity ordered. The **Builder** button can again be utilized to obtain help in entering the text for this field. Enter **Extension: [T Purchase Order Sub]![POInvQuantity]*[T Inventory]![InvCost]**. Next click **OK**.

10. Click on the **Run** icon to test the query. The result should include each of the fields listed above as well as the two new fields created in steps 6 through 9. Close and save this query as **Q Purchase Order**.

11. If you wish to quit *Access* at this time, simply close the program and your database will be saved with the name you used to create it.

CREATING A REPORT

The purchase order form you previously created is an internal form. Its intent was to provide a convenient, user-friendly form for employees, but it is not in a format that provides all the information needed by suppliers. Therefore, it will be necessary to create a **report** (using *Access* terminology) that can be sent to suppliers when Chateau Americana wants to make a purchase. You will use the query that you just created to build this report.

Requirements

1. Open your *Access* database and click on the **Report Design** 

icon in the **Reports** section under the **Create** tab. Click on the **Property Sheet** 

icon in the **Tools** section under the **Design** tab. Click on the pull-down menu in the **Record Source** field and select **Q Purchase Order**.

2. Click and drag the right edge of the report to the 6-inch mark on the top ruler. Click and drag the **Page Footer** and **Page Header** area edges up to reduce the height of each to zero. **NOTE: You will not enter anything into these sections!!!**

Figure 52

3. Click on the **Group & Sort** 

icon in the **Grouping & Totals** section under the **Design** tab. Then click on **Add a group** in the **Group, Sort, and Total** window.

Figure 53

Select **PONumber** as the first field to group on in the **Group, Sort, and Total** window.

4. Click on the **More** button to expand the options. Change "**without a footer section**" to "**with a footer section.**" Change the option "**do not keep group together on one page**" to "**keep whole group together on one page.**"

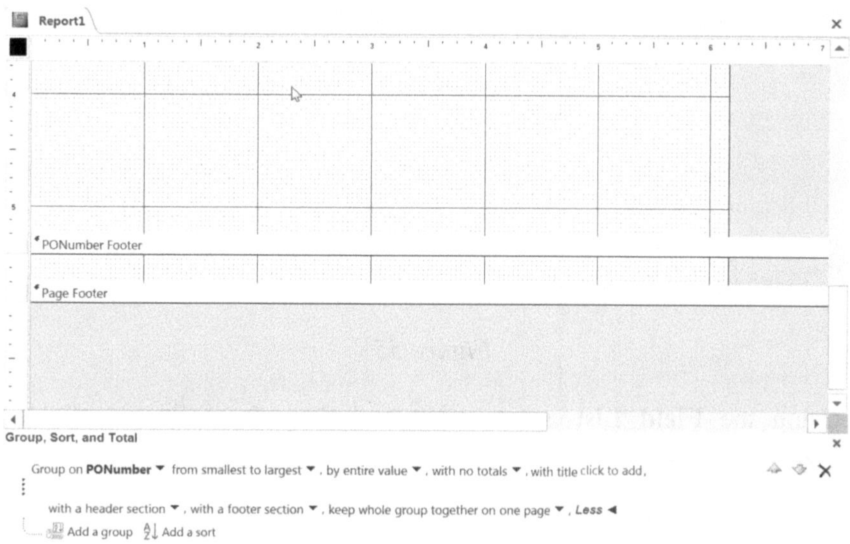

Figure 54

5. Click on the X on the **Group, Sort, and Total** menu line to close the **Grouping Dialogue Box**.

6. Click on the **Add Existing Fields** 

icon from the **Tools** section under the **Design** tab. Then click and drag the following fields to the **Detail** section.

- **InvCode**
- **InvDescription**
- **InvCost**
- **POInvQuantity**
- **Extension**

Each field will become a control on the report. Close the **Field List** window.

7. Click on the **Inventory Code** label (**NOT** the control box, just the label) and press Ctrl-X. This will cut the label away from the control box. Click on the **PONumber Header** bar, then press Ctrl-V to place the label in that section. Do the same for the remaining labels. Line the labels up horizontally just above the **Detail** bar line in the order above. Line up the control boxes just below their related labels.

8. Enlarge the **Header** section by dragging the **Detail** bar downward. Bring down the labels for the **Detail** section also.

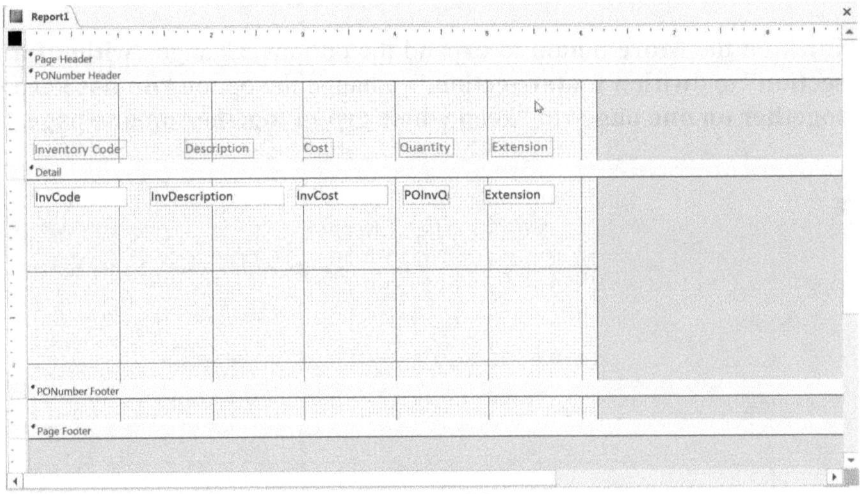

Figure 55

9. Using the **Field List** again, click and drag the following fields to the PONumber Header section:

   - **PONumber**
   - **PODate**
   - **SupplierNo**
   - **SupplierName**
   - **SupplierAddress1**
   - **SupplierAddress2**
   - **SupplierAddressComp**

   Delete the labels for everything but the purchase order number. Arrange the control boxes using good form design principles. Close the **Field List** window. Enlarge the **PONumber Header**.

10. Pull-down the **Controls** menu (found in the **Controls** section of the **Design** toolbar) and click on the **Label** Aa icon. Create a label for Chateau Americana's name, address and telephone number at the top of the purchase order by drawing rectangles with the **Label** tool. Use an appropriate font size (found in the **Home** tab) so that the supplier will know immediately who the buyer is.

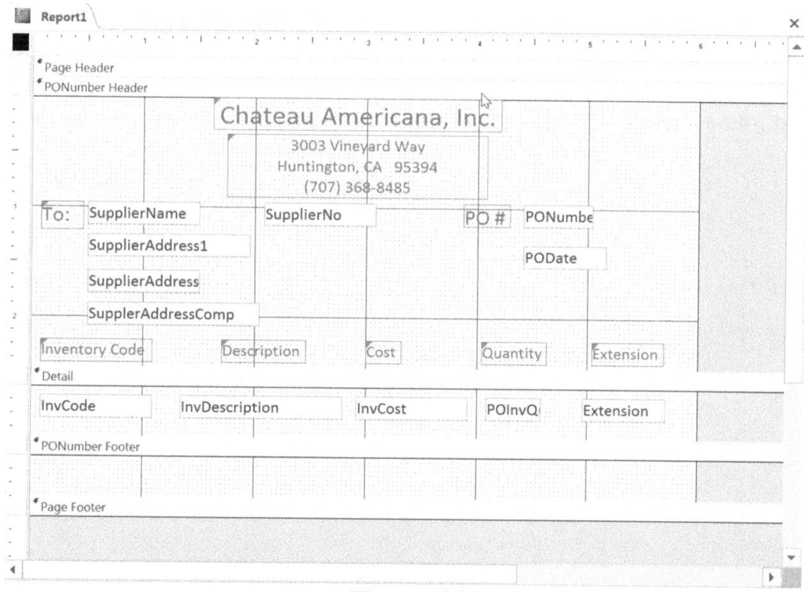

Figure 56

11. A **Control** box must be made to calculate the total of the extension amounts for each line of the purchase order. Pull down the menu for the **Controls** icon again and click on the **Text Box**  tool to create a control in the **PONumber Footer** section. Position the control box just below the **Extension** control box in the **Detail** section. Highlight the newly created control and click on **Property Sheet**. Set its **Control Source** property to **=Sum([Extension])** (found under the **Data** tab) and its format to **Currency** (found in the pull-down menu for **Format** under the **Format** tab).

12. Double click on the attached label and change the caption to **Total**.

13. Look at the report you have just created by clicking on the **View**  icon in the **Views** section under the **Design** tab and select **Report View.** Feel free to change the formatting (e.g., font sizes, bolding, italics, spacing, etc.) for any field you desire. The key is to utilize good form design principles to enhance the user's understanding of the purchase order.

14. Close and save the report as **R Purchase Order.**

15. You have now completed the *Access* assignment. Simply close the program and your database will be saved with the name you used to create it.

SUMMARY

In the preceding exercises, you have explored some of the power behind a database management system. You have created *Access* tables. You have learned the importance of primary keys and foreign keys. You have created queries to create composite fields and to combine fields from multiple tables into a single form or report. You have designed forms to display the information in a more user-friendly, intuitive manner and you have entered the data into those forms to see how they work. Finally, you have designed a report using the data from multiple tables. But this is just the beginning. There is much more to learn about database systems!